Please remember that this is a library book, and that it belongs only temporarily to each person who uses it. Be considerate. Do not write in this, or any, library book.

16.95

P9-DYY-508

A Resource Guide for Secondary School Teaching

WITHDRAWN

WITHDRAWN

A Resource Guide for Secondary School Teaching

Planning for Competence

Eugene C. Kim
Richard D. Kellough

California State University, Sacramento

3rd edition

Macmillan Publishing Co., Inc.
NEW YORK
Collier Macmillan Publishers
LONDON

Copyright © 1983, Macmillan Publishing Co., Inc.

Printed in the United States of America

All rights reserved. No part of this book may be reproduced
or transmitted in any form or by any means, electronic or
mechanical, including photocopying, recording, or any
information storage and retrieval system, without permission in writing from the Publisher.

Earlier editions copyright © 1978 and 1974 by Macmillan
Publishing Co., Inc.

Macmillan Publishing Co., Inc.
866 Third Avenue, New York, New York 10022

Collier Macmillan Canada, Inc.

ISBN   0-02-363810-9

Printing: 1 2 3 4 5 6 7 8   Year: 3 4 5 6 7 8 9 0

We Are One

Truth, love, peace, and beauty,
We have sought apart
    but will find within, as our
Moods—explored, shared,
    questioned, and accepted—
Together become one and all

    Through life my friends
    We can travel together,
    for we now know
    each could go it alone.

    To assimilate our efforts into one,
    While growing in accepting,
    and trusting, and sharing the
        individuality of the other,
    Is truly to enjoy God's greatest gift—
    Feeling—knowing love and compassion.

    Through life my friends
    We are together,
    for we must know
    we are one.

—R.D. Kellough

Preface

ABOUT THE COMPETENT TEACHER

What do we know about the competent teacher? For many years we have been led to believe that the competent teacher is one who has subject matter mastery. But is this statement really true or is it representative of the many existing untested hypotheses that educators so often accept as fact? The statement stands naked, unverified, and seemingly without real meaning. But subject mastery is included here as one of the characteristics of the competent teacher, although it is not necessarily the most important of the competencies if indeed these can be ranked at all. The statement means: *the teacher has a comfortable understanding of the subject matter, but, more important, can effectively guide the student through the learning process.* The competent teacher is afraid to say "I don't know the answer, but maybe we can look for it together," and then guides the student through the all-important process of searching for tentative truths.

More important than the teacher's knowledge of the subject is an understanding of the processes of learning. Many teachers' frustrations are caused by sole concentration on the subject matter when in fact their frustrations would be relieved and their teaching competency enhanced if they would concentrate more on the structure of the subject. That is, the competent teacher is really an "educational broker." He knows how and where to look for information. In short the teacher must (1) understand the skills of inquiry, (2) know how to mold the bits of information into a structural framework, and (3) be an expert in the technique of self-instruction. To repeat an overused but nevertheless true remark, "Competent teaching is more an art than a science." The concern of the teacher must be with the processes as well as with the products of learning.

Having analyzed many instances of what we consider to be effective teaching performances, the authors concluded that the main reason for this effectiveness is the teacher's ability to focus the attention of the class on the never-ceasing search for truth and understanding. This process is also dependent upon the student's comprehension and growing understanding of the structure of the subject matter, the structure itself being dependent upon the unifying concepts that are developed by the student under the guidance of a competent teacher. Finally, these concepts are molded and understood only when the theory of instruction is suitable.

An underlying concept of this book is that knowing *how* to teach is significantly important in competent teaching and that mastery of teaching style is the key. Therefore, this book is primarily concerned with techniques for understanding and developing your style and competence in classroom instruction. A practical approach is provided throughout the text by the introduction of discussion questions and exercises.

Factors that determine a teaching style come from three major sources: personal experience, tradition, and research evidence. Research evidence is the least influential in determining what a teacher does on a day-by-day basis. Many teachers teach according to the way they were taught by the teachers for whom they held the greatest admiration. Our own experiences with teachers during the past few years tell us that the gap between theory and practice is being narrowed.

There is much research on the importance of teacher personality as a major determinant of student learning. We are not sure just what the important personality traits are, but we believe that they have something to do with whether the teacher's style is consistent with the teacher's behavior.

We believe that if the teacher wishes to be authoritarian in orientation, he had better be consistent and good at it. Or, if the teacher wishes to be a facilitator rather than a director, he had better be good at that. Whatever the style, we hope that the tacher will be consistent and competent. And, just as students must learn to tolerate and accept those who may be different, teachers must also tolerate and accept other styles. We must develop our style from the most productive tradition, our happiest experiences, and the best that research has provided.

As we learn to recognize inconsistencies in our own behavior, we will learn to deal with them while continuing to develop our competence.

While we are sure there are others, we have identified four major characteristics of the competent teacher. These are

1. The teacher's understanding of the subject matter.
2. The teacher's understanding of the processes of learning.
3. The teacher's perceived role as an "educational broker."
4. The teacher's consistency in use of modeling behaviors.

Chapter one will expand this list and Section C of Chapter 17 provides forms for a detailed evaluation of these and other important competencies.

About This Third Edition

The intent and integrity of previous editions of our book have been maintained in this third edition as we strive to offer for both prospective and experienced teachers an organization of basic resource materials designed to improve teaching, while simultaneously attempting to exclude the lengthy and extrinsic explanations so often found in standard educational textbooks. Bibliographic entries have been updated and will direct the reader to further information on specific topics.

We were encouraged by the success of the previous editions of this resource guide and are grateful to those who offered suggestions helpful in our revision. Many of these suggestions have been incorporated. Some of the more significant changes are:

1. Nearly double the number of exercises from previous editions, including exercises in each chapter.
2. Increased emphasis in "planning for instruction."
3. Increased emphasis in the micro peer teaching content.

4. Increased content on legal guidelines.
5. Addition of chapter on test construction.
6. Expanded table of contents with easier exercise reference system.

As a matter of fact, changes were made throughout the text in every chapter of the second edition, in order to keep this guide relevant to today's professional teacher. However, for the sake of readability, we continue to use the masculine gender as an impersonal referrent throughout this text. Its use as a referrent in no way is intended to denigrate our female colleagues and students. However, until a sexless pronoun is established we will continue using the language as it has been used historically.

The employment opportunities for teachers have not been good, but we expect an improvement. When we look at the pupil-teacher ratios in public school classrooms today we become convinced that there is not really a current surplus of teachers but rather an urgent need to reassess economic and political priorities. If all the teachers were hired that are needed in the schools today, then we probably would not be adding material to this book on how to locate a job and how to handle disruptive students. Given the technology and knowledge that we in this country possess, it is embarrassing to witness the confusion and inefficiency that exist in so many of our public institutions today. The teaching profession is perhaps unique among professions in that the practitioner is expected to deal effectively with clients on something other than a one-to-one basis; frequently it is a ratio of 35 : 1 or 40 : 1. And since the teacher is typically assigned to teach five classes a day with perhaps an average of 30 students per class, five days a week, the entire issue of competence and accountability becomes nearly irrelevant. The youth of today are used to multi-million-dollar productions on television and the movie screen. When they come into a classroom and are subjected each day to something short of a high-budget production, they can be expected to react in a less than highly motivated fashion. There is no doubt that our youth are growing up in a highly stimulated instant-action society, a society that has learned to expect instant headache relief, instant turn-on television sets, instant dinners, and perhaps even instant high-paying employment. In the light of all this we are on the side of you the teacher, you who are on the firing line each day and who are expected to perform, perhaps instantly and entertainingly, but most certainly in a highly competent and professional manner in situations not even close to ideal.

In this book we continue to share with you what we and other teachers have found to work. We will attempt to assist you in building your confidence and competence as you develop your style and select those strategies that work best for you.

We wish to express our gratitude to all those students, secondary teachers, and college instructors who in their various ways continue to help us in improving this resource guide. We are indebted to the authors and publishers who granted their permissions to reprint materials acknowledged throughout the text. A most sincere appreciation goes to Lloyd Chilton for his continued encouragement. Very special thanks go to Sue and Noreen, both of whom are teachers, for their patience, support, and useful ideas shared during the years. And we are most appreciative of Jo Anne Breese, who was most talented in deciphering our handwriting and who typed the manuscript for us.

E.C.K.
R.D.K.

Contents

Part III *Choosing and Implementing Instructional Strategies*   103

A Resource Guide for
Secondary School Teaching

Part I

Orientation to Secondary School Teaching

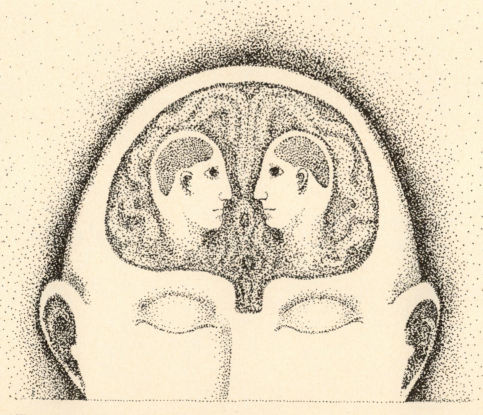

Drawing by Carol Wilson, unpublished material. Reprinted by permission.

157799

Part I is designed to provide you with the opportunity to look at your perceptions—what you feel about the teaching and learning situation; what your alternatives are as to the kind of teacher you would like to become—and then to establish goals and work toward the development of that style. Important to this process is the development of your perceptions about the profession and the aims, tasks, and functions of being a teacher, and how understanding you are of the behavior and personality of others.

In Part I we illustrate two opposing teaching styles, identified as styles A and B. We do not claim that one is better than the other. We believe that the effective and competent teacher is one who has style consistency, even if his style is identified as eclectic.

We hope that by the time you finish this book you will have gained new perceptions and will have made progress toward the development of teaching skills that are consistent with the style of teacher you are becoming.

As a competent teacher, you must remain open to change. From the moment you first set foot in a classroom you are a professional teacher; it takes time to become a skillful teacher. During your career you will undoubtedly change your style as you grow and master new skills, and as the needs of youth and society change. You will continue to develop your understanding of the dynamics of behavioral change. You will continue to examine the changing patterns explicit in your style, and to facilitate behavioral changes in your students and assist them in gaining new and more accurate perceptions of the world around them.

Do I Understand My Skills?
How Can I Improve My Weaknesses?
An Assessment of Where I Am

COMPETENCY IDENTIFICATION

Throughout this text we discuss competencies. The following is a compilation of those characteristics we believe to be most important for teacher competence. Some of these are addressed in this text; others are beyond its parameters. We suggest that you compile your own list as you go through this course and, with the help of exercises such as Exercise 1.1, keep an account of how you are doing in building your competencies.

Characteristics of the Competent Teacher

We believe that the competent teacher:

1. Has a comfortable understanding of the subject matter.
2. Understands the processes of learning.
3. Is an "educational broker," knows where and how to find information.
4. Practices modeling behaviors, behaviors consistent with his beliefs.
5. Is open to change, and willing to take risks and to be held accountable.
6. Is aware of his changing and emerging style.
7. Has a developing understanding of the dynamics of behavioral change (learning).
8. Is unbiased and unprejudiced with regard to race, color, creed, national origin, or sex.
9. Plans thoroughly, is resourceful, creative, and motivating.
10. Is protective of the health and safety of students.
11. Is optimistic and hopeful.
12. Continues to develop a strategy repertoire.
13. Is skillful and fair in assessment of learning.
14. Is skillful in working with colleagues and parents.

15. Provides a constructive and positive environment for learning.
16. Has a continued interest in professional responsibilities and opportunities.
17. Maintains ethical standards in professional relationships.
18. Has a wide range of interests, including those activities of students.
19. Has a wide range of coping skills.
20. Maintains a sense of humor.

No matter what grade level or what subject you want to teach, it is important to find out how much you know about yourself. This will help you (1) understand your students better in dealing with them, (2) help you understand your colleagues better in working with them and (3) help beginning teachers prepare better for a job interview. For these purposes let us begin with a personal assessment of yourself and share it with others in the class with respect to your secondary school teaching skills.

EXERCISE 1.1: UNDERSTANDING MY SKILLS—A PERSONAL ASSESSMENT

You are to list your perceived teaching strengths and the characteristics or skills you feel you need to improve. Be as specific and as candid as possible. Also list ways in which you might be able to share your strengths and help those classmates who might need improvement in those areas. Together with your weaknesses, list resources available for help in overcoming them and any constraints working against improvement. (See the examples shown on page 00).

For those who have not had regular teaching experiences we suggest that you recall your experiences when you were a teacher's aide, teacher's assistant, Sunday School teacher or a recreational leader for children, youth, or adults. You might be able to identify some strengths and/or skills to improve further on those things you have done in the past. For those who have no paraprofessional experiences at all, it is still possible to identify your strengths and/or areas to improve as a person; the way you perceive yourself, qualities that you see positive or strong and the characteristics you consider undesirable. We have provided in the following chart specific examples we obtained from novice and experienced teachers.

Now it is your turn to examine yourself following the format and examples shown in Exercise 1.

After completing the chart for Exercise 1, share your lists with members of your class. Exercise 1 might provide valuable data for organizing class activities for the remainder of your course. At periodic intervals during the course of your training you should comment on perceived advances being made toward the improvement of your teaching skills. You might wish to maintain a *journal* of your thoughts and progress. Repeating Exercise 1 several times during the course of a semester will provide useful information regarding progress being made.

EXAMPLES FOR EXERCISE 1.1: UNDERSTANDING MY SKILLS
A Personal Assessment

I. *Strengths:* *Characteristics/Skills* *I feel strong/positive:*	*How Can I Share These With Others?*
a. I don't give up too easily, and am anxious to learn.	Tell my friends more specifically about the qualities and experiences I feel strong or positive about.
b. I have background and experience in teaching young children in a Sunday School.	Convince them that they can do it, too, but it takes time and effort; keep trying; don't get discouraged even if they don't get it the first round.
c. I am open to different opinions.	Demonstrate a teaching skill in front of a small group of friends in class (Micro-peer-teaching).
d. I have a sense of humor and a positive outlook.	
e. I am unsure as to what to teach.	Ask my friends how they feel about teaching.

II. *Areas to be Improved:* *Characteristics/Skills:* *I need to change or improve:*	*Diagnosis and Evidences:* *What makes me feel or do this way?*	*Remedies:* *How could I possibly improve this?*
a. I am nervous in front of groups.	I feel frightened of strangers; I am not used to students in the classroom situation.	Meet more people; Practice speaking in front of small groups of friends or students.
b. I insist on my own way of doing things.	I think that my way is the best way all the time.	Learn to find some merits in other ways of doing things.
c. I talk too much about the subject matter.	I am always eager to tell students about what I know.	Let students tell what they know.
d. I use words that are too difficult for students to understand.	I want to impress students that I know such words.	Forget the college terminologies; lower vocabulary level.
e. I am too test oriented; often make it difficult.	I want to find out how much students have learned/remembered and to make up the grades; the test is difficult so that there won't be too many A's.	Use non-quiz/non-test methods. Don't bother as to how many A's, D's, and F's there should be.

EXERCISE 1.1: UNDERSTANDING MY SKILLS
A Personal Assessment

I. Strengths:	How Can I Share These?

II. Areas to Be Improved:	Diagnosis:	Remedies:

QUESTIONS FOR CLASS DISCUSSION

1. Compile separate lists from Exercise 1.1 with perceived strengths of all class members on one list and perceived weaknesses on the other. See how many categories each list can be narrowed down to. What are the common strengths? the common weaknesses?

2. Compare the lists from Question 1 above with the 20 competencies identified at the beginning of this chapter. Has your class identified other competencies not included by the authors?

2

What May Be Expected of Me
As a Secondary School Teacher?

Each profession in our society has a Code of Ethics of its own; so does the teaching profession. The code that follows is a standard that the teaching profession expects its members to honor. These do not constitute an exhaustive enumeration of all the acts or conduct considered to be professional; nevertheless, the members could adhere to them to make the teaching profession ethical and professional.

CODE OF ETHICS OF THE TEACHING PROFESSION[1]
Preamble

The educator believes in the worth and dignity of human beings. The educator recognizes the supreme importance of the pursuit of truth, devotion to excellence, and the nurture of democratic citizenship. The educator regards as essential to these goals the protection of freedom to learn and to teach and the guarantee of equal educational opportunity for all. The educator accepts the responsibility to practice the profession according to the highest ethical standards.

The educator recognizes the magnitude of the responsibility being accepted in choosing a career in education and engages individually and collectively with other educators to judge colleagues, and to be judged by them, in accordance with the provisions of this code.

PRINCIPLE 1—COMMITMENT TO THE STUDENT

The educator measures success by the progress of each student toward realization of potential as a worthy and effective citizen. The educator therefore works to stimulate the spirit of inquiry, the acquisition of knowledge and understanding, and the thoughtful

[1] Code of Ethics of the Teaching Profession, National Education Association. Reprinted by permission.

formulation of worthy goals. In fulfilling these goals, the educator:

a. Encourages the student to independent action in the pursuit of learning and provides access to varying points of view.
b. Prepares the subject carefully, presents it to the students without distortion and—within the limits of time and curriculum—gives all points of view a fair hearing.
c. Protects the health and safety of students.
d. Honors the integrity of students and influences them through constructive criticism rather than by ridicule and harassment.
e. Provides for participation in educational programs without regard to race, color, creed, national origin or sex—both in what is taught and how it is taught.
f. Neither solicits nor involves them or their parents in schemes for commercial gain, thereby insuring that professional relationships with students shall not be used for private advantage.
g. Shall keep in confidence information that has been obtained in the course of professional service, unless disclosure serves professional purposes or is required by law.

PRINCIPLE 2—COMMITMENT TO THE PUBLIC

The educator believes that democratic citizenship in its highest form requires dedication to the principles of our democratic heritage. The educator shares with all other citizens the responsibility for the development of sound public policy and assumes full political and citizenship responsibilities. The educator bears particular responsibility for the development of policy relating to the extension of educational opportunities for all and for interpretation of educational programs and policies to the public. In fulfilling these goals, the educator:

a. Has an obligation to support the profession and institution and not to misrepresent them in public discussion. When being critical in public, the educator has an obligation not to distort the facts. When speaking or writing about policies, the educator must take adequate precautions to distinguish the educator's private views from the official position of the institution.
b. Does not interfere with a colleague's exercise of political and citizenship rights and responsibilities.
c. Ensures that institutional privileges shall not be used for private gain. Does not exploit pupils, their parents, colleagues, nor the school system itself for private advantage. Does not accept gifts or favors that might impair or appear to impair professional judgment nor offer any favor, service, or thing of value to obtain special advantage.

PRINCIPLE 3—COMMITMENT TO THE PROFESSION

The educator believes that the quality of the services of the education profession directly influences the Nation and its citizens. The educator therefore exerts every effort to raise professional standards, to improve service, to promote a climate in which the exercise of professional judgment is encouraged, and to achieve conditions which attract persons worthy of trust to careers in education. In fulfilling these goals, the educator:

a. Accords just and equitable treatment to all members of the profession in the exercise of their professional rights and responsibilities.
b. Does not use coercive means or promise special treatment in order to influence professional decisions of colleagues.

c. Does not misrepresent personal professional qualifications.

d. Does not misrepresent the professional qualifications of colleagues, and will discuss these qualifications fairly and accurately when discussion serves professional purposes.

e. Applies for, accepts, offers, and assigns positions or responsibility on the basis of professional preparation and legal qualifications.

f. Uses honest and effective methods of administering educational responsibility. Conducts professional business through proper channels. Does not assign unauthorized persons to educational tasks. Uses time granted for its intended purposes. Does not misrepresent conditions of employment. Lives up to the letter and spirit of contracts.

THE TEACHER IS A CATALYST OF LEARNING[2]

If we define learning as the *changing of behavioral tendencies through experience*, we know that learning occurs in and is done by the learner. It is a function of his nervous system and involves the reorganization of his central nervous processes in response to stimulations. Learning is all IN the person—for school purposes it is all in his head—and the teacher cannot directly intrude without recourse to bone-chisel and scalpel or electrode. Consequently, the role of the teacher can only be catalytic; he is a director of learning, a contriver of stimulations. His role is to know *what changes* should occur: what information should be acquired, what concepts developed, skills learned, attitudes formed, etc. He may next determine *what experiences* are likely to produce the desired changes. Then he may contrive and arrange stimulating situations, which should provoke the desired experiences, which in turn should produce the desired changes. No more than these things can the teacher do. He is a director of learning only—a catalyst, and not a mechanic.

To be the proper sort of catalyst and thus to have students learn appropriate things in the most effective way, the following items seem to be essential:

1. Understanding of the learning process and the adolescent who is to learn.
2. Knowing what to teach (the subject), in what amounts, in what sequences, at what rates, with what expectancies and standards of achievement.
3. Studying students with respect to their background, goals, readiness and aptitude, intelligence, adjustment problems, etc.
4. Planning and executing the teacher's activities and planning and directing those of students so as to ensure appropriate motivation, control and educative experiences, and in this connection to select and prepare instructional materials and equipment.
5. Measuring and evaluating student achievement.
6. Using all appropriate facilities and services of the school and community to facilitate any of these ends.

Toward the Improvement of Classroom Interaction

Before leaving the theory and proceeding to methodology, it would seem helpful to specify some of the aims that encourage professional teachers to take the time to improve interaction in the classroom.

[2] H. Orville Nordberg, James M. Bradfield, and William C. Odell, *Secondary School Teaching* (New York: Macmillan, 1962), p. 5. Reprinted by permission.

What is sought . . .

in the area of teaching and learning is a movement[3] :

From	*Toward*
Teacher domination	Teacher as special member of group
Teacher as sole leader	Group-centered shared leadership
Extrinsic control in hands of teacher	Intrinsic control in hands of individuals (including teacher)
Active membership of teacher plus two or three verbal students	Active membership of total group
Stress on subject with inclusion of personal social needs	Stress on both cognitive and affective elements
Almost total dependence on teacher as planner, initiator, and evaluator	Student self-direction and independence
Formal recitation by small percentage of students	Spontaneous participation by all
Selective inattention by students	Careful listening with feedback
Aggregate of noncohesive individuals	Cohesive group of interacting individuals
Student learning with intent of passing tests and getting good grades	Student learning with aim of satisfying personal needs to know and to grow

. . . in the area of emotional growth is a movement:

From	*Toward*
Guarded, hidden feelings	A norm of openness and spontaneous expression of feelings
Unchecked assumptions	Positive feelings that assumptions should be checked
Neutral feelings toward the meaningfulness of the learning experience	Positive feelings that the experience has personal meanings and values
Neutral feelings toward the class group	Positive, warm response toward others ("my group" feeling)
Vague student anxiety: "Who am I in this group?"	Personal security: "I am I, accepted and valued"
Preoccupation with self and with projection of "good" self-image	Sensitivity to verbally and nonverbally expressed needs of others
Student fear of speaking in a group situation	Confidence in expressing feelings, knowledge, and direction
View of teacher as nonhuman	View of teacher as human being with feelings similar to those of students

Gorman gives an identification of the functions that people perform in groups. The essence of inclusion here is to point out the importance of the potential of each student's contribution within a class, whether the individual's behavior falls under the classification of a task or a maintenance function, contributing or hindering.

[3] Alfred Gorman, *Teachers and Learners: The Interactive Process of Education,* (Boston: Allyn, 1969), pp. 40-41. Reprinted by permission.

TASK FUNCTIONS

Gorman explains that with the development over the years of what might be called the American Cult of Efficiency, there is a great individual anxiety within aggregates over the possibility of wasting time. A typical committee called for the purpose of accomplishing a particular task rarely takes the time that would be required for the members to get to know each other or to deal in any way with its process level. Each individual is much too intent on making decisions and taking quick action. It is as if we are an instant action society, and in getting the work done, one or more of the members must contribute behaviors that Gorman refers to as *task functions*.[4]

1. *Initiating:* stating or defining the group task or goals, suggesting action, proposing plans, supplying ideas for the accomplishment of the task, making suggestions for the use of resources.
2. *Supplying Information:* giving facts, providing data relevant to concerns of the group.
3. *Giving Opinions:* stating feelings as to the workability of plans, giving ideas as to whether they may or may not be accepted.
4. *Requesting Information:* identifying areas where facts and concepts are needed, asking for suggestions and ideas.
5. *Providing Information:* listing possible resource people or materials, bringing in solutions developed in other places, using one's own background and expertise.
6. *Requesting Opinions:* calling for member expression of feeling about procedures or ideas, asking for acceptance or rejection of objectives or proposals.
7. *Clarifying:* restating ideas of others in one's own terms, questioning proposals, interpreting.
8. *Elaborating:* building on ideas of others, restating one's own ideas in more complex form.
9. *Summarizing:* restating main ideas proposed at any point, combining ideas of others in single form.
10. *Consensus Testing:* stating conclusion or decision and asking for group commitment, calling for vote or general agreement.
11. *Evaluating:* reminding group of deadlines, keeping minutes.
12. *Orienting:* keeping discussion relevant and on the track.

Maintenance Functions

While the supplying of task functions by the leader and/or members should lead to effective task accomplishment, it does not always succeed and quite often the work of the members is slow and inefficient. Such blocks to progress and member satisfaction are common in an aggregate where the social needs of members are ignored. What seems needed are behaviors that act to build more of a group feeling—an intragroup respect and rapport. Such group building maintenance functions are:

1. *Recognizing:* use of names in group discussions, giving credit for good ideas or actions.
2. *Accepting:* expressions of friendliness and warmth, smiling and head nodding, indicating that one's absence is regretted and that one's presence is noted and welcome.
3. *Harmonizing:* helping others to understand the basis of their disagreements, reconciling conflicts, helping members to see the other fellow's point.

[4] *Ibid.*, pp. 58–59.

4. *Compromising:* helping others to combine their ideas into a mutually satisfactory proposal, giving ground on one's position in favor of a more generally acceptable statement, giving consent or commitment to an experimental tryout of a not yet personally acceptable idea.
5. *Norm Testing:* trying out procedures seemingly agreed upon by the group to find out if they are really acceptable.
6. *Communication Facilitating:* helping others to participate, making process-level comments, exploring personal feelings, voicing perceptions of the group feeling.

EXERCISE 2.1   RECOGNITION OF TASK AND MAINTENANCE BEHAVIORS

For this exercise we suggest that you visit a secondary school to observe one or more classrooms for patterns of interaction. Use the tally sheet provided and bring the collected data for class discussion. The focus for this exercise is to improve your understanding of the 18 behaviors listed below, not to critique the classes visited.

TASK AND MAINTENANCE FUNCTION BEHAVIORS

Task Function Behaviors

Tally Sheet

	Teacher Initiated	Student Initiated
1. Initiating		
2. Supplying information		
3. Giving opinion		
4. Requesting information		
5. Providing information		
6. Requesting opinion		
7. Clarifying		
8. Elaborating		
9. Summarizing		
10. Consensus taking		
11. Evaluating		
12. Orienting		
Maintenance Function Behaviors		
1. Recognizing		
2. Accepting		
3. Harmonizing		
4. Compromising		
5. Norm testing		
6. Communication facilitating		

OPENNESS IN TEACHING

Many references have been made during the past decade to openness in teaching. Indeed, entire textbooks have been written on the subject. Within such references we are apt to find such related terms as "open classroom," "student-centered," "student-structured curriculum," "people-oriented," and even the term "unstructured teaching." Experience tells us that when using such terms, people are talking about what we like to refer to as *open-structure teaching*. To teach in this kind of atmosphere requires as much, if not more, planning than does teaching in situations in which the more traditional "teacher-centered" approaches are used. In an atmosphere of openness, the structure is left open, and much of the specific planning is done *with* the students rather than for the students.

A competent teacher does not walk into class each day and say to the students, "OK, what would you like to do today?" As a parent of a student of that teacher's class, we would not appreciate that inept style any more than we would appreciate driving our car into a service station for gasoline and hearing the attendant say: "The last time you were here we put the gas into the rear of the car; this time why don't we try the front?" A competent teacher does plan and does possess skills that will assist others in their search for knowledge and skill development.

The talented, creative people of Essentia of Tiburon, California developed a list of some of the "characteristics of open classrooms, open learning, and people who accept openness." This list was developed as a result of their experiences during the late 1960s and early 1970s with their test-center schools, which were primarily large metropolitan schools throughout the United States. With their permission we have borrowed the items from their list and introduce them here as characteristics of an open environment for learning and/or student-teacher response in an atmosphere of openness.[5]

Characteristics of an Open Environment for Learning	*An Atmosphere of Openness: Student and Teacher Responses*
Freedom of movement	Self-discipline and self-control
Free choice of involvement	Comfort with visitors
Diversity of expressed emotions	Comfort with silence
Excitement, discovery, exploration	High spontaneity
Nonsterile, pregnant environment	Unpredictability
Absence of coercion, of competition	Low conformity
Freedom to do what you want but not without responsibility (not to be confused with anarchy)	High self-esteem, good self-image
Student control of the environment	High serendipity*
Highly aesthetic environment	Low embarassment
Student planning	Help without directions
Student concern for learning	Self-initiated activities
Diversity of types of space, of time, use of activity, of activity, of resources	Play
Freedom of grouping	Laughter
Free access to all materials	Low formality—students and teacher on first-name basis, no dress code
Attitude of empathy	Free communication
Atmosphere of invention	Decisions made by individuals rather than groups
Few rules	No contracts
Compassion	Emphasis on self-evaluation
Strengths, not weaknesses, emphasized	Failure seen as positive feedback
Tolerance and acceptance	Peer teaching
Trust	Invention, creativity
	Trust

[5] Essentia, P.O. Box 129, Tiburon, CA 94920. Reprinted by permission.
*Serendipity is the opportunity to make fortunate discoveries, accidentally.

The following summary points regarding openness in teaching might provide guidelines for class discussion.

1. Openness requires planning, conviction, self control, cooperation, and trust.
2. Openness allows for the suddenness of discovery.
3. Openness places a value on mistakes, cooperation, and diversity.
4. Openness is not to be confused with "permissiveness."
5. Openness is not to be confused with "sloppiness."
6. Openness is not limited to sensory curiosity and satisfaction.
7. Openness does not imply that all should discover fire for themselves.

A NEW CATECHISM[6]

While the *Code of Ethics of Teaching Profession*, *Toward the Improvement of Classroom Interaction*, and *Openness in Teaching* afford a diversified viewpoint on teaching, *A New Catechism*, which follows, sheds yet another insight on teaching.

A New Catechism

Who is the pupil?
    A child of God, not a tool of the state.
Who is the teacher?
    A guide, not a guard.
What is the faculty?
    A community of scholars, not a union of mechanics.
Who is the principal?
    A master of teaching, not a master of teachers.
What is learning?
    A journey, not a destination.
What is discovery?
    Questioning the answers, not answering the questions.
What is the process?
    Discovering ideas, not covering content.
What is the goal?
    Opened minds, not closed issues.
What is the test?
    Being and becoming, not remembering and reviewing.
What is a school?
    Whatever we choose to make it.

NONINSTRUCTIONAL DUTIES OF SECONDARY SCHOOL TEACHERS

Teacher responsibilities most certainly do extend beyond the use of awareness and skill in the implementation of various classroom instructional strategies. It is the objective of this section to identify some of those responsibilities.

[6] Reprinted by permission from Allan A. Glatthorn, *Dynamics of Language*, D.C. Heath & Company, 1971.

We assume that you have completed a course such as Principles of Education in American Society, and thus will have an understanding of the philosophical assumptions underlying the fact that there is much to be learned in a secondary school which is not taught in the classroom. You probably have had fourteen or more years of experience in the public schools (as a student) and are aware of what is being emphasized in this section. However, our experiences with preservice teachers tell us that frequently they are subject-matter oriented and are not sufficiently aware of the time required for these out-of-class activities; on the other hand, if you have served as a paraprofessional (Chapter 20) you probably are aware. Here are some noninstructional responsibilities of secondary school teachers:

A. Responsibilities related to *clerical* and *maintenance* functions:
   1. Attendance checking and reporting.
   2. Preparation of budgets and schedules.
   3. Ordering, using, and maintaining audiovisual materials and equipment.
   4. Ordering, using and maintaining textbook and curriculum materials and supplies.

B. Responsibilities related to *advising, supervision,* and *sponsorship:*
   5. Supervision of halls, cafeteria, and assemblies.
   6. Supervision of homerooms and activity periods.
   7. Supervision of intramural contests.
   8. Advising and sponsoring student clubs.
   9. Advising and sponsoring student government.
   10. Advising and sponsoring plays, concerts, graduation exercises, or other events and productions.
   11. Support of the athletic program (for example, ticket taker, serving as scorer, supervision of stands).
   12. Sponsoring and arranging for guest speakers and campus visitors.
   13. Advising, guiding, and counseling of students.
   14. Responsibility for student safety.
   15. Chaperoning student dances and bus trips.

C. Responsibilities related to *school-community* activities:
   16. Attendance and participation at PTA.
   17. Attendance and participation in community events.
   18. Support of local bond issues.
   19. Parent conferences.
   20. Representing the school at social gatherings.
   21. Establishing rapport with other adults (for example, administrators, teachers, paraprofessionals, clerical and custodial staff).

D. Responsibilities related to *professional* activities:
   22. School and district-wide committee work.
   23. Continued study and development in your field.
   24. Support of professional associations, local, state, and federal.
   25. Responsibility to professional Code of Ethics.

This list of 25 noninstructional teacher responsibilities is by no means exhaustive. It does represent the kinds of things that can exhaust a teacher. Many of these tasks are unavoidable and necessary for each teacher to perform, others are negotiable. The new teacher must first concentrate on the classroom instruction, then move cautiously into those other necessary but more or less optional kinds of activities. Generally speaking, here is a list of eight DOs for the new teacher.

1. Get to know your students out of class.
2. Get to know your community.
3. Stay on the right side of administrators.
4. Be supportive of other teachers' programs.
5. Get to know and establish rapport with the noninstructional staff.
6. Maintain good records.
7. Stay up to date in your field through professional periodicals and meetings.
8. Support your profession.

EXERCISE 2.2   THE LIFE OF A FIRST-YEAR TEACHER

For discussion:

1. One 24-hour day in the life of a first-year teacher can be safely divided into four major categories:
   a. Time spent in actual classroom teaching.
   b. Time spent in reading papers, preparing lessons, and generally readying for classes.
   c. Time spent in noninstructional activities as found in the list of 25 responsibilities.
   d. Time spent in personal life task and maintenance functions.

   Have your class divide into small groups and have each group discuss and make a prediction of how much of a beginning teacher's (24-hour day, 7-day week) is spent in each of the four categories. Compare your group's predictions with those of other groups.

2. Visit some first-year teachers and ask them to give an estimate (in hours/day, hours/week) of how their time is spent in each of the four categories. Compare their estimates with your class predictions.

3. From the 25 responsibilities, list those you think you would enjoy doing the most; the least. Compare your list with others in the class. Which items on the list seem to be the most popular; the least?

4. See if your class can add items to the list of 25 noninstructional responsibilities of a classroom teacher.

CHART FOR EXERCISE 2.2

*Estimated Number of Hours Spent
in One Seven Day Week*

A. Time spent in clerical and maintenance functions
   1. attendance checking and reporting. . . . . _____
   2. preparation of budgets and schedules . . . . _____
   3. ordering, using, and maintaining AV materials and equipment . . _____
   4. ordering, using and maintaining textbook and curriculum
      materials and supplies . . . . _____
   5. other (specify) . . . . _____

B. Time spent advising, supervising, sponsoring
   6. supervision of halls, cafeteria, assemblies . . . . _____

7. supervision of homerooms and activity periods . . . . _____
8. supervision of intramural contests . . . . _____
9. advising and sponsoring student government . . . . _____
10. advising and sponsoring plays, concerts, other events and productions . . . . _____
11. support of athletic program (e.g., ticket taker, supervision, serving as scorer . . . . _____
12. sponsoring and arranging for guest speakers and campus visitors . . . . _____
13. advising, guiding, and counseling of students . . . . _____
14. responsibility for student safety . . . . _____
15. chaperoning student dances and bus trips . . . . _____
16. other (specify) . . . . _____
17. advising and sponsoring student class . . . . _____

C. Time spent in school-community activities
18. attendance-participation at PTA . . . . _____
19. attendance-participation in community events . . . . _____
20. supporting local bond issues . . . . _____
21. parent conferences . . . . _____
22. representing the school at social gatherings . . . . _____
23. establishing rapport with other adults (e.g., administrators, teachers, paraprofessionals, clerical and custodial staff) . . . . _____
23a. other (specify) . . . . _____

D. Time spent in professional activities
24. school and districtwide committee work . . . . _____
25. continued study and development in your field . . . . _____
26. support of professional associations, local, state and federal . . . . _____
27. other (specify) . . . . _____

E. Time spent in actual classroom instruction . . . . _____

F. Time spent in daily preparation for instruction . . . . _____
   includes lesson planning, paper reading, grading, preparing classrooms for instruction

QUESTIONS FOR CLASS DISCUSSION

1. In an interview for a secondary teaching position you are asked to express your philosophy of education/teaching. What would be your reply?
2. Have you ever been a student in an "open classroom?" Did you learn? Why, or why not?
3. Would you like to be a teacher of "open-structure teaching?" Why or why not? How would you have to change? How would you go about making those changes?
4. Does "openness" fit into the concept of "performance-based" teaching?
5. Have members of your group select items from the chapter that are difficult to achieve in teaching and prepare an analysis for discussion at the next class meeting.
6. Can you form an eclectic teaching philosophy of your own which would combine major ideas conveyed in this chapter?

7. Are there limits to the provisions that a teacher in your subject field can make for serendipity?
8. Is "openness" more a characteristic of private than public schools?
9. Do you believe that as a teacher you should encourage or allow students to call you by your first name?
10. How possibly can failure be viewed by a student as positive feedback?
11. How much are you willing to trust? To risk?

What Kinds of Styles and Patterns Shall I Look for in My Teaching? An Analysis

In Chapter 1 you analyzed and shared your perceptions of teaching strengths and areas for further improvement. In Chapter 2 we introduced information regarding what is sought in teaching–learning interactions. In Chapter 3 we present two distinct and consistently different teaching styles. Compare the teacher and student behaviors and use the dichotomy for small-group and class discussion. Suggested discussion questions follow.

Style A Teacher Behaviors

1. The teacher asks questions that require specific answers dependent upon prior knowledge.
2. The teacher discourages insightful jumps.
3. The teacher lectures on subject matter for entire period.
4. The teacher performs a demonstration, supplying the related principles.
5. The teacher is uncomfortable with silence.
6. The teacher puts problems in focus.
7. The teacher promotes competition.

Style A Student Behaviors

1. The learner seeks an authoritative answer to a problem.

Style B Teacher Behaviors

1. The teacher directs processes designed to facilitate students answering their own questions.
2. The teacher encourages insightful jumps; high serendipity.
3. The teacher lectures when students request more data. Minilectures are frequent.
4. The teacher may perform a demonstration, allowing the students to ask questions to facilitate their discovery of generalizations.
5. The teacher is comfortable with silence.
6. The teacher facilitates student focusing on problems.
7. The teacher facilitates cooperation.

Style B Student Behaviors

1. The learner seeks data to effect a solution to a problem; his experience and knowledge are largely self-appropriated.

Style A Student Behaviors	*Style B Student Behaviors*
2. The learner performs experiments about which he possesses prior knowledge of desired outcomes, conclusions, and generalizations.	2. The learner performs experiments with no prior knowledge of desired outcomes and forms his own conclusions and generalizations.
3. The learner reads about new subject matter previously presented by the teacher.	3. The learner realizes the importance of facts and reads to expand upon prior knowledge of principles, the formulation of which he has pursued actively.
4. The learner does not engage in free discussion with his peers.	4. The learner engages in free discussion of pertinent subjects with his peers, even on topics that involve morality, values, and ethics.
5. The learner is engaged in repetitive "drill" exercises.	5. The learner engages in drill when attempting to improve skills. More importantly, he knows the value of mistakes and shows confidence in trying "new" ways.
6. The learner is reluctant to suggest *his* ideas, to express *his* feelings.	6. The learner accepts and shares his own ideas and feelings.
7. The learner plays a passive role in his classroom environment.	7. The learner is an active participant in the development of a responsive classroom environment designed to facilitate the acquisition of data.

Style A above is what we call *didactic* and style B is *inquiry*. The didactic style is consistent with the delivery mode of strategy design. The inquiry style is consistent with an access mode. In the *delivery mode*, information is delivered to the learner, while in the *inquiry mode*, the learner is provided access to information. We believe that most teachers utilize the didactic style most of the time, and some others may be more eclectic in their style, utilizing behaviors from both columns.

In this chapter we do not intend to imply that one style is better than the other. We do believe that learners should be exposed to competent teachers of various styles, rather than to all didactic teachers. Consequently, we encourage you to explore the options we present in this and other chapters.

QUESTIONS FOR CLASS DISCUSSION

1. Can you describe in your own words what is meant by the term "teaching style"?
2. With which style (A or B) do you feel more comfortable as a teacher? As a student?
3. Could a competent teacher be legitimately eclectic in style?
4. Compare styles A and B with teachers you have had in the past. Where do most fit?
5. Can you fit the instructor of this course into one or the other style?
6. Does what you have learned from this chapter change any of your responses in Exercise 1.1?
7. Can a teacher's teaching style change? If so, what forces might affect this style change? (*Hint:* refer to Preface)
8. Are there likely to be differences between the styles of an art teacher and a mathematics teacher? What about a physical education teacher and an English teacher?
9. What reasons can you provide that might explain why inquiry teaching, as defined in this chapter, is not readily found in public secondary schools today?
10. When, if ever, should our teaching be designed to lead to divergent thinking?

EXERCISE 3.1 EXPLORING UNDERSTANDINGS OF YOUR OWN STYLES AND PATTERNS

Follow these steps:

1. Identify three questions that you have regarding material presented in this chapter.
2. Share these with members of your class.
3. Identify a final list of unanswered class questions.
4. With the help of your instructor and the Selected References on page 32 devise a plan for finding tentative answers to the questions identified in step three.

My questions:

1. _____

    _____

2. _____

    _____

3. _____

    _____

What Do I Know About Today's Secondary School Students? Toward a Better Understanding

Is there a discrepancy between what students do and learn in school and what they experience in the world outside school? Can you recall what your high school life was like? What was the quality of the relationship between you and your parents? What peer influences affected you most? What kinds of teachers did you have? How did they teach? Do you have a good understanding of today's youth and their views on the major issues in their world? In this section we present straightforward expressions by young people of their thoughts on school and society.

ABOUT VALUES AND INFLUENCES[1]

"We high school kids get pretty cynical. A lot of our values have been cracked. We're in a transitional period and we can't believe it all the way we used to. And one thing is for sure: our parents aren't our main influence anymore. Sometimes it seems like a battle—us kids against our parents. The influences are going to come from some place else now."

"I feel that during the junior high school years most parents want their children to learn and explore and grow. The marks are quite secondary. But during those final three years, parents get desperate about 'the right college,' and about the things they read about college admissions competitions in the papers and magazines. And the whole emphasis on marks and competition suddenly becomes dramatic and loaded with pressure."

[1] David Mallery, *High School Students Speak Out* (New York: Harper & Row, 1962), pp. 3 and 79. Reprinted by permission.

ABOUT SCHOOLS[2]

"We're out for a real drive on marks—the city tests and the national tests, not just the school tests."

"Yes, and we work for all it's worth."

"And so do the teachers!"

"You know, sometimes I wonder if it's really worth it, being in the advanced course and getting all this terrific pressure."

"Yes, you really have to convert yourself into a machine."

"Well, you wouldn't except for the school's neurotic obsession with college admissions and national tests."

"Who's the school, though? Is it the teachers or is it us?"

"It's both. But we're in the fight and they know it, and they know they have us over a barrel."

"The only way you can exist and actually grow as a human being in this setup is to convert yourself into a machine—no, a supermachine—so that you can knock off all the work, hit the high marks, and have time left over to think and question and explore."

"We figure that our class once had three social strata. I'd call them the Untouchables, the Middle Group, and the Upper Echelon (the Nobility). At least this was the way I saw it in the tenth grade. And I know, because I spent time in each group."

"Well, it was a matter of who went with whom, what kids you cut classes with, what teachers you were rude to, things like that."

ABOUT TEACHERS[3]

"I think there are three kinds of teachers: (1) the kind that teach the subject—really get it into you; (2) the kind that really make it interesting—tie it up with something you know about, seem to want you to care about it; and (3) the kind that put it in front of you—they don't care whether you get it or not—just put it on the blackboard and say Good luck!"

"The really influential teachers around here have a lot of status with the students. They are the teachers who seem to get into our thinking. The students influence each other in things like what clothes to wear and how to comb your hair and all that. But these teachers seem to be in on the big things."

"Mr. Sullivan in music—there's a marvelous man. He teaches us about life. I've got a whole new set of standards for myself because of being in his choir!"

"Miss Mahoney will stop and talk about things. Sometimes it's philosophical or it's about the way people behave. But it's interesting, you know what I mean. With some teachers it would be horrible—a real bore. But with her, it's good."

[2] *Ibid.*, p. 25 and p. 11.
[3] *Ibid.*, pp. 50, 47, 48.

"I have a math class—it's really something. The teacher once wanted to be a psychiatrist. I think he's a teacher because he likes people. He's really an interesting guy. It doesn't matter that he teaches math, particularly. Whatever he was teaching would be interesting."

"I know a teacher who could take the best book ever written and kill it dead as a doornail in one class period!"

ABOUT TESTS[4]

"We know what kind of testing there will be. We do our reading for the teacher's purposes, not ours. We can chase through those chapters, pamphlets, and articles, and crack the test. We know how to do that by now. Yet it's possible that you might really get involved in the thing for your own reasons and then God knows what you might do on the test. I guess the idea would be to be able to read for your own purposes AND for the teacher's, once you figure out what his purposes were. But it's easier to read just for the teacher's purposes—and the test's—they're the same. It's easier and it pays off."

ABOUT CLASS DISCUSSION[5]

"I like the student-to-student discussion better than the teacher drawing out the student. There is more freedom—you don't have to stick to the teacher's questions."

"We waste a lot of time in discussion. I wish the teacher would just cut it out and give it to us straight. It would save a lot of time."

"I get pretty lost when the teacher lectures. Like in science and mathematics, even though they're my best subjects. We talk more in English. You feel it matters more, as if you were important to the learning—as if your way of seeing things counted."

"We try to have discussions now and then, but you make a 30-second comment and the teacher gives a 10-minute development of it!"

"You know, in physics last week, it was really great. We got into a discussion of something, and we suddenly realized that there was no answer to the question we were talking about. We went on and talked about possibilities, about things we couldn't know yet, on the basis of the information we had now—and about things we needed to explore this century. And it was exciting to see that the teacher didn't know the answer—that he was talking about possibilities, about unknown regions, with us!"

Another Source of Insight

For greater understanding of what it's like to be a present-day high school student, the authors recommend reading *Inside High School* by Phillip A. Cusick (New York: Holt, Rinehart and Winston,

[4] *Ibid.*, p. 25.
[5] *Ibid.*, p. 49 and 19.

Inc., 1973). Mr. Cusick, in gathering data for this book, attended high school daily for a six-month period, went to class with the students, ate with them, took part in their formal and informal activities, became accepted by them and learned how they behaved, felt, and thought. His observations and thoughts are worthwhile reading for anyone who is considering teaching in the secondary school.

EXERCISE 4.1 ANALYZING YOUR OWN HIGH SCHOOL EXPERIENCES

We hope the foregoing has provided you with some realistic insights and viewpoints of secondary school students about their school and society. Although these were the expressions in the 1960s we still hear the same in the 1980s. Will they still be prevalent in the 1990s or in the year 2000?

How would you analyze your own high school experiences? Use the suggested format below for analysis and discussion.

WHAT I LIKED AND WHAT I DIDN'T LIKE ABOUT MY HIGH SCHOOL EDUCATION

What I Liked	*What I Didn't Like*
About Schools	
About Teachers	
About Friends	
About Parents	
About Tests	
About Class discussions, lab work, etc.	
About Rules and Regulations (School or class)	
Society in General	

EXERCISE 4.2 FURTHER INSIGHT DATA—SCHOOL VISIT

In many teacher-training institutions, a school or classroom visit is required of candidates prior to student teaching.

In case such a visit is not required or if you have not been in a public secondary school for a number of years, this exercise visit is intended to assist you in obtaining first-hand insight pertaining to today's secondary school students. Your objective for this exercise is to *visit a secondary school in your area,* perhaps more than one school, say a junior high school as well as a high school. Our suggestion for this exercise: use the format for Exercise 4.1 to interview students. Student teachers may ask their own students to respond to the questions. Share with other members of your class the results of your visit and observations.

QUESTIONS FOR CLASS DISCUSSION

1. What were your feelings about the dialogues of students as reported at the beginning of this chapter? How did the comments of those students compare with those of students you interviewed during your visit(s)?
2. Have the values of youth changed during the past decade? What is your evidence?
3. Who was the most influential teacher in your life? Why?
4. What factors in our society influence the values and behaviors of youth? Do teachers have an influence?
5. In a high school today what activities have the greatest positive influence upon a student? Which have the least?
6. Can you find evidence to support the feeling that your subject should be offered (or required) in the secondary school curriculum?
7. Are high school students today involved in any way in curriculum evolution?
8. What are the major purposes of secondary schools in this country? Are the schools accomplishing these purposes? What evidence is there of this?
9. Is there still a student-perceived emphasis on "marks and competition?" Do you believe the emphasis is too great or insufficient?
10. Do you believe students should be required to pass basic competency examinations prior to high school graduation? If yes, in which subjects?
11. Should non-English speaking students be taught in their native languages or should they be taught English first?

Selected References

Ausubel, David P., Joseph D. Novak, and Helen Hanesian. *Educational Psychology, A Cognitive View.* Second Edition. New York: Holt, Rinehart and Winston, Inc., 1978.

Butts, Freeman, R. *The School's Role as Moral Authority.* Association for Supervision and Curriculum Development. Washington D.C., 1977.

Cusick, Phillip A. *Inside High School.* New York: Holt, Rinehart and Winston, Inc., 1973.

Duck, Loyd. *Teaching with Charisma.* Allyn and Bacon Co., 1981.

Feldhusen, Erik. "Behavior in Secondary Schools," *Yearbook,* 1978, Part II. Washington D.C.: National Society for the Study of Education, 1979.

Henson, Kenneth T. *Secondary Teaching Methods.* D.C. Heath and Co., 1981.

Howes, Virgil M. *Informal Teaching in the Open Classroom.* New York: Macmillan Publishing Co., Inc., 1974.

Kellough, Richard D. *Developing Priorities and a Style: Selected Readings in Education for Teachers and Parents,* 2nd ed. New York: MSS Information Corp., 1974.

Lapp, Diane, Hilary Bender, Stephas Ellenwood, and Martha John. *Teaching and Learning: Philosophical, Psychological, and Curricular Applications.* New York: Macmillan Publishing Co., Inc., 1975.

LeFrancois, G.R. *Psychological Theories and Human Learning: Kongor's Report.* Monterey, California: Brooks/Cole, 1976.

Lucas, Christopher J. Challenge and Choice in *Contemporary Education: Six Major Ideological Perspectives.* Macmillan Publishing Co., Inc., 1976.

MacMillan, Donald L. *Behavior Modification in Education.* New York: Macmillan Publishing Co., Inc., 1973.

Novak, Joseph D. *A Theory of Education.* Ithica, New York: Cornell University Press, 1977.

Palardy, Michael J. *Teaching Today; Tasks and Challenges.* Macmillan Publishing Co., Inc., 1975.

Silvernail, David L. *Teaching Style as Related to Student Achievement.* Washington, D.C.: National Education Association, 1979.

Travers, Robert M.W. and Jacqueline Patricia Dillon. *The Making of a Teacher: A Plan for Professional Self-Development.* New York: Macmillan Publishing Co., Inc., 1975.

Van Til, William. *Secondary Education: School and Community.* Houghton Mifflin, 1978.

Wadsworth, Barry J. *Piaget for the Classroom Teacher.* New York: Longman, 1978.

Part II
Planning for Instruction

Our experience tells us that the competent teacher knows *what* he is going to teach, *why* he is going to teach, and *how* he is going to teach. Part II is designed to assist you in *organizing* the what and how of your teaching. Part III is concerned with implementation and specific teaching strategies, and is the largest portion of the book. However simple logic would tell us that organizational planning and knowledge of implementation strategies cannot be separated. Consequently, the reader is advised to become aware of the material in Part III as he pursues the activities of Part II.

Competent teachers plan carefully. They are willing to take risks and to be held accountable for what they are doing. There is no magic formula for how lesson plans should be done. We know that the most effective novice teachers give considerable thought to what they are going to do on a daily basis and to the nature of their long-range goals as well.

In this section we provide various plans and forms for short- and long-range planning. We are convinced from our own experiences that one of the reasons that some teachers have difficulty in lesson planning is that they do not clearly communicate their objectives to others. If students are confused as to what is to be done, they will not learn it well. There should be no secret regarding what the students are expected to know and what they should be able to do as a result of the instruction. In the past there have been too many classrooms in which the teacher played a guessing game with the students. The teacher had objectives in mind and kept them hidden from the students. The student that could guess best what these objectives were usually scored highest on the teacher's exams. We do not doubt that there are things taught in school for which no objectives could have been written. There is a strong possibility that on occasion the easiest time to write behavioral objectives is after the lesson has been taught. We want the new teacher to know how to write and to communicate good teacher *and* student objectives. We believe that the kind of learning that is most lasting is that which is self-appropriated, but we do not adhere to the belief that each and every one of us needs to discover everything for himself.

We wish to stress the importance of having the teacher provide concrete learning activities as frequently as possible, *of using the most abstract symbolization* (for example, verbal lectures and/or written symbols) *as infrequently as possible,* of providing experiences whereby all the senses are used, and of individualizing instruction to the greatest extent possible. For the latter we provide samples and instructions for developing self-instructional packages.

Why Plan?
The Need for Lesson Plans

Professionally minded teachers do not question the need to plan lessons but may differ to the *what* and *how* questions concerning the format of the plan itself. From a very realistic point of view, the *why* of a lesson plan can be considered from two standpoints: from the administrator's point of view and from the teacher's point of view.

A. From the administrator's point of view:
   1. To obtain evidence, especially from first-year teachers, of a teacher's ability to prepare a professional teaching plan.
   2. To evaluate how well a teacher can prepare and implement a plan in actual teaching situations. (See the sample forms in Section D of Chapter 17).
   3. To use the plan as a guide for substitute teachers, especially when the need for a long-term substitute is anticipated.

B. From the teacher's point of view:
   1. To visualize and prepare oneself in terms of *what* instructional activities to emphasize and *how* they should be directed.
   2. To avoid "instant planning," "impromptu," or "off-the-cuff" teaching, which, because it lacks a good foundation, often results in poor teaching.
   3. To use as future reference; to reinforce the strengths and improve the weaknesses revealed in the previous plan and the teaching of it.
   4. To earn respect from the students for the fact that the teacher prepares his work.
   5. To insure coherence with respect to content.

EXERCISE 5   LESSON PLANNING PRETEST

Instructions: Without looking ahead to subsequent chapters, we ask you to list five major components of a daily lesson plan.

1. _____

2. _____

3. _____

4. _____

5. _____

Now look at the suggested inclusions inverted at the bottom of this page. How did you do? The chapters that follow will aid you in planning for your teaching. But before you can plan you need to know how one decides what to teach. Chapter 6 will provide this information.

Did you include the following? objectives; set induction; lesson content procedure with time planning; closure; materials and audio-visual needs.

6

Where Do I Discover What I Should Teach? Resources for Instructional Planning

SOURCE I—TO DISCOVER WHAT ONE SHOULD TEACH:[1]

1. The new teacher talks with other professionals. (a) He learns what the school presumably expects him to teach, and (b) he considers the nature of the students he is to teach and something of the community in which they live.
2. He examines available school and other public documents for traditional, legal, and ethical obligations. These are discussed in Source II.
3. He probes and analyzes his own knowledge, nature, and convictions.
4. He thinks through his own philosophy of education; that is, why do we have schools and teachers?
5. He reshapes his thinking and begins to translate it into assimilable elements by expressing things in terms of behavior.
6. He arranges for learning in depth, emphasizes that learning should lead to more learning, endeavors to make certain that goals and content have intrinsic motivational value, and weighs the issues of education versus indoctrination.
7. He learns that working out what he should teach in his classroom is a process which parallels that followed in long-range curriculum development.

SOURCE II—RESOURCE UNIT MATERIALS

Resource unit materials are also called curricular documents; these include almost any resource materials teachers can use such as courses of study, curriculum guides, curriculum handbooks, teaching guides, and learning activity packages. These materials can be located in the school district office and/ or in individual schools. Your university library may have a collection. Ask your instructor.

[1] H. Orville Nordberg, James M. Bradfield, and William C. Odell, *Secondary School Teaching* (New York: Macmillan, 1962), p. 60. Reprinted by permission.

Common Ingredients of Curriculum Resource Units:

1. An introduction or a statement about the educational philosophy of the school that corresponds with that of the community.
2. Objectives for the courses: Some schools list general goals and specific instructional objectives or teacher objectives and student objectives separately. Some schools designate this area as Educational Outcomes or Expected Learning Outcomes.
3. Topics, units, or areas of study are listed indicating approximate time allotment, scope (how much coverage), and sequence (in what order).
4. A statement about provisions for individual differences, grouping system, alternative plans for differentiated learning, and facilities for learning are introduced. Some administrative guidelines to facilitate these provisions may be included here.
5. Suggested activities, procedures, or methods for each topic or segment of subject-matter units are outlined.
6. Instructional aids or resources that are available within or outside of the school are listed. Materials include audio-visual media, primary texts and supplemental materials, game materials, laboratory equipment, tools and machines, guest speakers and community resources, etc.
7. Evaluation procedures, progress report outlining kinds of tests (subjective, objective, pre- and post-test), distribution of weights, grading policy, report cards, etc., are stated here. In the context of these dimensions, evaluations of the student's habits, attitudes, participation, and progress made are also included.

EXERCISE 6.1 CURRICULUM GUIDES SURVEY

Obtain from your library or from a public school several copies of curriculum guides or courses of study that include the subject(s) you are preparing to teach. Examine how closely they follow the curricular elements listed under Source II above and analyze the strengths and weaknesses of each document. You will gain new ideas as to what you can teach and what you are expected to teach. Compare documents in similar subject fields from various school districts.

Use the following format for recording your survey:

Name/Title of Document: _____

School/School District: _____

Year Written/Published: _____

I. Does the document contain the following elements?

		Yes	*No*
1.	Statement of Educational Philosophy	( )	( )
2.	Course Objectives	( )	( )
3.	Arrangement of Topics, Units w/time allotment suggested	( )	( )
4.	Provisions for individual differences, Grouping, Alternative Plans, etc.	( )	( )
5.	Suggested Activities. Procedures, Methods and Approaches	( )	( )
6.	Instructional Aids and Resources (Texts, Audio-visuals, Game Materials, Lab Facilities)	( )	( )
7.	Evaluation Procedures (Report Cards, Grading Policy, Testing)	( )	( )

II. A. Does this document help you find what the school expects you to teach or what you can plan to teach? If so, identify them.

   B. If the document does not help you, what are some of the improvements to be made? Identify them.

EXERCISE 6.2   TEXTS AND TEACHER'S MANUAL SURVEY

Secondary school textbooks are often accompanied by a teacher's manual or teacher's edition, which contains specific objectives, methods, approaches, activities, and some test items.

Instructions

1. Select one or two high school textbooks for your teaching field(s) that are accompanied by a teacher's edition or manual. Frequently these are obtainable from the textbook section of the curriculum materials center in the college or university library.
2. If there are no standard textbooks available for your teaching field, then select a field in which there is a possibility you might teach. Beginning teachers are often assigned to teach in more than a single field.
3. Examine the contents of the books following the guidelines suggested below:

Author: _____

Name/Title: _____

Publisher: _____

Year: _____

		Yes	No
I.	Does the manual contain the following?		
A.	Specific goals/objectives/concepts for which the lessons are developed,	( )	( )
B.	Units/lessons systematically developed with suggested time allotment and some provisions for individual differences,	( )	( )
C.	Suggested activities which include motivational techniques, methods of teaching and approaches,	( )	( )
D.	Media utilization for teaching aids and resource materials (A–V, lab, teacher references), and	( )	( )
E.	Specific guidelines for measurement and evaluation of the lessons.	( )	( )
II.	Would you use this text and the teacher's manual for teaching your subject?	( )	( )

Your reasons: _____

_____

_____

_____

_____

EXERCISE 6.3 STATE CURRICULUM FRAMEWORK

Find out if your State Department of Education publishes a curricular *framework* for your subject field. Addresses are located on page 271 of this text. If a state framework exists we suggest that you obtain a copy, for it will specify the content to be taught in your field. Other useful information may also be found.

Some of the State Frameworks found in the state of California, for example, are:

The Social Sciences Education Framework for California Public Schools
Art Education Framework
Bilingual-Bicultural Education and English-as-a-Second Language Education: A Framework for Elementary and Secondary Schools
Drama/Theatre Framework for California Public Schools
English Language Framework for California Public Schools
Foreign Language Framework for California Public Schools
Framework for Health Instruction in California Public Schools
Mathematics Framework for California Public Schools
Music Framework for California Public Schools
Physical Education Framework for California Public Schools
Framework in Reading for the Elementary and Secondary Schools of California
Science Framework for California Public Schools

SUMMARY OF CHAPTER 6

A teacher's decisions as to what to teach are guided by:

1. State curriculum documents.
2. District curriculum documents.
3. Local school courses of study.
4. The individual teacher's best thinking.
5. The nature and the ability of the students.

After discovering what you are expected to teach comes the process of preparing the plans. Chapter 7 will guide you through this planning process.

7

How Do I Go About Making Lesson Plans? Unit and Lesson Planning Forms and Illustrations

Before you begin to work on a specific unit plan or on a daily lesson plan, you need to understand the following elements of instructional planning.

Range	Units	Definitions/Descriptions	Illustrations
Long range	Resource unit	Curriculum guides, courses of study, or teacher's guide written by the state, school district, or the subject-matter department outlining recommended contents, approaches or procedures for each subject for the whole school year.	California Social Studies Framework: San Juan Unified School District Courses of Study: Ethnic Contributions—Detroit Public Schools; *Land of the Free* (Teacher's Manual); *Drug Decisions* (Teacher's Guide).
Intermediate	Teaching unit (unit plan)	Teacher-made plan for a given unit based on the suggested outline in the resource unit; study guide or worksheets, which include reference materials, projects, assignments, and the like; unit duration varies depending on the topic, the ability, and interest of students	See sample unit plans on pages that follow.
Immediate (short range)	Daily unit (daily lesson)	Teacher-made lesson plan for each day based on the teaching unit above	See sample daily plans on pages that follow.

FORMS

There is no single best form of lesson plan for all teachers. You can make your own intelligent and practical choice from the forms presented in this section ranging from lecture lessons to performance lessons. In selecting a form, you should keep in mind (1) the subject or content you want to teach, (2) the methods or approaches you are considering using, and (3) the interest and ability of your students. With these factors in mind, you should:

1. Know what you are expected to teach by consulting the "course of study" within the school district where employed.
2. Prepare long range plans for the course. Samples are provided throughout this chapter.
3. Prepare a unit plan for the course you intend to teach. Samples are provided in this chapter as shown on page 45.

EXERCISE 7.1   UNIT PLAN PREPARATION

Instructions:

Prepare a unit plan for the course you intend to teach. Samples are provided in this chapter.

DAILY LESSON PLANNING

As you prepare your first daily lesson plan keep in mind three key ingredients: the set induction, the lesson itself, and your closure. These are identified as follows:

1. *Set induction:* This is what you do at the very outset of the lesson to set the mood for the day. Your set induction sets the climate, motivation, or whatever you want to call it. A joke to lighten the anxiety or a period of role-playing to set the scene prior to a lesson of reading the novel *Lord of the Flies* may be in order. The set induction may be used for only a few minutes or for an entire period, but it is important to consider and prepare it for each day and for each new lesson.
2. *The lesson:* This is the content. Here you must consider not only what you want to teach but how best to do it—your methods and strategies.
3. *The closure:* This is the summary or wrap-up, in which you make sure that each student has learned. It compliments the set induction.

Give as much consideration to the preparation of your set induction and closure as you do to the lesson itself. This will help you to bring the lesson together for the students to insure their learning. Prepare each lesson as carefully as if you were a surgeon preparing for an operation or a trial lawyer preparing a court case.

Daily Lesson Plans

Experienced teachers often use the short form or lesson plan book (layout) as shown on page 46.

Conventional Unit Plan Form

Grade: _____ Course/Subject: _____ Teacher: _____

Unit Topic: _____ Duration: _____

1. *Introduction:* State briefly the nature and scope of the unit; include the significance or justification of the problems, concepts, issues, skills, or activities that will be specified in the unit.

2. *Instructional Objectives:* (anticipated outcomes stated in behavioral or performance terms— cognitive, psychomotor and affective):
   a. What do I, the teacher, expect the students to accomplish?
   b. What changes in the students' behavior do I intend to bring about?
   c. What would each student be doing which would demonstrate that he has achieved the objective?

3. *Unit Content Problem/Concept/Skills:*
   a. When and what am I going to teach or do? (Dates and topics)
   b. List the topics, subtopics, problems, concepts, issues, information, or skills involved.
   c. The activities should be identified and an approximate time indicated for each (e.g. 1 week, 2 sessions).

4. *Procedures/Activities/Approaches/Methods:*
   a. How am I going to teach?
   b. Instructional procedures to be used should be identified; informal lecture, discussion (large or small groups), oral or written reports, panel or committee work, audiovisual activities, educational games, guest speaker, field trip, and so on.

5. *Instructional Aids or Resources:*
   a. List the materials or equipment that you will need.
   b. List all materials that the students will need except conventional teaching aids such as chalk, chalkboard, and pencil and paper.
   c. Identify the textbook or reference materials in a standard bibliographical form (author, title, publisher, and year published).

6. *Evaluation:*
   a. In what ways am I going to measure and evaluate the students' progress or achievement?
   b. How am I going to find out whether or not I have achieved the stated objectives?
   c. How am I going to find out whether I have successfully communicated with the students?
   d. What evaluation devices could I use besides quizzes, tests and classroom participation?

CONVENTIONAL LESSON PLAN—SHORT FORM

Grade: _Junior_   Subject: _English literature_   Teacher: _Walter_

Date	Learnings	Materials Needed	Procedures	Evaluations
Mon.	Introduction to Hemingway Biographical sketch	Biography of American novelists	Lecture	—
Tues.	Read *The Old Man and the Sea*, Parts I and II, pp. 15–40.	Textbook	Silent reading	A quiz?
Wed.	Discussion of Parts I and II	—	Open discussion	—
Thurs.	Movie: *The Old Man and the Sea*	Movie	Smith's class will join	—
Fri.	Test on Parts I and II	—	—	—

Novice teachers may also use the short form after they have familiarized themselves with the mechanics of the standard form that follows and have successfully demonstrated the ability to implement the plan in teaching. The standard form may be filled out as shown in the following:

Conventional Daily Lesson Plan—Long Form

Date: _____ Grade Level: _____ Teacher: _____

Subject: _____ Unit Topic: _____

Topic for this lesson: _____

1. *Instructional objectives:* Approximately the same as stated in the unit plan except that the objectives here should be for this lesson exclusively.

2. *Contents:* Major problems, concepts, skills, or activities to be taught or demonstrated for this lesson.

3. *Procedure* (progression of the lesson, but not necessarily in the following order):
   a. Introduction or motivation: How do you plan to begin or motivate the learners?
   b. Major activities: What do the teacher and students do?
   c. What questions would you ask to clarify the problem or to promote further learning? (summary or conclusion)
   d. How do you plan to close the lesson? (summary or conclusion)
   e. Assignment: What would students do to review the lesson for today or to prepare the lesson for tomorrow?

4. *Instructional Materials and Resources:* Approximately the same as illustrated in the unit plan except that the materials and aids here are for this lesson only.

5. *Evaluation:* A brief statement about whether or not the teacher has accomplished the objectives stated for this lesson. Self-evaluation or evaluation by someone else in terms of strengths and points for improvement, based on this lesson.
   a. What did I do well?
   b. What could have been done better?
   c. Classroom routine/management—discipline/group control.
   d. Adequate activities—materials used? Meet the needs of the class?
   e. Timing: Too fast—too slow?

The Modified Lesson Plan forms that follow are for your consideration depending upon your subject for teaching, type of activities, and assignments for your students. Review each form and choose the one that will best serve your instructional purposes. You need not use the same form throughout the unit.

MODIFIED LESSON PLAN I: LECTURE LESSON
For any subject for which the lecture method
(formal or informal lecture) is used primarily.

Grade: _____   Subject: _____

Date: _____   Teacher: _____

Unit Topic: _____

Topic for this lesson: _____

Instructional objectives: _____

_____

_____

_____

Introduction or motivation: _____

_____

_____

_____

Outline of problems, issues, or events: _____

_____

_____

_____

Examples, Definitions, or Analogies: _____

_____

_____

_____

Summary or Conclusion: _____

_____

_____

_____

MODIFIED LESSON PLAN II: DISCUSSION LESSON
For any subject (social studies especially) for which the discussion is the major activity of the lesson.

Grade: _____   Subject: _____

Date: _____   Teacher: _____

Unit topic: _____

Topic for this lesson: _____

Instructional objectives: _____

_____

_____

Procedures for discussion: _____

_____

Key questions:

1. _____

   Possible answers: _____

   _____

   Summary: _____

   _____

2. _____

   Possible answers _____

   _____

   Summary: _____

   _____

Conclusions: _____

_____

MODIFIED LESSON PLAN III: PROBLEM-SOLVING LESSON
For any subjects (especially science) for which the problem-solving, critical-thinking, or the inquiry method is used primarily.

Grade: _____ Subject: _____

Date: _____ Teacher: _____

Topic for this lesson: _____

_____

Instructional objectives: _____

_____

_____

Procedures or steps:

1. Problem identification: _____

_____

2. Acquisition of data or materials: _____

_____

3. Formulation of hypothesis or assumption(s): _____

_____

4. Analysis of data or materials: _____

_____

5. Testing hypotheses or assumptions: _____

_____

6. Conclusion or judgment: _____

_____

MODIFIED LESSON PLAN IV: PERFORMANCE LESSON
For performance subjects (physical education, art, music,
typing, speech, industrial arts, etc.) for which the mastery
of skill is the primary objective.

Grade: _____ Subject: _____

Date: _____ Teacher: _____

Topic for this lesson: _____

Instructional objectives: _____

_____

_____

_____

Skills to be learned: _____

_____

_____

_____

Specific teaching points: _____

_____

_____

_____

Materials or equipment needed: _____

_____

_____

_____

Unit and Daily Lesson Plan—Illustration[1]

Grade: __8th__   Course/Subject: __Social Studies__   Teacher: __Therese Feeney__

Unit Topic: __The Energy Crisis and Your Environment__   Unit Duration: __5 days__

Introduction:

Americans today are realizing that the nation has been facing an environmental and energy problem since the 1950s. To combat these problems, several measures have been implemented. With these in mind, this five-day unit will focus on the following:

a. The students will identify the general nature of the energy crisis and how it has influenced their world.
b. The students will be able to compare and contrast personal ideas and opinions about the energy crisis with classmates, the teacher and the guest speaker.
c. The students will be able to initiate and evaluate the energy-saving device that they set up in their homes.

Day 1: Objectives and Activities

a. The students are asked to define the term energy crisis in their own words (content).
b. Students will tell the class what they have heard and/or know about energy crisis (content).
c. The students are asked to list ten terms they might use to describe oil companies, and place a plus sign next to each term which has a positive connotation, a minus sign next to each negative term, and a zero next to each term that is neutral. The results are tabulated on the chalkboard totaling the plus, minus and zero symbols. They are then asked to analyze their results and write a paragraph explaining what the exercise reveals about their own attitudes towards oil companies (inquiry).

Day 2: Objectives and Activities

a. The students will openly discuss the ways in which the energy is used in their homes (content).
b. The students will decide on an appropriate energy-saving device for their homes (decision-making).
c. Students will be able to decide in their own minds what energy-saving devices that they like and might use in their future in their community (inquiry).

Day 3: Objectives and Activities

a. The class will have the opportunity to hear about the need for conservation from a State Official, a guest speaker (content).

[1] Therese A. Feeney, unpublished material, 1981. Reprinted by permission.

b. The students will be able to ask questions about the energy crisis and other areas of concern that the guest speaker is able to answer and explain (inquiry).

Day 4: Objectives and Activities

a. The students will be able to critique and apply the lecture presented by the guest speaker to what they are studying in class and at home while carrying out an energy-saving program (content).
b. The students will be able to evaluate the information and experience the guest speaker shared with the class. They will also make suggestions that they can use in their home projects and in their future contacts in the real world (inquiry).
c. Through the use of the simulation game (Recycling the Resources) the students will be able to express their own feelings, emotions and values when placed in the various roles within the context of the game (valuing).

Day 5: Objectives and Activities

a. The students will listen carefully to their fellow classmates when they explain and discuss their home energy-saving devices (content).
b. Students will do the follow-up exercise which essentially involves the comparison of history with the energy crisis and conservation (inquiry).

Reading Assignments

1. Go to the library and consult the book reviews of the following books: *Silent Spring* by Rachel Carson and *The Quiet Crisis* by Stuart L. Udall.

    After reading the reviews you are asked to decide if the book would be worth your while to read. Does it appear to relate to our topic of discussion this week?

or

2. Review the section in your textbook about the Native Americans. Then tell me if you think they had a drastic so-called "energy crisis" in their time.

Evaluation

1. The homework from Day 1. (10% of your grade)
2. Group participation and sportsmanship (15% of your grade). It will basically measure how well you work with your fellow classmates and how cooperative you are within the group setting.
3. The Home Energy-Saving Project (50% of your grade). This is based on the fact that you decide on a certain project and then set it up within your home environment. Lastly, you will be asked to explain your project to the class and turn in a brief summary.
4. The follow-up exercise (25% of your grade).

UNIT AND DAILY LESSON PLAN—ILLUSTRATION[2]

Unit Plan

Subject: _____Biology_____   Teacher: _____D. Grobman_____

Unit Topic: _____Microorganisms—Viruses and Bacteria_____

Text: _____Biological Science, An Inquiry Into Life_____

Topics	Time Estimates in Periods	Learning Activities
A. Viruses		
1. Discovery	$\frac{2}{5}$	T lectures
2. Electron microscope	$\frac{3}{5}$	Ss read Chapter 9 in class and complete at home.
3. Structure	1	Lab—Inquiry 9–1 Microbiological techniques.
4. Life Cycle	1	Lab—Inquiry 9–2 A disease of bacteria.
5. Diseases	$\frac{3}{5}$	Oral participation, Q/A on previous labs.
	$\frac{2}{5}$	T goes over Quiz questions for tomorrow, Ss read and study for Quiz.
6. Review	$\frac{3}{5}$	Written Quiz.
	$\frac{2}{5}$	Ss Oral Q/A at end of Chapter 9. Ss to read Chapter 10 at home.
7. Epidemic—Bubonic Plague	$\frac{1}{10}$	T explains approach and assigns groups.
Occurrence Today	$\frac{1}{10}$	Role-playing by students. T conducts Q/A on results.
B. Bacteria		
1. Discovery	$\frac{1}{5}$	T lectures on Chapter 10.
	$\frac{1}{10}$	T introduces Lab—Inquiry 10–1. Distribution of Microorganisms.
	$\frac{7}{10}$	Ss work on lab.
2. Structure		
3. Shapes		

[2] Deborah Grobman, unpublished material, 1981. Reprinted by permission.

Topics	Time Estimates in Periods	Learning Activities
4. Reproduction Growth, Colonies	1	Ss do lab—Inquiry 10–2. Staining and observing Bacterial cells.
5. Cultures	$\frac{9}{10}$	Ss work on Labs—Inquiry 11–1.
6. Diseases		Descendents of a single cell and inquiry 11–2 War on bacteria.
	$\frac{1}{10}$	Q/A on quiz tomorrow.
7. Evaluation	1	Written quiz.

Unit Plan for Microorganisms—Viruses and Bacteria

OBJECTIVES AND SAMPLE TEST ITEMS

Instructional Objectives	*Test item*
A. Viruses	
1. Describe the discovery.	What is the piece of equipment that made it possible to study viruses?
2. State evidence for the hypothesis that viruses are similar to the earliest forms of life.	Propose a theory explaining why viruses could not have been the first life on earth.
3. Identify the structure of a virus.	Draw and label the parts representing a typical virus.
4. Diagram the reproductive cycle of a virus.	Draw and label the stages in reproductive cycle of a virus.
5. Explain how a virus infects and affects another living cell.	Predict what would happen when a virus enters a healthy cell.
6. Identify equipment used in dealing with micro-organisms.	Given various pieces of lab equipment: microscope, petri dishes, agar, inoculating loop, etc., identify each item and state its use.
7. List aseptic techniques in handling and growing microorganisms.	List aseptic techniques in handling and growing microorganisms.
8. State diseases caused by viruses, their prevention, and cure.	What are some of the diseases caused by viruses. Do these have cures? How can you be protected against them?
9. Postulate the occurrence of a viral epidemic happening today.	See Lesson Plan that follows.
10. Describe the discovery of bacteria.	List several conditions under which bacteria survive. What helps them survive these conditions?

(continued)

Instructional Objectives	*Test item*
11. Identify the structure of a generalized bacterium.	Given a diagram of a generalized bacterium, label the parts.
12. Identify 3 bacterial shapes.	Shown various bacteria, classify each according to correct shape.
13. List the principal steps of the Lederberg-Tactum experiments of the effects of X-rays on bacteria.	List the principal steps of the Lederberg-Tactum experiments of the effects of X-rays on bacteria.
14. Explain the transforming principle.	Fill in the partially completed chart on transduction in bacteria.
15. Explain Koch's postulates.	State Koch's postulates in your own terms.
16. List ways bacteria benefit us.	Name several ways man benefits from bacteria.

A Daily Lesson

Unit Topic—*Microorganisms, Viruses and Bacteria*
Topic for this lesson—*Plague today, A reality?*
Class/Period—Biology 10, Period 4

Instructional Objectives

1. Postulate the occurrence of a viral epidemic happening today.
2. Identify the steps leading to the identification of the disease.
3. Explain the difference between bubonic and pneumonic plague.
4. State the animal vectors of the disease.
5. Recall and state symptoms of the plague.
6. List the defense systems of the body.
7. Trace the spread of the epidemic.
8. Propose the procedures for containment and elimination of the plague.
9. Criticize the public's reaction to the epidemic.

Routines:

1. Take attendance via seating chart as students enter.

Content Item	Special Material or Equipment	Instructional Strategies	Feedback Strategies		Time Est.
			Get	*Give*	
Recall concept of viruses, pathogens		T reviews Chapter 9 and conducts Q/A on viruses and diseases. "How many cases of Bubonic Plague were there in U.S. this year, 10 years ago, 50 years ago, and 100 years ago?" "Can viral diseases be controlled?"		Ss raise hands to answer. T calls on several to confirm replies.	5 min.
Bubonic Plague is thought to be a disease of the past. Is this a true statement?		T explains that the class will be simulating an outbreak of Bubonic Plague in New York City. T breaks Ss up into groups and assigns each for role-playing.			

(continued)

57

58

Content Item	Special Material or Equipment	Instructional Strategies	Feedback Strategies		Time Est.
			Get	Give	
	Prepared profiles on specific roles: 1. Initial single plague victim. 2. Police-found victim and try to trace where it was contracted.	T hands out character sketches to each group and asks for questions.	T takes straw vote to confirm understanding of assignment.	Ss break into groups and ask questions.	5 min.
Role-playing cont.	3. Health Dept. and Disease prevention and control. 4. People victim contacted. 5. Nurses and Doctors associated with the case. Try to trace victims contacts. 6. Government officials: Mayor, etc.		Tour and look for errors. Answers Qs.	Ss start working in groups and try to solve their particular problem.	30–40 min.
Comparing results and generalizing in their cases.		T leads Q/A on class results. T asks for class agreement of proposed actions of the various T shares group progress with class.	T writes results on board. T takes straw vote.	Ss respond and vote on feasibility of each groups conclusions.	5 min.
Relating a similar model.		T relates the theory proposed by Gwyneth Cravens and John S. Marr in *The Black Death*, a novel.	T asks Ss to list the similarities and differences and to justify their theory.	Ss discuss the results. T confirms correct proposals. T praises thoughtful responses.	5 min.
Look ahead		T instructs Ss to work on the write-up of the results of their groups and the classes activity.	Compliment class on good work of today (to extent this proves true)	Ss write their parts up and bring to class the next day.	5 min.

If the Role-playing part of the lesson takes longer than the time allotted, the remainder of the lesson plan can be carried over to the next class period and finished then.

Unit and Daily Lesson Plan—Illustration[3]

Subject: _____Spanish 4_____ Teacher: _____Gloria Rodriguez_____

Unit Topic: _____The Uses of *Ser* and *Estar*_____ Unit Duration: ____8 days____

1. *Introduction: Ser* and *estar* are verbs which both mean "to be." These two verbs, however, are widely different in their concepts, and they can never be interchanged without a basic change of meaning. It is important that a student automatically know when to use these two verbs, considering the frequency with which they are used in the language. This unit is designed as an extensive review of the uses of these two verbs.

2. *Instructional Objectives:*
   The student will be able to:
   a. Identify the rules governing the uses of *ser* and *estar*.
   b. Complete substitution and fill-in oral and written drills involving the uses of the two verbs.
   c. Translate correctly the English sentences containing forms of "to be" into their Spanish equivalents.
   d. Spell correctly the vocabulary words presented in the chapter.
   e. Compose short oral presentation correctly using the new vocabulary and using the correct forms of *ser* and *estar*.

3. *Content Outline:*
   a. Read and discuss the *Enfoque* at the beginning of the chapter (3 days).
      1. New vocabulary words (Estudio de vocabulario).
      2. Topic for discussion (the law).
   b. *Estructura* (3 days).
      1. General view of *ser* and *estar*.
      2. *Ser* and *estar* with adjectives.
      3. Other uses of *ser* and *estar*.
   c. Read and give presentations on *"Creación"* to reinforce vocabulary words and grammatical concepts (2 days).

4. *Procedures/Activities:*
   a. Read and discuss *"Enfoque-Usted y la ley."*
   b. Handouts on vocabulary words to be learned and *ser* and *estar* drills.
   c. Have students prepare short oral presentations about their opinions and solutions to the situations given in the *"Creación"*

5. *Instructional Aids or Resources:*
   a. Zenia Sacks da Silva, *On with Spanish*, Harper & Row, 1977.
   b. Handouts on *ser/estar* drill.

6. *Evaluation.*
   a. Student's answers to oral and written homework drills.
   b. Content of student's oral presentation.
   c. Vocabulary quiz.
   d. Unit test.

[3] Gloria Rodriguez, unpublished material, 1981. Reprinted by permission.

Daily Lesson Plan

Grade: ___12___ Subject: ___Spanish 4___

Unit Topic: ___The Uses of *Ser* and *Estar*___ Topic for this lesson: ___Other Uses of *Estar*___

1. *Instructional Objectives:*
   The student will:
   a. Complete the exercises, both oral and written, on the uses of *ser* and *estar* with a minimum of teacher help.
   b. Identify circumstances other than those already studied in which the verb *estar* is used.

2. *Assignment:*
   Finish worksheet. Read "Creación" on pp. 148–149 and be prepared to discuss in class.

3. *Procedure:*
   a. Review previously learned uses of *ser* and especially *estar*.
   b. Review homework on "Other uses of *ser*."
   c. Explain other uses of *ser*.
   d. Give oral drills, including Ejercicio 1 (drill on other uses of *ser*).
   e. Have class work on worksheet in class.

4. *Instructional materials:*
   On with Spanish text, ditto.

5. *Evaluation:*
   Student answers to homework, performance on drills and on worksheet.

Unit and Daily Lesson Plan—Illustration[4]

Grade: ___7th___ Course: ___English___ Teacher: ___Ms. Sue Morgan___

Unit Topic: ___How to Correctly Punctuate With Commas___

Duration: ___Three weeks; two sessions each week___

1. *Introduction:* The purpose of this unit is to introduce the correct use of the comma through student application of the comma use rules found in the grammar text to practice sentence exercises, assigned literature readings, and most importantly, to their own writing.

2. *Instructional Objectives:*
   a. Students will correctly punctuate with commas in test exercises and passages with at least 70% accuracy.
   b. Students will correctly punctuate with commas in their own writing compositions with at least 80% accuracy.
   c. Students will recognize the value of correct comma use to produce clear and comprehensible writing.

[4] Sue Morgan, unpublished material, 1981. Reprinted by permission.

3. *Unit Content Concepts:*
   a. Comma use in specific occasions (Rules 1–6). Two class sessions.
   b. Comma use to separate words in direct address (Rules 7–10). One class session.
   c. Comma use to separate appositives. (Rule 11) One Class session.
   d. Comma use in compound and complex sentences. (Rules 13–15) Two class sessions.

4. *Procedures:*
   a. Students complete pre-test of ten sentences (Grammar text, p. 19).
   b. Students write descriptive compositions, letters, narrative paragraphs and a dialogue.
   c. Informal lectures introducing comma use rules.
   d. Students practice sentence and paragraph exercises orally and in writing.
   e. Students edit classmates' compositions.
   f. Class discussion of application of comma rules to the practice exercises and to student compositions.

5. *Aids:*
   a. Text: Dawson, Elwell, Johnson, and Zollinger, *Language for Daily Use,* Silver Level (New York, Harcourt Brace Jovanovich, Inc., 1973).
   b. Students' compositions.
   c. Dittoes of sentence and paragraph exercises.
   d. Overhead projector.

6. *Evaluation:* Three objective tests and three student compositions
   a. Pre-test: Ten test sentences; One student-written letter
   b. Midterm: Review of comma use skills, rules 1–10.
   c. Final: Review of comma use skills, rules 1–15.
   d. Writing: Narrative paragraph, Descriptive paragraph, and Dialogue

Lesson Plan—Daily

Subject: ___English___   Unit Topic: ___Correct Comma Use___

Lesson Topic: ___How to Use Commas to Separate Words or Phrases Within a Series___

1. *Instructional Objectives:*
   a. Students will apply the comma use skill requiring the separation of items in a series by commas to their classmates' descriptive paragraphs.
   b. From the above editing activity, the students will recognize the need for proper comma use to achieve sentence clarity in their own writing.

2. *Contents:*
   a. Teacher explanation of the comma rule.
   b. Examples.
   c. Practice application of rule with sentence exercises.
   d. Application of rule to student writing.
   e. Group review for correction.

3. *Motivation:*
Reading and editing their classmates' writing will stimulate the students' interest and appreciation for the value of this lesson.

4. *Procedure:* Teacher will:
   a. Give short lecture introducing grammar rule regarding comma use within a series of words or phrases.
   b. Lecture using test examples and exercises displayed on the overhead projector.
   c. Assign ditto of three student paragraphs and request the class to edit the paragraphs for proper comma use within items of a series. Paragraphs done day before.
   d. Lead class discussion of the correct answers to Exercise D. Stress to the class that commas are necessary to produce clear, easily understood sentences.

5. *Instructional Aids and Materials:*
   a. Overhead projector.
   b. Copy of grammar text for each student.
   c. Student copies of classmates' descriptive paragraphs.

6. *Evaluation:* Objective Test:
   a. Given two descriptive passages from two already assigned short stories, in which the commas between series of items have been removed. Students will correctly punctuate with commas with at least 70% accuracy.

Unit and Daily Lesson Plans—Illustration[5]

Grade: ___7 and 8___   Subject: ___Art (ceramic)___

Unit Topic: ___Forming clay—hand building___   Duration: ___three weeks___

1. *Introduction*
   The purpose of this unit is to acquaint the students with the methods of forming clay through hand-building techniques.

2. *Behavioral Objectives:*
   a. The students will be able to name five different techniques for forming clay with the hands.
   b. The students will be able to demonstrate forming clay over objects to create an interior form.
   c. The students will be able to demonstrate forming clay inside objects to create an exterior form.
   d. The students will be able to demonstrate creating a form by pushing objects into the clay.
   e. The students will be able to demonstrate creating a form using hand-rolled clay coils.
   f. The students will be able to demonstrate creating a form using clay slabs.

3. *Content Outline:*
   a. Using objects to create a form with clay (1st week)
      (1) Forming clay over objects (2 sessions).
      (2) Forming clay inside objects (2 sessions).
      (3) Pushing objects into clay (2 sessions).

[5] John Meeks, unpublished material, 1977. Reprinted by permission.

  b. Coil technique of handbuilding (2nd week): rolling coils; making small pots; making large objects.
  c. Slab technique of handbuilding (3rd week): making slabs; making small boxes; making larger objects.

4. *Procedures and Activities:*
   Informal lecture combined with demonstration by teacher;
   Studio experiences working in classroom studio or home studio;
   Studio demonstration.

5. *Materials and Equipment:*
   clay, objects, sticks, rocks, molds, equipment, wheel, kiln, glazes, wedging table.

6. *Evaluation:*
   a. Each student will show a representative sample of each technique in forming clay, rolling coils and making slabs.
   b. Each student will demonstrate at least one other technique.

Daily Lesson Plan

Class: ___Art Grade 7 & 8___   Topic: ___Handbuilt Coil Pots___

1. *Objective:* The students will make a small pot using hand-rolled clay coils.
   Skills to be learned: how to determine clay consistencies; to roll coils; to adhere clay coils to make pot shape; to score clay coils for strengthening pot; to burnish clay for a surface.

2. *Teaching points:* Teacher will demonstrate and give an informal lecture about each step of construction. Students will then recreate sequences with individual help from teacher.

3. *Materials needed:* Each student will need:
   1 lb. of clay, fork for scoring, sponge for dampening;
   smooth block of wood for burnishing.

Unit and Daily Lesson Plan—Illustration[6]

Grade: ___10___   Subject: ___Mathematics___

Unit Topic: ___Polygonal Regions and Their Areas___   Duration: ___5 days___

1. *Introduction:* This unit will familiarize students with area postulates and area theorems of common polygonal regions.

2. *Instructional Objectives:* The student will be able to
   a. State the definition of a general and specific polygonal region, i.e., triangle, parallelogram, rectangle, etc.

[6] Steve McLain, unpublished material, 1977. Reprinted by permission.

b. State in his own words the five area postulates.
c. State in his own words the eight area theorems for triangles and quadrilaterals.
d. Prove the eight area theorems.
e. Solve miscellaneous problems that are related to the areas of triangles and quadrilaterals.

3. *Unit Content:*
   a. Polygonal definitions (1 session): General polygonal region and triangle; trapezoid; parallelograms.
   b. Five area postulates (1 session).
      (1) a is a function $\gamma - R$; $a\, R > 0$.
      (2) Congruence, additivity, square postulates.
   c. Area theorems (2 class sessions).
      (1) Area of rectangle, triangle, and parallelogram.
      (2) Ratio of triangle bases and areas versus corresponding altitudes.
      (3) Ratio of any two corresponding sides of triangles with the same area.
   d. Problem solving (1 session).
      (1) Compute area of various polygonal regions.
      (2) Determine values of unknown altitudes and bases when given area.
      (3) Verify with geometric proof congruence and ratio relations.

4. *Procedures and Activities:*
   a. Informal lecture following main contents as above.
   b. Chalkboard activities: students will perform proofs, write definition, and work on area problems at the board.
   c. Student recitation: during and throughout the lecture, students will be asked to state in their own words theorems and definitions presented in the lecture.
   d. Using a prepared overlay transparency, the students will see how polygonal regions can be formed by the union of triangles.
   e. Group effort in proof theorems: two students at the chalkboard will be given a theorem to prove with the assistance of all the students in the class; one student will be the recorder while the other will acquire the information from the class in an orderly manner.

5. Instructional Aids and Resources: Overhead projector and student text.

6. Evaluation: Review quizzes; daily oral questioning review; unit test; chalkboard participation.

Daily Lesson Plan

Class: _____10_____   Topic: Area Theorems for Triangles and Quadrilaterals (3rd lesson of unit)

1. *Instructional Objectives:* The student will
   a. State in his own words four area theorems.
   b. Prove these four theorems.
   c. Solve problems asking for unknown values in basic polygonal regions using these four theorems.

2. *Content:* Explanation, proof, and problem solving.

3. *Procedure:*
   a. Review five area postulates.
   b. Give short lecture explaining area theorems.
   c. Give oral quiz asking students to restate theorems.
   d. Have class prove at least one of theorems.

4. *Instructional Materials:* Overhead projector and students text.

5. *Evaluation:* Random oral questioning and observation of students in discussion and at chalkboard.

Unit and Daily Lesson Plan—Illustration[7]

Grade: **9**   Subject: **Physical Education**

Unit Topic: **Beginning Track and Field**   Duration: **2 weeks, 55 min/day**

1. *General Objective:* For students to realize and experience an increased level of cardiovascular efficiency through skill instructions and drills in the track and field unit.

2. *Specific Objectives:* The student will be able to:
   a. Demonstrate proper techniques in each of the following areas: springs, long jump, high jump, distance runs.
   b. Observe the proper safety procedures during class while pursuing the objectives above.

3. *Unit Content:* see master calendar that follows.

4. *Evaluation:* written test and skill demonstrations.

5. *Equipment:* (for 32 students) 3 sets of high jump standards; 3 cross bars; 2 18 lb. shots; 2 12 lb. shots; 4 flights of hurdles.

MASTER CALENDAR

Monday	*Tuesday*	*Wednesday*	*Thursday*	*Friday*
First Week				
Introduction to unit and class procedures WU: stretch and jog SI: running form SD: form running CA: 20 yd sprints	WU: stretch and jog SI: sprint start SD: start CA: 10 yd sprints	WU: Astronaut drill SI: relay techniques SD: hand-offs CA: relay race 100 yd 4 × 25	WU: stretch and jog SI: long jump SD: pop-ups CA: group jump relay	WU: stretch and form running SI: review with station work SD: stations 1. start 2. hand-offs 3. long jump 4. form running

[7] David Shipp, unpublished material, 1977. Reprinted by permission.

MASTER CALENDAR (*continued*)

Second week

WU: astronaut drill	WU: stretch	WU: stretch and short jog	WU: upper body stretching	WU: upper body stretching
SI: distance running	SI: high jump	SI: high jump	SI: short put	SI: discuss
SD: 100 yd runs with correct form	SD: approach and take-offs	SD: jump & landing	SD: circle moves; put itself	SD: circle moves throw
CA: 1320 run for time	CA: low jump	CA: jump for maximum height	CA: group relay	CA: group relay

KEY: WU: warm up   SI: skill instructions   SD: skill drills   CA: culminating activity

Daily Lesson Plan

Class: __Physical Education__   Topic: __Beginning Track and Field—day 1__

Objectives:

1. Students will be able to demonstrate correct arm movement while running.

2. The students will be able to demonstrate correct leg action while running.

Procedure	Time	Formation	Teaching points
1. Introduce unit and class procedures	5 min.	x x x x x x x x x x x x x x x x	1. Listen attentively to teacher: follow instruction.
2. Warm up	5 min.	x x x x x x x x	2. Static stretching.
3. Gather students and demonstrate form running	4 min.	same	3. Arms moving up and down. High knee action. Push off toes.
4. Have students find a place and practice form running	3 min.	same	4. High knee action. Arms moving up and down.
5. Have students line up in 8 lines and stride out	5 min.	x x x x x x x x x x x x x x x x x x x x x x x x x x x x x x x x	5. High knees. Point out students with this and up and down arm motion.
6. Remain in same formation and bound out 10 yds.	5 min.	same	6. Exaggerate points in step 5.

Unit and Daily Lesson Plan—Illustration[8]

Subject: __Typing I__ Teacher: __Christy Scofield__

Unit Topic: __Business Letter—Modified Block__ Duration: __5 days__

1. *Introduction:* Relate business letter to personal letter which students have already written. Show similarities and differences. Talk about the importance of proper form in a business letter.

2. *Instructional Objectives:* Given a business letter in an unorganized form, the student will be able to produce it in the proper form in 20 minutes.

3. *Unit Content:* Introduction of the 60-space line; use of the bell cue; proper spacing in the rest of the letter; use of typist's initials.

4. *Procedures and Activities:*
    a. Show example of proper format in book.
    b. Review by drawing letter and format on chalkboard.
    c. Give practice by doing letters in typing book.
    d. Have papers turned in for suggestions and corrections.
    e. Work with individuals as necessary.

Lesson Plan—Daily

Subject: __Typing I__ Date: __March 20, 1981__

Teacher: __Christy Scofield__ Duration: __55 minutes__

1. *Warm-up:* Conditioning practice, p. 86, 55A.

2. *Topic for this lesson:* Business letter in modified block form.

3. *Instructional Objective:* The student will produce two letters with proper format by the end of the period.

4. *Skills to be Learned:* Correct form of a business letter; correct setting of right margin by listening for bell cue.

5. *Specific Teaching Points:*
    Review bell cue,
    Review use of typists initials,
    Review centering and use of 60-space line.

6. *Assignment:* Type letter problems 1 and 2 on page 87.

7. *Evaluation:* The letters completed and turned in at the end of the period should have the proper format; maximum errors 12.

[8] Christy Scofield, unpublished material, 1981. Reprinted by permission.

UNIT PLAN CONTRACT ILLUSTRATION—BIOLOGY[9]

Growing in popularity in recent years has been the use of "teacher-learner contracts." Here is a sample Unit Plan Contract.

Unit Plan Contract: Photosynthesis

Read through the following items and check those you would like to do. Then decide what grade you would like to contract for. Grades will be given as follows:

D—The starred items plus one more from each group
C—The starred items plus two more from each group
B—The starred items plus three more from each group
A—The starred items plus four more from each group

Discuss your choice with your teacher and then sign your name in the proper place on the other side of this sheet.

Prepare a title page for the section on photosynthesis in your notebook.
Introduce your unit with a brief description of the energy conversion process that takes place during photosynthesis.
Write a paragraph explaining why photosynthesis is a vital process in regard to life on earth.

Group I:

Diagram a "typical" chloroplast and identify its organelles and components.

1. Explain why a high percentage of photosynthesis occurs in the ocean. State what organisms make this possible.
2. Read about Van Niel's experiment with photosynthetic bacteria. Explain where the liberated O_2 comes from during photosynthesis.
3. Set up an experiment to show how different wavelengths of light affect the rate of photosynthesis.
4. Examine *Spirogyra, Mougeotia*, and *Zygnema* under the light microscope. Locate the chloroplast in each and make a drawing of it.

Group II:

State the probable origin of the chloroplast in the higher plants.

1. Identify the "process" that replenishes the CO_2 content of the atmosphere.
2. Explain why Ruben used $^{18}O_2$ (a stable isotope of oxygen) in his famous experiment in 1941. Write a chemical equation showing the reaction Ruben proved.

[9] Targe Lindsay, Jr., unpublished material, 1973. Reprinted by permission.

3. Extract and separate by paper chromatography the photosynthetic pigments from fresh spinach leaves. Identify the pigments on the chromatogram.
4. Examine *Mougeota* under a microscope. Move a bright light source around the microscope in different positions and write down what you observe about the chloroplast.

Explain the role of chlorophyll in photosynthesis.

1. Tell how stomatal activity and CO_2 concentrations are related to photosynthesis.
2. Make a collection of leaves from different plants. Examine the stomatiferous areas of the leaves. Try to draw some conclusions regarding the size, number, and location of stomata on the different leaves.
3. Identify five accessory pigments and explain their role in photosynthesis.
4. Explain the manometric method of detecting photosynthesis.

_____   _____
Date   Pupil's signature

_____   _____
Grade Contracted   Teacher's signature

EXERCISE 7.2 PRELIMINARY EXERCISE FOR LESSON PLANNING

The purpose of this exercise is to start your thinking about planning. You might find this exercise useful in getting your thoughts together prior to specific lesson planning.

Process Development

1. List specific objectives for the subject you intend to teach. _____

_____

_____

_____

_____

2. List the major learning experiences that you will attempt to provide. _____

_____

_____

_____

3. What teaching strategies will you use. _____

_____

_____

_____

4. Identify materials needed for the lesson. _____

_____

_____

_____

5. What set induction will you use? _____

_____

_____

_____

6. Identify how you will determine whether these objectives have been met. _____

_____

_____

_____

7. How will you bring the lesson to a close? _____

_____

_____

_____

EXERCISE 7.3 LESSON PLAN PREPARATION

Now prepare a lesson plan you are likely to teach. Follow these steps:

1. After reviewing your plan developed in Exercise 7.2, select from this chapter a suitable lesson plan form.
2. Develop a detailed lesson plan following the form chosen.
3. Have your plan evaluated by members of your class or by your instructor using the Check List for Lesson Plan Evaluation that follows.

EXERCISE 7.4   LESSON PLAN EVALUATION

(check one)

	good	weak	poor	none

1. Is it clear for what grade level, subject and topic the lesson plan is designed?

2. Are the objectives clear?

3. Are the content and procedures spelled out clearly enough that a substitute teacher would be able to follow the plan?

4. Is it clear as to what materials and instructional aids are to be available?

5. Is there a clear—
   a. introduction (set)?
   b. summary (closure)?

6. Is there a time plan (sequence)?

7. Is there allowance (plan) for what to do if time remains following completion of lesson?

8. Does the procedure (item 3 above) clearly lead to attainment of objectives (item 2)?

+ + +   + + +   + + +

      (to be completed by author)   (this space for evaluator's comments)

Lesson Plan Author _____

Lesson Plan Type (check one or more)

Conventional Long Form   ____

Modified Lecture   ____

Modified Discussion   ____

Modified Problem Solv.   ____

Modified Performance   ____

Modified Laboratory   ____

Contract   ____

LESSON PLAN EVALUATION CODE
(To be completed after evaluation)

	(circle one)			
	good	weak	poor	none
1. Subject, topic, grade level designation	1	0	−1	−2
2. Objectives	2	1	0	−1
3. Content/Procedures	6	3	0	−6
4. Materials/Aids	2	1	0	−1
5. Introduction (set)	1	1	0	−1
Summary (closure)	1	1	0	−1
6. Time plan	2	1	0	−1
7. Allowance for time remaining	3	2	1	0
8. Procedure Match Objectives	2	1	0	−1

TOTAL ____

Scoring: 18–20 = excellent lesson plan—"A"
          16–17 = good lesson plan—"B"
          14–15 = acceptable—"C"
  Less than 14 = unacceptable, do again

How Do I Prepare a Self-Instructional Learning Activity Package? Development and Models

There exist today many devices and commercially produced materials designed to individualize teaching programs, such as UNIPAC, Learning Activity Packages, self-paced materials, etc. Although many of these require an expenditure of money, there is one technique that has grown rapidly in popularity because it requires little or no expenditure and provides the teacher with an opportunity to create. An equally important reason for its success is that it is fun for the student and assures his learning. The name of this concept is the self-instructional package (S.I.P.), which was developed by Johnson and Johnson.[1] While it would take a considerable portion of this book to fully treat the rationale, theory, and developmental techniques of the S.I.P., we introduce here the essentials of what the S.I.P. is and how you can develop one.

The S.I.P. is designed for an individual student and usually requires 15–50 minutes of learning time. Teachers have found the S.I.P. to be useful in the following ways:

1. As enrichment for the student who is ahead of the class.
2. As a method of makeup for the student who is behind the class.
3. As a means of allowing each student to move at his own pace.
4. As a means other than a lecture of introducing basic information, thus freeing the teacher to work with individual students and so better utilize teaching time.

The S.I.P. is most successful when coordinated with audio and visual materials such as cassette tapes, pictures, filmstrips, and film loops. *The most important single ingredient of the package is the use of small sequential steps with immediate feedback for the learner.*

[1] Rita Johnson and Stuart Johnson, *Assuring Learning with Self Instructional Packages* (Chapel Hill, North Carolina: Self Instructional Packages, Inc., 1971).

DEVELOPING YOUR FIRST SELF-INSTRUCTIONAL PACKAGE

Although development of a good package is a time-consuming process, we have found from experience that students feel it to be a very worthwhile activity. It teaches one to plan activities in small steps, to write objectives clearly, and to plan and individualize in such a way that the student receives immediate feedback and assurance that he is learning. And how exciting it is when you actually try out your package on students for the first time!

As you begin to prepare a package, the following points should be kept in mind:

1. Prepare a package designed to take about 30 minutes or less of time.
2. Remember: you are writing for *a* student. Write as if you are talking to him in person.
3. Use humor, cartoons, pictures, and anything else that will make your package attractive and interesting for the learner.
4. Use the other members of the class as resource persons—try out your ideas on one another as you prepare the objectives, test items, and first draft of the package.
5. The package should involve many small and sequential steps, with frequent practice and feedback—*it should not read like a lecture.*
6. Write post test items in such a manner that the student could actually evaluate it himself—try to avoid many subjective items.
7. There is no subject for which the S.I.P. cannot be used.
8. Look at the models provided to get a better idea of what the S.I.P. might look like. The sample S.I.P.s are provided here as they were prepared by former methods students. Go through each of them as if you were the student for whom the package was intended.
9. The S.I.P. is always open for revision, just as if it were any other kind of lesson plan.
10. The well-written package will assure learning.

Now you are ready to begin production of your own S.I.P. Follow the steps suggested in Exercise 8.1. Good luck!

EXERCISE 8.1   STEPS IN DEVELOPING YOUR PACKAGE FOR INDIVIDUALIZED INSTRUCTION

1. *Prepare the package cover sheet:* List the title of the package, author, intended students. (See the models.)
2. *Prepare the objectives:* There will be a tendency here toward difficulty in getting objectives into behavioral terms, and in trying to cover too much material in a single package. The objectives should tell the student what he is to know and how he will demonstrate this knowledge. Include at least one attitudinal objective.
3. *Share items 1 and 2 with the other members of the class.*
4. *Rework the objectives* (if necessary).
5. *Prepare a pretest:* If the learner does well on the pretest, there is probably no need for him to continue with the package. Some packages may not include a pretest, although we think it is good practice to include one in your first package.
6. *Share the pretest with the other members of the class* to check whether the test items match the stated objectives.

7. *Prepare a posttest:* Make sure the posttest really does test the objectives. Include at least one attitudinal objective, but try to keep most items objective, as if the learner himself would check the results.
8. *Share the posttest with your classmates* to check whether the items match the stated objectives.

(If items 1 through 8 are successfully completed, you are now ready to prepare the text of your package.)

9. *Prepare the text of your package:* Remember, the student should be able to work through the package without additional help from you. Use small steps with frequent practice and feedback for the learner. (Refer to the models.)
10. *Test your package on a few of the other members of the class:* Have a few of your classmates go through your package as if they were the students for whom it was intended. Have them make notes, using the following guidelines:
    a. Errors?
    b. Comments on clarity?
    c. Suggestions for improvement?
    d. Other data for revision?
11. *Revision of package* (if necessary): You might wish to keep a journal of package tryouts and suggestions for revision.
12. *Congratulations:* You have just completed your first self-instructional package and are now ready to give it its first real test. Try it out during your practice teaching.

(*Note:* The authors' experience suggests that about 4–6 weeks be given for completion of steps 1–10.)

FACTOR

SELF-INSTRUCTIONAL PACKAGE—ILLUSTRATION[2]

Instructor's Name: <u>Bob Peterson</u> $3 \times 3 = 9$

Institution: <u>Nevada Union High School</u>

Class or Course Title: <u>Pre-Algebra II</u>

Intended Students: <u>Ninth and Tenth Grades</u>

Topic: <u>Factoring—Simplified</u>

Estimated Working Time: <u>30–45 minutes</u>

$2 \cdot 2 \cdot 5 = 20$

[2] Bob Peterson, unpublished material, 1977. Reprinted by permission.

Objectives

Up until now, you've heard teachers and other students use the term factoring, and you've used the distributive property in several ways. But, now you are going to learn how to factor, beginning with some very simple numbers.

When you are finished with this package, you will be able to tear numbers apart like never before, and most important of all, you will be enjoying it.

Remember, the fun in math depends on how well *you* understand it, so be sure to finish each section as you come to it and be ready to go on with the next.

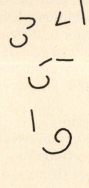

H A V E

F U N ! ! ! !

Pretest:

Factor each of the following terms in as many different ways as you can.

1. 18
2. 12z
3. 14m
4. 5cd
5. 3ac

6. abc
7. 2m/7
8. bmk
9. 3rst
10. 1/5 rh

Now check to see if your answers agree with those listed on the fold-out page that is attached to your answer sheet. (Fold-out and answer sheet are omitted here in order to conserve space.)

If you find some answers to your questions are not included on the answer sheet, re-check your work to see if you are sure your answer is correct, then show your instructor.

If you missed some of the problems or if you want more practice, the following instructions should be read carefully as you continue through this package.

First, you may not see what is taking place in factoring, so take a look at some examples. Factors are two or more numbers that, when multiplied, make up another number, like:

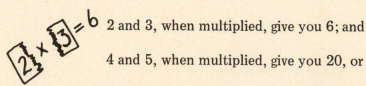 2 and 3, when multiplied, give you 6; and

4 and 5, when multiplied, give you 20, or

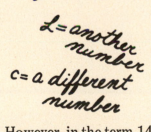

2 and 10, when multiplied, give you 20, or

2, 5, 2, when multiplied, give you 20.

In these problems, 2 and 3, 4 and 5, 2 and 10, and 2, 5, and 2, are the factors.

Now, take a look at it from the other way. Given the number 20, right away, if you were asked for the factors, you would probably be able to say "4 and 5," or "10 and 2," or "2, 5, and 2." But, if you saw the number 25, what would you say the factors were? Well, ask yourself, "What numbers multiplied by each other would give me 25?" And, your answer would be "5 and 5" wouldn't it? But remember 1 and 25 are also factors!!

Why not try a few of these, and check your answers below.

a. 15
b. 14
c. 30

Before checking your answers, go back and see how many different answers you can get for each problem, then check.

a. 5·3 1·15
b. 2·7 1·14
c. 6·5 15·2 10·3 2·3·5 30·1

Got them all right? Good for you!!!

If you'll look at the next examples, you'll see how close they are to the last problems you just finished.

a = some number

b = another number

c = a different number

3a   14a   5ab

Do you remember you've worked before with variables (letters used in place of numbers). Therefore, you probably can think of how to factor numbers like 3a. 3·a = 3a, so we call "3" one factor and "a" the other factor.

However, in the term 14a, this is a little different, because we can find a number of factors. 14·a = 14a, 7·2·a = 14a, 7·2a = 14a, 7a 2 = 14a, and 14a·1 = 14a. You can see where multiplying each of these factors results in the product 14a.

Why not try the other number above, 5ab, and see if you agree with the answers listed below.

If you got all of these, you're doing great and are more than likely ready and anxious to go on to the next page.

5a·b 5b·a 5·ab 5·a·b

So far, you've worked on whole numbers and variables, but to finish this package you should also consider fractions. Just a reminder!! Fractions are just another form of numbers, so think of them in that way.

   The following examples give you a look at a number or term containing a fraction and one or more variables.

$\dfrac{ab}{2}$ also written $\dfrac{1}{2}ab$ can be factored:

$$\dfrac{1}{2}\cdot a \cdot b \qquad \dfrac{1}{2}ab\cdot 1 \qquad \dfrac{1}{2}a\cdot b \qquad \dfrac{1}{2}b\cdot a$$

$\dfrac{3}{5}a$ also written $\dfrac{3a}{5}$ can be factored:

$$\dfrac{3}{5}\cdot a \qquad 3\cdot\dfrac{a}{5} \qquad 3\cdot a\cdot\dfrac{1}{5} \qquad \dfrac{3}{5}a\cdot 1$$

and $\dfrac{1}{5}\cdot 3a$

So, you can see how many factors this one term has.

Try the numbers below, and then check your answers listed at the bottom of the page.

1. $\dfrac{1}{3}a$

2. $\dfrac{bc}{11}$

3. $\dfrac{5mn}{13}$

3. $\dfrac{5mn}{13}\quad \dfrac{5m}{13}n \quad \dfrac{5n}{13}m \quad 5\cdot m\cdot n\cdot\dfrac{1}{13} \quad \dfrac{1}{13}\cdot 5m\cdot n \quad \dfrac{1}{13}\cdot 5\cdot m\cdot n \quad \dfrac{1}{13}\cdot 5mn$

2. $\dfrac{bc}{11}\quad \dfrac{b}{11}c \quad \dfrac{c}{11}b \quad \dfrac{1}{11}\cdot b\cdot c \quad \dfrac{1}{11}\cdot bc$

1. $\dfrac{1}{3}a\quad \dfrac{a}{3} \quad \dfrac{3}{1}\cdot a\cdot 1$

Aren't sure yet??????

Now that you've worked with all kinds of terms in this package, here are a few more problems to work on if you think you need them. Check your answers at the bottom.

If not, go right on

and complete the Posttest — — — — — — — —

1. 12

2. 18

3. 6z

4. 5ct

5. $\dfrac{3xy}{5}$

Answers:

1. 4·3   6·2   12·1   2·2·3
2. 18·1   9·2   3·6   3·3·2
3. 6z·1   3z·2   2z·3   3·z·1
4. 5ct·1   5c·t   5t·c   5·ct
5. $\dfrac{3xy}{5}$·1 $\dfrac{3xy}{5}$·x $\dfrac{3x}{5}$·y $\dfrac{3y}{5}$·x $\dfrac{1}{5}$·3xy
   $\dfrac{1}{5}$·3·x·y $\dfrac{x}{5}$·3·y $\dfrac{y}{5}$·3·x $\dfrac{y}{5}$·3x $\dfrac{y}{5}$·3·x·x

(After finishing, turn package in to the instructor.)

Posttest:

Factor the following terms in as many ways as you can:

1. 8

2. 18s

3. 25m

4. 7mn

5. 3ac

6. rst

7. $\dfrac{3d}{5}$

8. 5uv

9. 5uvw

10. $\dfrac{7}{11}x_y$

SELF-INSTRUCTIONAL PACKAGE—MODEL II[3]

Instructor: <u>Gerri O'Connell</u>

Institution: <u>El Camino High School</u>

Course: <u>French I</u>

Intended students: <u>Freshmen</u>

Topic: <u>The Time of Day</u>

Estimated working time of student <u>20–30 minutes</u>

Objectives

Upon completion of this self-instructional package, you will be able to:

1. Write correctly in French the different times of day.
2. Identify correctly the words relating to time that have been added to your vocabulary.
3. Increase your desire to speak, read, and write more fluently in French.

Pretest

Write the following times of day correctly in French:

1. 3:15
2. 10:10
3. 6:45
4. noon
5. 2:30
6. 11:00
7. 1:00

[3] Gerri O'Connell, self-instructional package, unpublished material, 1972. Reprinted by permission.

Put your answers here. (Use complete sentences, please.)

1. _____
2. _____
3. _____
4. _____
5. _____
6. _____
7. _____

Your answers to the pretest should have been:

1. Il est trois heures et quart.
2. Il est dix heures dix.
3. Il est sept heures moins le quart.
4. Il est midi.
5. Il est deux heures et demie.
6. Il est onze heures.
7. Il est une heure.

If you have answered them all correctly, please see me for another package. However, if you have missed any of the answers, complete this package.

Learning to tell time in French is not difficult if you can count to *soixante* and learn the little tricks presented in this self-instructional package. Proceed slowly, and if you answer any practice exercises incorrectly, repeat that section of the packet.

Good Luck!!

Instructional Activities

Quelle heure est-il?

This phrase is used in French to ask the time of day.

How would you translate this question into English?

Quelle heure est-il? = _____

_____

Was your answer "What time is it?" If it was, you're right! Actually, "heure" translated exactly means "hour." But, in this case, the sentence "Quelle heure est-il?" is an idiom always used to ask the time of day.

Quelle heure est-il?

Il est une heure.

Il est deux heures.

Note: heure is feminine, so the number one is feminine also.

What's the difference in the word *heure* in the two times of day shown above? Do you know why there's a difference?

Answer here: _____

_____

_____

_____

Warning: Never change the singular *il est* to the plural *ils sont* when telling time. You must always start with *il est.*

If you said that *heure* has an "s," in the second case, you were absolutely right! *Heure* is plural when the number preceding it is plural.

NOW—try to write the following times in French

Quelle heure est-il?

_____

Answers: Il est six heures.
Il est neuf heures.
How did you do?

Quelle heure est-il?

Il est deux heures cinq.

Il est trois heures vingt.

See if you can do the next two!

   Quelle heure est-il?

_____   _____

Il est dix heures dix.
Answers: Il est huit heures vingt-cinq.

That wasn't so hard, but take a look at what's coming up!!!

   Quelle heure est-il?

Il est sept heures *et quart*.   Il est cinq heures et *demie*.

Notice the *et* between *heure* and *quart* or *demie*.
Also note that *demie* is feminine (*demie* + *e*) in order to agree with the feminine word **heure**.

What do you think that *quart* means? _____

How would you translate *demie*? _____

demie means half.
quart means quarter.
Answers:

Try a couple by yourself!

   Quelle heure est-il?

_____   _____

Il est quatre heures et demie.
Il est onze heures et quart.
Answers:

Now for the TRICKY part . . .

Quelle heure est-il?

Il est douze heures *moins le* quart.

Il est une heure *moins* vingt.

Important: The French use a subtraction method in telling time after the second hand of the clock has passed the half-hour. The French name the approaching hour first and then subtract the number of minutes needed to reach that hour.

Can you figure out the meaning of the French word *moins*?

Answer here: _____

Answer: *Moins* means "minus" or "less."
Congratulations if you got that right!

Try the following times yourself.

Quelle heure est-il?

_____   _____

Answers: Il est trois heures moins dix. (Best)
Il est six heures moine le quart. (Acceptable)
Be sure you remembered the *le* before the *quart!*

Quelle heure est-il?

Il est midi.

Il est minuit.

From the pictures, can you tell the meanings of the words *midi* and *minuit*?

midi = _____ minuit = _____

Answers: midi = noon   minuit = midnight

You have now completed the sequence for telling time in French. Let's see how much you have learned as you take the posttest. Good luck!

Posttest

Write the following times in French, using complete sentences. *Quelle heure est-il?*

1. 3:30 _____

2. 4:15 _____

3. noon _____

4. 2:45 _____

5. 9:29 _____

6. 1:00 _____

7. midnight _____

8. 5:45 _____

9. 11:10 _____

10. 10:30 _____

Translate the following into French:

1. hour _____

2. midnight _____

3. quarter _____

4. noon _____

5. half _____

6. What time is it? _____

7. minus _____

Have you benefited from this self-instructional package? Has it increased your confidence in your fluency in French and your desire to learn more? Please comment.

_____

_____

_____

_____

SELF-INSTRUCTIONAL PACKAGE—MODEL III[4]

Instructor: _____Shawn Netherda_____   Institution: _____Sutter High School_____

Course: _____Physical Education_____   Intended students: _____9–12 graders_____

Topic: _____Artificial Respiration_____   Estimated working time of student _____30–45 minutes_____

Objectives

Inhale deeply! Now exhale. You are about to learn how to breathe for someone else. This is a skill to be used any time it is needed, not only in a water accident case. Artificial respiration is used to make air flow in and out of a person's lungs when breathing is inadequate to support life.

At the end of this unit, you will be able to:

1. Go through the basic procedures of artificial respiration.
2. Go through the procedures after determining a blockage.
3. Go through the procedure for a stoma.

Pretest

Before beginning this unit, I want you to try a simple test to see if you have any knowledge of what artificial respiration is all about. You'll need a piece of paper and something to write with, so go and get them.

Any time you are ready you can begin.

1. What are the two basic steps of artificial respiration?

   _____

   _____

2. What is an obstructed airway?
3. What is respiratory failure?
4. What is a head tilt?
5. "LOOK" at what?
6. "LISTEN" to what?
7. "FEEL" what?
8. What are some signs of stopped breathing?

   _____

   _____

   _____

9. What is a laryngectomee?
10. What is a stoma?

[4] Shawn Netherda, unpublished material, 1981. Reprinted by permission.

Check your answers with the answers at the end of this packet. If you have answered all the questions correctly, see me. If you have missed part of one answer or more than one answer, continue with the packet.

The Packet:

Go to the cabinet and take out a resuscitation dummy, or a doll will do.

Take a deep breath, deeper. Now you have performed the first step in artificial respiration. Let's set up a situation to work through.

While walking through a campground, you come across a camper who is unconscious and appears not to be breathing. The steps for artificial respiration are:

1. Ask the person if he is okay.
   If no response then
2. Give the person a slight shake and ask again.
   If still no response then
3. Open the mouth gently, with the index finger sweep the mouth clear of any foreign particles.
4. Place one hand under the neck and gently lift up on it, place the other hand on the forehead and tilt the head back. Sometimes this is all that is needed to restore breathing. If not, then:
5. Look for the raise and fall of the chest, listen for the sound of air escaping from the chest, feel the air escape against your ear.
   If these are not present then:
6. Begin artificial respiration (breathing).

Now that we have a procedure to follow, let's break the steps down and discuss them.

Using your resuscitation dummy, or a doll, practice the following steps.

Step 1:

You want to ask the person if he is all right just to make sure that he is not just taking a nap or sleeping. This should only take a couple of seconds.

Step 2:

The shake and asking if he is all right just insures that the person is not just sleeping.

Step 3:

Open the mouth of the victim and with your index finger gently sweep the victim's mouth. This is done to make sure that there are no foreign particles in the mouth—gum, food, etc. (False teeth may be left in place if they are secure, because they help make the seal tighter.)

Step 4:

The head tilt. Place the hand under the neck and gently lift up. Place the other hand on the forehead and tilt the neck back. By tilting the head back the tongue is moved away from the back of the throat, thus opening the airway. Sometimes this is all that is needed to help a person resume breathing on his own.

Step 5:

The "look, listen, feel" is your check that the person is or is not getting air. This step will be used each time a breath is given to the victim.

You "look" for a rise and fall of the chest cavity after each breath. You "listen" for the air to escape after each breath. You "feel" the air escape against your ear after each breath.

Step 6:

The artificial respiration. Artificial respiration means actually breathing for someone else. As the rescuer, you will be breathing for yourself and for the victim. You make a tight seal around the victim's mouth with your own mouth and pinch the victim's nose closed with the fingers of the hand on the forehead. Then begin breathing. Turn your head to the side, as in Step 5, after each breath.

The first of the breathing should be a series of four *quick* breaths in which you do not allow the air to escape between the breaths. This ensures full ventilation of the lungs. After that you should deliver one breath approximately every 5 seconds or at a rate of approximately 18 breaths per minute for an adult (the breathing rate is different for small children and infants—this is covered in a smaller packet). After each breath you should repeat Step 5, the "*look, listen, feel.*" This allows for some feedback as to whether the victim is getting any air or not.

If the victim is not getting any air—if the stomach is filling up instead of the chest—then reaccess the head position. Try again. If the victim still does not appear to be getting any air, then return to Step 3, sweep the mouth, and begin again from there.

Here I should note that it is not uncommon for the victim to vomit. If this happens, return to Step 3 and start over again—do not repeat the four quick breaths in step 6, instead just begin the regular breathing pattern.

Now that you have read through the steps, practice on the dummy. Please refer to the packet notes as often as you need to.

You are an expert now, right? Good—now you list the steps in order, with a small description of each. *Do not* use the packet notes this time.

1. _____

   _____

2. _____

   _____

3. _____

   _____

4. _____

   _____

5. _____

6. _____

_____

_____

Check your answers with the answers at the end of this packet.

There is one more procedure I feel that I should mention. This is used on laryngectomees. *Laryngectomees* are people who have had their larynx removed for some reason or another, they are no longer able to breathe through their mouth or nose. If for some reason you are breathing but no air seems to be getting in and you have checked and rechecked the head position and seal, then look at the base of the throat for a small hole. This hole or *stoma* is usually covered with a scarf or a t-shirt or a sweater. This hole is covered with a screen that should be removed only if it is loose. The steps for mouth-to-stoma are easier than for mouth-to-mouth.

Step 1:

Locate the stoma. See if the screen is secure.

Step 2:

Keep the victim's head straight. Do not use the head tilt.

Step 3:

No need to check for foreign particles.

Step 4:

Make a tight seal with your mouth over the stoma. Use the breathing rate of 5 breaths per second or 18 per minute. Turn your head to the side to "look, listen, and feel" the air.

Now list the differences between mouth-to-mouth and mouth-to-stoma.

Well, you have made it to the end of the packet. Take a few more minutes to review the packet notes and then prepare to take the test. When you are ready, begin the test. Remember that this packet must be completed before the end of the period, so don't take all day.

Posttest

You will need a piece of paper and something to write with. This test is going to be given using situation questions. Answer the questions using the steps given in the packet. Include as many steps as you need. After you finish the questions, turn your answers in to me.

1. You have been trying mouth-to-mouth for several times. You have checked and rechecked the head position and the seal. What do you do now?

2. While in the park you find an unconscious jogger who is not breathing. What should you do?
3. Your unconscious jogger has just vomited. What should you do next?
4. What is a laryngectomee?
5. Why sweep the mouth?
6. Why pinch the nose closed?
7. What does artificial respiration mean?
8. What is the rate of breathing used during artificial respiration?

Pretest Answers

1. What are the two basic steps of artificial respiration?

   Open the airway

   Restore breathing

2. What is an obstructed airway?
   The air passage is blocked by a foreign particle and the breathing intake is inadequate to support life.
3. What is a respiratory failure?
   All breathing has stopped.
4. What is a head tilt?
   The position used to open the airway.
5. "*look*" at what?
   The rise of the chest cavity during inhalation and the fall of the chest cavity during exhalation.
6. "*listen*" to what?
   The air escaping between breaths.
7. "*feel*" what?
   The air rush out against your ear during exhalation.
8. What are some of the signs of stopped breathing?

   lips and fingers turn blue

   unconscious

   pupils are dilated

9. What is a laryngectomee?
   A person who has undergone a laryngectomy, and who now breathes through a stoma at the base of his throat.
10. What is a stoma?
    A hole cut in the voice box through which a person who has had a laryngectomy breathes.

Packet Fill-in Answers:

List the steps in order, with a small description of each.

1. Question the victim. This is to be sure he is not sleeping.

2. Shake the victim and question him. This insures that the victim is not just taking a nap.

3. Sweep the mouth. This removes all foreign particles.

4. The head tilt. This opens the airway.

5. LOOK, LISTEN, FEEL. This gives feedback on where the air is going.

6.   Artificial respiration. The actual breathing for the victim, using the mouth-to-mouth method. _____

7.   Repeat any of the above steps if needed. (extra credit) _____

List the differences between mouth-to-mouth and mouth-to-stoma.

There is no need to clear the mouth.
There is no head tilt used.
Mouth seals over a hole in the throat (stoma) rather than over the victim's mouth.

Posttest Answers:

1.   You have been trying mouth-to-mouth for several times. You have checked and rechecked the head position and seal. Still nothing. What do you do now?
     a. Check for a stoma.
     b. Keep the victim's head straight.
     c. Make a tight seal over the stoma with mouth and breathe at an approximate rate of 5 per second or 18 per minute.

2.   While in the park you find an unconscious jogger who is not breathing. What should you do?
     a. Ask if he is okay.
     b. Gently shake him and ask if he is alright.
     c. Sweep the mouth clear.
     d. Tilt the head back to open the airway.
     e. Look, listen, and feel for breathing.
     f. Begin artificial respiration with four quick breaths. Continue breathing after that at a rate of 5 per second or 18 per minute.

3.   Your unconscious victim has just vomited. What should you do next?
     a. Clear mouth.
     b. Tilt head back.
     c. Look, listen, feel.
     d. Artificial respiration. Leave out the four quick breaths.

4.   What is a laryngectomee?
     A person who has undergone a laryngectomy, and who now breathes through a stoma at the base of his throat.

5.   Why sweep the mouth?
     To clear the mouth of any foreign particles so that they do not become lodged in the throat.

6.   Why pinch the nose closed?
     To make a seal. No air can escape then.

7.   What does artificial respiration mean?
     Actually breathing for someone else.

8.   What is the rate of breathing used during artificial respiration?
     one breath/5 seconds or 18 breaths/min.

9

What Are Instructional Objectives?
How Do I Write Them?

In the previous four chapters, you have noticed that *objectives* (interchangeably called *Instructional Objectives, Behavioral Objectives,* or *Performance Objectives*) have been mentioned as an essential and a critical component of any lesson planning. In this chapter we direct your attention exclusively to stating the objectives for your lesson planning.

An objective is an *intent* communicated by a statement describing a proposed change in the learner—a statement of what the learner is to be able to do when he has successfully completed a learning experience. It is a description of a pattern of behavior (performance) we want the learner to be able to demonstrate. The statement of objectives of a training program must denote *measurable* attributes observable in the graduate of a program; otherwise it is impossible to determine whether or not the program is meeting the objectives.

A distinction must be made between the *description* of a course and the *objectives* of the course. A course description tells something about the content and the procedures of a course; a course objective describes a desired outcome of a course. *An objective tells what the learner is to be like as a result of some learning experiences; the course description tells only what the course is about.*

THE QUALITIES OF MEANINGFUL OBJECTIVES[1]

A meaningfully stated objective is one that succeeds in communicating the intent of the writer; the best statement is the one that excludes the greatest number of possible alternatives to the goal. There are many "loaded" words which are open to a wide range of interpretation. If only these words are used, the statements which include them are left open to misinterpretation.

[1] Robert F. Mager, *Preparing Instructional Objectives*, 2nd ed. (Belmont, Calif.: Fearon, Publishers, 1975). pp. 19, 20. Reprinted by permission.

Words Open to Many Interpretations	*Words Open to Fewer Interpretations*
To know	To write
To understand	To recite
Really to understand	To identify
To appreciate	To differentiate
Fully to appreciate	To solve
To grasp the significance of	To construct
To enjoy	To list
To believe	To compare
To have faith in	To contrast

There are a number of schemes for writing objectives. The one that follows has been successfully used and has proved to be fairly uncomplicated.

First, identify the terminal behavior by name: the kind of behavior which will be accepted as evidence that the learner has achieved the objective. The way to write an objective which meets the first requirement is to write a statement describing an educational intention and then modify it until it answers the question: "What is the learner *doing* when he is demonstrating that he has achieved the objective?"

For example, the statement "to develop a critical understanding of the operation of the Target Tracking Console" could be worked to read: "When the learner completes the program of instruction, he must be able to identify by name each of the controls located on the front of the Target Tracking Console." "To be able to write a summary of the factors leading to the depression of 1929" is stated in performance terms and would be an acceptable objective. "To know the rules of logic" does not tell what the learner does to demonstrate that he has achieved the objective. The writer must decide what he will accept as evidence of "understanding" and then describe this intent in terms of his objective.

Second, the instructional objectives must be student-centered rather than teacher-oriented (teacher goals or purposes). The following examples are teacher-oriented purposes stated in ambiguous and nonbehavioral terms which we have often found in teacher's objective statements.

1. "To develop critical thinking."
2. "To instill good language usage."
3. "To improve study habits."
4. "To provide useful experiences for the children."
5. "To provide for individual differences of the learner."
6. "To provide opportunity for the enjoyment of life."

Although they may sound noble and educational, they do not convey a meaning in its full context, and they are quite remote from what the teacher expects the learners to accomplish.

Third, state instructional objectives in an infinitive form and be consistent throughout.

Consistent and Recommended	*Inconsistent and Not Recommended*
Students will (be able to):	
1. Differentiate propaganda from the truth about the life of people in the Soviet Union.	1. To differentiate [infinitive] . . .
2. Express greetings in French.	2. Exchange of greetings in French [noun]
3. Demonstrate proper skill for backstroke in tennis.	3. Demonstrating proper skill [noun] . . .

CLASSIFICATION OF INSTRUCTIONAL OBJECTIVES

For the purpose of classification of what it is that a student is to be able to do as a result of instruction, objectives have been categorized in three domains: *cognitive, psychomotor,* and *affective.* In simple terms, these are defined as follows:

1. *Cognitive:* objectives that emphasize simple recall to complex synthesis and creation of new ideas.
2. *Psychomotor:* objectives that emphasize manipulation and/or control of objectives, principally through motor control.
3. *Affective:* Objectives that emphasize emotional feelings and attitudes.

Most of the objectives written to date have been cognitive, although educators have been addressing increased attention to affective principles.

Emphasis in the early 1970s on accountability has found many teachers burning the midnight oil in an effort to learn how to write instructional objectives in behavioral terms. We only hope that the issue of accountability proves to hold true for all credentialed personnel, not only teachers, and that the process becomes a cooperative effort rather than an individual one.

Each of the three domains has been further broken down into hierarchies of subcategories. There is no doubt that there is much overlap among these.

Cognitive Domain

The major cognitive subcategories of instructional objectives are as follows:

1. *Knowledge.* Example: The student will be able to define the terms "osmosis," "plasmolysis," and "diffusion."
2. *Comprehension.* Example: The student will be able to give his own examples of recent Supreme Court decisions on man's protection under the law.
3. *Application.* Example: When provided with unknown numbers, the student will be able to apply the formula necessary to solve geometry problems.
4. *Analysis.* Example: The student will be able to detect discrepancies between television commercials and the true quality of an expensive vacuum cleaner.
5. *Synthesis.* Example: The student will be able to create an environment for a hypothetical animal.
6. *Evaluation.* Example: The student will be able to evaluate objectively the best of two student essays on Hemingway.

Psychomotor Domain

We have identified the three major psychomotor subcategories as follows:

1. *Accuracy.* Example: Students will be able to demonstrate the ability to catch and pass the ball accurately while on the move during a basketball game.
2. *Coordination.* Example: Students will be able to blow the trumpet skillfully to produce a high F for a duration of 1 minute.
3. *Manipulation.* Example: Students will use the power saw safely to cut out a desired form for a bookstand.

Affective Domain

The four affective subcategories are as follows:

1. *Attending.* Example: The student will illustrate an awareness of the importance of ecology by supplying pertinent newspaper clippings.
2. *Responding.* Example: The student will demonstrate enjoyment of the subject by volunteering to join in the role playing of King Arthur.
3. *Valuing.* Example: The student will demonstrate a continuing desire to learn to use the microscope by volunteering to work with it after school hours.
4. *Value Development.* Example: The student will, in a class discussion, freely express his opinion about the importance of sex education.

ILLUSTRATIVE VERBS FOR THE STATEMENT OF SPECIFIC LEARNING OUTCOMES[2]

Creative Behaviors

Alter	Paraphrase	Reconstruct	Rephrase	Rewrite
Ask	Predict	Regroup	Restate	Simplify
Change	Question	Rename	Restructure	Synthesize
Design	Rearrange	Reorder	Retell	Systematize
Generalize	Recombine	Reorganize	Revise	Vary
Modify				

Complex, Logical, Judgmental Behaviors

Analyze	Conclude	Deduce	Formulate	Plan
Appraise	Contrast	Defend	Generate	Structure
Combine	Critize	Evaluate	Induce	Substitute
Compare	Decide	Explain	Infer	

General Discriminative Behaviors

Choose	Detect	Identify	Match	Place
Collect	Differentiate	Indicate	Omit	Point
Define	Discriminate	Isolate	Order	Select
Describe	Distinguish	List	Pick	Separate

Social Behaviors

Accept	Communicate	Discuss	Invite	Praise
Agree	Compliment	Excuse	Join	React
Aid	Contribute	Forgive	Laugh	Smile
Allow	Cooperate	Greet	Meet	Talk
Answer	Dance	Help	Participate	Thank
Argue	Disagree	Interact	Permit	Volunteer

[2] This list was developed by Calvin K. Claus, Psychology Department, National College of Education, Evanston, Ill., and appears in Norman E. Gronlund, *Stating Behavioral Objectives for Classroom Instruction* (New York: Macmillan, 1978), pp. 53–56. Reprinted by permission.

Language Behaviors

Abbreviate	Edit	Punctuate	Speak	Tell
Accent	Hyphenate	Read	Spell	Translate
Alphabetize	Indent	Recite	State	Verbalize
Articulate	Outline	Say	Summarize	Whisper
Call	Print	Sign	Syllabify	Write
Capitalize	Pronounce			

"Study" Behaviors

Arrange	Compile	Itemize	Mark	Record
Categorize	Copy	Label	Name	Reproduce
Chart	Diagram	Locate	Note	Search
Circle	Find	Look	Organize	Sort
Cite	Follow	Map	Quote	Underline

Music Behaviors

Blow	Compose	Hum	Pluck	Strum
Bow	Finger	Mute	Practice	Tap
Clap	Harmonize	Play	Sing	Whistle

Physical Behaviors

Arch	Face	Jump	Push	Step
Bat	Float	Kick	Run	Stretch
Bend	Grab	Knock	Skate	Swim
Carry	Grasp	Lift	Ski	Swing
Catch	Grip	March	Skip	Throw
Chase	Hit	Pitch	Somersault	Toss
Climb	Hop	Pull	Stand	Walk

Arts Behaviors

Assemble	Dot	Illustrate	Press	Stamp
Blend	Draw	Melt	Roll	Stick
Brush	Drill	Mix	Rub	Stir
Build	Fold	Mold	Sand	Trace
Carve	Form	Nail	Saw	Trim
Color	Frame	Paint	Sculpt	Varnish
Construct	Hammer	Paste	Shake	Wipe
Cut	Handle	Pat	Sketch	Wrap
Dab	Heat	Pour	Smooth	

Drama Behaviors

Act	Display	Express	Pass	Show
Clasp	Emit	Leave	Perform	Sit
Cross	Enter	Move	Proceed	Start
Direct	Exit	Pantomime	Respond	Turn

Mathematical Behaviors

Add	Derive	Group	Number	Square
Bisect	Divide	Integrate	Plot	Subtract
Calculate	Estimate	Interpolate	Prove	Tabulate
Check	Extract	Measure	Reduce	Tally
Compute	Extrapolate	Multiply	Solve	Verify
Count	Graph			

Laboratory Science Behaviors

Apply	Demonstrate	Keep	Prepare	Specify
Calibrate	Dissect	Lengthen	Remove	Straighten
Conduct	Feed	Limit	Replace	Time
Connect	Grow	Manipulate	Report	Transfer
Convert	Increase	Operate	Reset	Weight
Decrease	Insert	Plant	Set	

General Appearance, Health, and Safety Behaviors

Button	Dress	Fasten	Taste	Unzip
Clean	Drink	Fill	Tie	Wait
Clear	Eat	Go	Unbutton	Wash
Close	Eliminate	Lace	Uncover	Wear
Comb	Empty	Stop	Untie	Zip
Cover				

Miscellaneous

Aim	Erase	Lead	Relate	Stake
Attempt	Expand	Lend	Repeat	Start
Attend	Extend	Let	Return	Stock
Begin	Feel	Light	Ride	Store
Bring	Finish	Make	Rip	Strike
Buy	Fit	Mend	Save	Suggest
Come	Fix	Miss	Scratch	Supply
Complete	Slip	Offer	Send	Support
Consider	Get	Open	Serve	Switch
Correct	Give	Pack	Sew	Take
Crease	Grind	Pay	Share	Tear
Crush	Guide	Peel	Sharpen	Touch
Designate	Hand	Pin	Shoot	Try
Determine	Hang	Position	Shorten	Twist
Develop	Hold	Present	Shovel	Type
Discover	Hook	Produce	Shut	Use
Distribute	Hunt	Propose	Signify	Vote
Do	Include	Provide	Slide	Watch
Drop	Inform	Put	Slip	Weave
End	Lay	Raise	Spread	Work

EXERCISE 9.1   HOW KNOWLEDGEABLE AM I ABOUT BEHAVIORAL OBJECTIVES? A DIAGNOSTIC TEST

I. Write an X before any of the following objectives that are stated in performance or behavioral terms.

_____ 1. The student will learn the major parts of speech.
_____ 2. The student will appreciate the significance of the Gettysburg Address.
_____ 3. The student will be able to construct an isosceles triangle with a protractor.
_____ 4. Given a model of a hypothetical cell, the student will identify the cellular structures.
_____ 5. The student will read and understand the chapter on civil rights.
_____ 6. The unit on chemical oxidation-reduction reactions will be reviewed.
_____ 7. The student will write an essay in which he develops an argument for or against family planning.
_____ 8. The student will volunteer to visit a pre-school program.
_____ 9. The student will become aware of the significance of supermarket shelving practice.
_____ 10. The students will translate the song "Hey Jude" into Spanish.
_____ 11. The student will correctly operate the duplicating machine.
_____ 12. From a list of ten substances, the student will identify those that are compounds and those that are mixtures.
_____ 13. The student will write the Spanish alphabet from memory.
_____ 14. The student will know the Mendelian laws.
_____ 15. The learner will show an appreciation of outdoor sports.
_____ 16. The learner will list the major causes of the Civil War.
_____ 17. Given three hypothetical situations, the student will decide which one best represents the posture of the Republican Party.
_____ 18. The student will learn to recognize differences between the music of Beethoven and Bach.
_____ 19. The student will learn ten French verbs.
_____ 20. The student will create in minature a model environment for an imaginary animal.

II. Classify each of the following objectives by writing the correct letter in the blank provided according to the following domains: Cognitive (C); Affective (A); or Psychomotor (P). Answers at the end of the test. Check your answers (after).

_____ 1. The student will correctly focus the microscope.
_____ 2. The student can summarize the histories of the origin of the two major political parties.
_____ 3. The student will identify from a list those items that are Spanish cognates.
_____ 4. The student will anonymously indicate in writing that this course has improved his confidence.
_____ 5. The student will volunteer to remain after class to help clean up the classroom.
_____ 6. The student will be able to identify the respective poets after reading and analyzing several poems.
_____ 7. The student will translate a French poem into English.
_____ 8. The student will accurately predict the results of combining equal quantities of any paired combination of secondary colors.
_____ 9. The student will voluntarily read outside material related to current events.
_____ 10. The student will make a goal in basketball a minimum of seven times in ten attempts.

III. For the following cognitive objectives, identify by the appropriate letter the highest level within that domain (one sub-domain which will be the highlight within a given objective): Knowledge (K); Comprehension (C); Application (Ap); Analysis (An); Synthesis (S); Evaluation (E).

_____ 1. When given a new poem, the student will recognize it as one of Shelley's.
_____ 2. The student will underline from a list those words that are spelled correctly.

Part I: The following objectives should be marked X: 3, 4, 7, 8, 10, 11, 12, 13, 16, 17, and 20. Part II:

(1) P, (2) C, (3) C, (4) A, (5) A, (6) C, (7) C, (8) C, (9) A, (10) P. Part III: (1) C, (2) K, (3) Ap, (4) S, (5) E.

—— 5. The students will write critical appraisals of their essays on capital punishment.
—— 4. The student will create a poem using the style that is designated.
—— 3. The student will read a pattern and correctly select the amount of material and equipment necessary to make a dress.

Selected References _____

Bergeson, John B., and George S. Miller. *Learning Activities for Disadvantaged Children*. New York: Macmillan Publishing Co., Inc., 1971.

Bloom, B., J.T. Hastings, and G.F. Madans. *Handbook on Formative and Summative Evaluation*. New York: McGraw-Hill Book Company, 1971.

Bruner, J.S. *The Process of Education*. Cambridge, Mass.: Harvard University Press, 1962.

Clark, Leonard. *Secondary and Middle School Teaching Methods*. Fourth Edition. Macmillan Publishing Co., Inc., 1981.

Gayles, Anne R. *Instructional Planning in the Secondary School*. New York: David McKay Co., Inc., 1973.

Georgiades, William, et al. *New Schools for a New Age*. Santa Monica, CA: Goodyear Publishing Co., 1976.

Gronlund, Norman E. *Stating Behavioral Objectives for Classroom Instruction*. New York: Macmillan Publishing Co., Inc., 1978.

Gronlund, Norman E. *Preparing Criterion-Referenced Tests for Classroom Instruction*. New York: Macmillan Publishing Co., Inc., 1973.

Horton, Lowell. *Mastery Learning*. Bloomington, Indiana: Phi Delta Kappa, 1981.

Nelson, Clarence H. *Measurement and Evaluation in the Classroom*. New York: Macmillan Publishing Co., Inc., 1970.

Plowman, Paul D. *Behavioral Objectives: Teacher Success Through Student Performance*. Chicago: Science Research Associates, Inc., 1971.

Popham, W., and E. Baker. *Establishing Instructional Goals*. Englewood Cliffs, N.J.: Prentice-Hall, Inc., 1970.

Tanner, Daniel. *Using Behavioral Objectives in the Classroom*. New York: Macmillan Publishing Co., Inc., 1972.

Part III
Choosing and Implementing Instructional Strategies

Drawing by Carol Wilson, unpublished material. Reprinted by permission.

Personally I am always ready to learn,
although I do not always like being taught.
—Sir Winston Churchill

We have asked you to assess your skills and perceptions (Part I). We have guided you through the process of deciding what to teach and in preparing plans for implementation (Part II). But to effectively implement a plan one must carefully decide a strategy choice.

This section of the book is concerned with *how* one might teach. It is important to again emphasize that there is no "magic bag of tricks," no singular magic formula. Teaching involves human interactions; and, because people differ, situations differ. What works for one teacher will not necessarily work for another in a similar situation. This means that the teacher must develop a large repertoire of strategies from which to choose.

As a secondary school teacher you will most likely be working with five or six classes a day with an average of approximately thirty students per class. You will need to develop your resourcefulness in awareness and use of a variety of motivational techniques or devices. Student intrinsic motivation is certainly not always evident to the teacher. "How can I motivate my students?" is a frequently overheard question teachers ask. "How can I interest them to study?" "How can I 'turn them on'?" These are questions of concern to almost every teacher we have known. We trust that what follows will further assist in finding answers to your own questions. In order to teach you must gain their attention (motivate them). We begin Part III with ideas for doing that.

10

What Are Some Motivational Strategies? An Annotated List of 166 Ideas

YOU MUST GAIN THEIR ATTENTION BEFORE YOU CAN TEACH

In this chapter we identify many potential motivators. We identify first those general to all fields; then we list motivators more specific to certain subject fields. You would do well to read all of the entries for each field, for although an entry might be identified as specific to one field it may well be useful in other areas or it might stimulate a creative idea for your own stock of motivational strategies.

General Ideas for Motivation

1. Your students should clearly understand the objectives of your class activities and assignments.
2. Show enthusiasm and interest in what you have planned and are doing.
3. Present the proper quantity of content at the proper pace.
4. Vary the teaching procedures and the activities. Let students follow the activities of their choice with responsibility for change.
5. Use familiar examples in presenting your materials. Don't just teach definitions, principles, theorems, or rules. Be certain to explicate these with concrete examples that can be understood by students.
6. Use audiovisual materials—but do not assume that films or filmstrips have "built-in motivation." Select those that would be relevant and interesting to the students on the topic or subject matter that is under consideration.
7. Use objects for the lesson—foreign stamps, coins, models, antiques, toys, and so on.
8. Plan your set induction (what you do the first few minutes of a class period) with care.
9. Keep students informed of their progress. Don't keep them in the dark as to where they stand.
10. Remember that students need to be recognized by you, their parents, and their peers.

11. Remember that students need steady awareness of progress being made, of "How am I doing?", "What can I do better next time?"
12. Talk with individual students, about their problems and their interests.
13. Go down your roll book periodically and ask yourself what you know about each individual in the class.
14. Students are sometimes motivated by extrinsic devices such as tests. Use this technique judiciously, not as a weapon for punishment.
15. Give praise or reward for jobs well done.
16. Utilize a modified version of the elementary show-and-tell activity.
17. Have the students make a movie or slide show of class activities (e.g., a role-playing lesson). Let them plan and write the narration.
18. Word naming in various categories—such as synonyms, same initial letters, various uses of a term—becomes an indicator of ideational fluency.
19. Invite guest speakers when and where appropriate. Perhaps some of the parents can be resource persons. (See also number 22)
20. Hold small-group discussions in class. These often are more beneficial than are large-group or all-class discussions.
21. Utilize Mondays or day following holidays to share with class an exciting or enjoyable experience.
22. Have students prepare a potential guest speaker resource file.
23. Try playing music in your classroom for mood setting.
24. Use educational games in your teaching. Many are being made available all the time. (Refer to Chapter 14 for sources)
25. Try role playing to enhance the reality of material being learned.
26. Try Unit Contract or contract teaching.
27. Write individual and personalized notes to students, on their papers, rather than merely letter grades or point scores.
28. Try video taping an activity and replaying to the entire class.
29. Use games and microlab exercises (Chapter 12) to provide a change of pace.
30. Have students plan with you the "open house" and/or "back-to-school-night" activities. This helps in getting parents out, too.
31. Let the class help plan a field trip.
32. Have the students create and design a simulation game for a specific subject area or controversial issue in your field.
33. Create student mailboxes out of ice cream cartons for distribution of papers. Be sure to have one for yourself. Everyone likes to receive mail. You may wish to limit mail delivery time to the first few minutes of the class period.
34. Recycle old textbooks by removing all text material but leaving pictures and diagrams, then have students create their own texts.
35. Get permission from the administration to redecorate your classroom with colorful walls, drapes, and stuffed furniture.

Art:

36. Use lyrics from popular music to influence class work, such as putting the lyrics into pictures.
37. Bring in examples of instructor's work, both current and beginning. This would enable students to easier relate their own beginning frustrations with instructors.
38. Going outside into school yard for free drawing experience.

39. Have them draw with the hand they never use.
40. Do a class mural on a piece of quarter-inch plywood.
41. Let them make their own kites and paint them. Demonstrate.
42. Arrange field trip for class to dig up natural clay. In class, sift and refine it, soak in water and work it into usable clay. Follow with hand-built clay project.
43. As part of a unit on the creative process, have each student draw on a piece of paper, then pass it on to the person next to him, and that person will make additions to the paper. Instructions could include "improve the drawing," "make the drawing ugly," "add what you think would be necessary to complete the composition."
44. As part of a unit on design or creativity, have students construct, design, and decorate their own kite. When the projects are complete, designate a time to fly them. Make necessary arrangements.
45. Listen to a musical recording and try to illustrate it.
46. Imagine that you're a bird flying over the largest city you have visited. What do you see, hear, smell, feel, taste? Draw a "sensory" map.
47. Assign a different color to each student. Have them arrange themselves into warm and cool colors and explain their decision (why blue is cool, etc.). (Include emotional responses to the color).
48. Make a class visit to local galleries to observe works of contemporary artists.

Business Education:

49. Choose a sentence or paragraph everyone has typed several times already. The instructions are for the students to type until they make an error, whether it be not capitalizing a word, typing a wrong letter, or whatever. The last one typing is the winner.
50. For production work, such as typing letters in a second semester typing class, you, the teacher, take on the role of the "boss." Therefore, when a letter is typed the "boss" will receive it for signing. In this way the students are not just typing a letter for a grade, but typing it for the "boss," which will mean the letter will be set up according to his instructions.
51. Make a field trip to the front office to observe and talk to the office workers. Those included in the interviews would be the principal's and the vice-principal's secretary, the registrar, and attendance clerks. This field trip would interest some students to seek student jobs in the office. In addition, there are other jobs on campus that they can find out about and investigate for possible employment. Back in the classroom, have each student report their findings to the rest of the class.
52. Have office (administration) personnel come into class and dictate some "real" letters and have students experience office-style dictation.
53. Compose crossword puzzles and newspaper cartoon strips in shorthand.
54. Arrange for students (on a rotational basis) to be "aides" to administration or free teachers to take, transcribe, and type dictation.

English (Including Speech, Drama, Journalism):

55. For a unit such as Elizabethan English, a wall-to-wall mural depicting a village of the times may be a total class project. Students can research customs, costumes, and architecture. Others may paint or draw.

56. For the holidays students can design their own holiday cards, creating their own poems for their cards.

57. To enhance understanding of parts of speech, set up this problem: Provide several boxes containing different parts of speech. Each student is to form one sentence from the fragments chosen from each box, being allowed to discard only at a penalty. The students then nonverbally make trades with other students to make coherent, and perhaps meaningfully amusing sentences. A student may trade a noun for a verb but will have to keep in mind what parts of speech are essential for a sentence. Results may be read aloud as a culmination to this activity.

58. Try this for an exercise in objective versus subjective writing. After a lesson on descriptive writing bring to the class a nondescript object, such as a potato, and place it before the class. Ask them to write a paragraph either describing the potato in detail, that is, its color, size, markings and other characteristics, or to describe how the potato feels about them.

59. Set up a special communications board somewhere in the room where students may write anonymously or post sealed comments addressed to particular individuals including the teacher.

60. Read to the class a story without an ending, then ask the students to write their own endings or conclusions.

61. Ask the students to create an advertisement using a propaganda device of their choice.

62. Ask the students to each create and design an invention and then to write a "patent description" for the invention.

63. Establish a "mini-library" in a corner of your room.

64. Ask students to write a physical description of some well-known public figure, such as a movie star, politician, athlete, or musician. Other class members may enjoy trying to identify the "mystery" personality from the written descriptions.

65. A bulletin board may be designated for current events and news in the world of writers. Included may be new books and record releases as well as reviews. News of poets and authors may also be displayed.

66. Start a paperback book library in your classroom. Set aside some time each week for reading. Perhaps one of your students would volunteer to serve as your "librarian."

67. Ask your students to maintain a daily "journal," with emphasis on expressing their feelings and unedited thoughts. Journals should be accepted as personal statements, which are to remain unjudged.

68. Provide students a choice as to which novel they will read next.

69. Design a "game" where students give original names to stories or captions to cartoons.

70. Remove the text from a Sunday newspaper comic strip and have the students create the story line.

71. Use popular recordings to introduce vocabulary words. Use for analysis of antonyms, synonyms, listening, writing, comprehension and other skill development.

72. Use newspaper want ads to locate jobs, as a base for completing job application forms and creating letters of inquiry.

73. Use video tape equipment to record employer-employee role-play situations, interviews for jobs, or child-parent situations, to develop language and listening skills.

74. Have students choose a short story from a text and write it into a play.

75. Use a round robin type of oral exercise to practice different kinds of sentence development.

76. Design an antonym game such as: have one student write a word on the board, then a student who correctly guesses the antonym goes to the board.

77. Have students look in newspapers and magazines for examples of the type of writing being studied in class. Give points for correct examples brought in.

78. When beginning a poetry unit ask students to bring in the words to their favorite songs. Show how these fit into the genre of poetry.

79. Once in a while dress yourself in costume and makeup and role-play the character your class is studying.
80. Have your students look for commercial examples of advertisements that might be classed as "eco-pornographic," i.e., ads that push a product that is potentially damaging to our environment.
81. Change the environment and ask students to write poetry to see if the change in surroundings stimulate or discourage their creativeness. For example, take your class to a large supermarket to write (you are advised to make arrangements first).
82. Bring a television set to class and have your students analyze advertisements for the emotions they appeal to, techniques used, and their integrity. Try the same thing with radio, teen magazines, and other media.

Foreign Languages:

83. Draw a large outline of France on cardboard and have students fill in the major cities, rivers, and mountains. They can illustrate products of different regions, costumes, and other significant characteristics of the country.
84. Translate the school menu into French each day. This could be the daily project of selected groups from within the class.
85. Perhaps your class could earn money and go to a French restaurant as an end-of-the-year activity. You could obtain copies of the menu in advance so that students could select and practice ordering in French.
86. Organize a spelling bee in French, using the French alphabet.
87. Play "Password" in French.
88. Begin a game by saying "I went to France and took a radio" in French. The next person repeats the sentence adding another item, e.g., "I went to France and took a radio, a raincoat." If a student misses an item then he is out; this continues until only one person remains.
89. Show the students a tray containing several or many items that they know how to say in French. Allow them a few minutes to study it, then remove it and ask them to list each of the items on the tray.
90. Use puppets in native costume for students to use in practicing dialogue.

Home Economics:

91. Take still photos of class members at special events such as dinners, fashion shows, field trips, and special projects. Build a scrapbook or bulletin board with these and display on campus or at Open House.
92. Encourage students to enter their projects in outside contests such as county fairs.
93. Collect cartoons related to food costs, consumer problems, and family relationships.
94. Instruct students on the means of obtaining and completing consumer complaint forms.
95. Set up authentic food tasting booths; set up campus tasting contests.
96. Establish a play school or nursery in conjunction with a Child Development class.
97. Use a large box wrapped as a gift to open a lesson on toy safety or toy purchasing.
98. Allow the students to plan and do the shopping for a food lab assignment.
99. Plan a unit on cultural foods, using the traditions, costumes, and music of a particular culture. Have the students decorate the room. Invite the principal for a meal and visit.
100. Take a trip to Small Claims Court. (Plan ahead and obtain permission.)

101. Plan a color and grooming unit. Ask students to match their personal colors closely to magazine photos. Match to color schemes to determine the most complimentary colors to wear or to use in household furnishings.
102. Try these nutrition-related games:
    a. Bring a bag full of all types of foods. Ask students to group them into the four basic food types. Let them eat the food as a reward for correct classifications.
    b. Pen the name of a food on a student's back. The student must ask another student questions until he guesses which food he is. Only "yes" or "no" response questions may be asked.
103. Plan a bulletin board displaying pictures of 100-calorie portions of basic nutritional foods and popular fad foods that contain only empty calories. The display can motivate a discussion on foods with calories and nutrients versus foods with empty calories.
104. Try this for motivation toward a unit on laundry: Pin the names of different garments on the back of students. The students are then to sort themselves into different wash loads. This is a fun game that motivates and involves an entire class.
105. For a clothing unit hold an "idea day." Ask each student to bring in an idea of something that can be done to give clothes a new look, a fun touch, or an extended wearing life. Ideas they may come with include: appliques, embroidery, tie-dye, batik, colorful patches, and restyling old clothes into current or creative fashions.
106. Have the students write, practice, and present skits, perhaps for video tape presentation, on consumer fraud.
107. Take the class on a field trip to the school cafeteria, a nearby supermarket, or a large restaurant. (Make necessary arrangements.)
108. Students should become familiar with shelving practices in stores and supermarkets.

Mathematics:

109. Plan an in-class mathematical debate.
110. Try a game of mathematical baseball. Divide the class into two teams. Arrange the room as a baseball field. The "pitcher" fires content questions to the "hitter." This can be a fun way to review for an examination.
111. Arrange mathematical tournaments with other schools.
112. Do a mathematical survey of your school campus.
113. Plan with your class a role-play unit where members role-play the solar system. Students calculate their weights, set up a proportion system, find a large field, and on the final day actually simulate the solar system using their own bodies to represent the sun, planets, and moons. Arrange to have it photographed.
114. Have your students build mathematical models. Pyramids can be of special interest to the students.
115. Encourage your students to look for evidence of Fibonacci number series* in nature and in man-made objects. Here are some examples of where evidence may be found: piano keyboard, petals on flowers, spermatogenesis and oogenesis, and many places in mathematics. Perhaps your students might like to organize a Fibonacci Club.
116. Become familiar with the many games available for teaching mathematics.

*Fibonacci numbers are a series of numbers, each of which is the sum of the preceding two; i.e., 1, 1, 2, 3, 5, 8...

Music:

117. Hang a cloth bag on the wall. Buy a sack of potatoes. For every song that students learn to sing, get a potato, write a date and a title of the song learned, and put the potato in the bag. At the end of the semester, buy a McDonald's certificate for each potato and divide them among the students.

118. Take the class to a concert. They can observe others playing their instruments.

119. Have students find ways in which music is used around them, i.e., for television.

120. Periodically during the school year, after the students are very familiar with a certain piece (have memorized it or can play it perfectly) switch the band or orchestra around by not putting any two of the same instruments together. For example, put no flutes next to each other, put a cello by a trumpet, a violin beside a drummer, or a saxophone next to a viola and bass. This ensures that each person knows his own part and can carry his own weight in terms of performance. This can also be done in chorus, mixing sopranos with altos, tenors, and basses, etc.

121. Find a popular song on the radio the students like. Transpose the melody into unfamiliar keys for each instrument. This makes the student want to learn the song, but in the process he will have to become more familiar with his instrument.

122. Set aside one weekend morning a month and hold small informal recitals (workshops) allowing students to participate/observe the performance situations(s) among their peers and themselves. (Students might be told previously about these "special days" and encouraged to prepare a selection of their own choosing.)

123. Listen to current popular musical recordings and discuss them as to musical content and performance techniques.

124. As an extra credit project, have students prepare brief oral reports on past composers and give an example of their music by recording, performance. (The student may even enjoy dressing the part of the composer.)

125. Trumpet Clinics: A. With trumpet teachers; B. With trumpet performers (all styles of music); C. With other students from other schools.

126. Plan different money-making projects such as singing telegrams.

Physical Education:

127. Students will choose a famous athlete whom they most admire. A short report will be written about the athlete. The student will then discuss the attributes and/or characteristics that they admire in the athlete, and how they feel they can emulate those qualities.

128. Students will make up an exercise routine to their favorite record, and share it with the class.

129. Have class divide into groups. Given the basic nonlocomotive skills, have each group come up with a "people machine." Each student within the group is hooked up to another demonstrating a nonlocomotive skill and adding some sort of noise to it. Have a contest for the most creative people machine.

130. Have a special talent day—where students may demonstrate an individual talent or group talent, relating it to physical education. (Might have them keep this in mind, practice on rainy days, and present it on a rainy day.)

131. Have a mini-Olympic day, where students help create the various events to be used, and give honors to winners.

132. Students are given a chance to design a balance beam routine that has two passes on the beam and that must include: front support mount, forward roll, leap, low or high turn, visit, chasse,

and cross support dismount. These routines will be posted to show the variety of ways the different maneuvers can be put together.

133. Divide the class into groups. Have them create a new game or activity for the class, using only the equipment they are given. Let the class play these newly created games.

134. Use Fridays as a game day—do not introduce anything new. Review what was taught earlier in the week. Have some kind of competitive games or relays related to the skills previously learned.

135. Videotaping is a good device to show students their errors and their improvements in a skill such as batting. It helps them see what they are doing and helps them develop a kinesthetic awareness of their movement.

136. Organize and make available to your students a trip to a professional, collegiate or any highly-skilled team's game. This usually will motivate them if they are at all interested in the sport.

137. Engage a guest speaker, preferably a professional athlete or coach in the sport you are teaching, to talk or demonstrate specific skills.

138. Exercises done to popular music. Let students take turns bringing in music and leading the exercises. The teacher will furnish a general outline to follow.

Science:

139. Have your students create microscopes with bamboo rods and drops of water at each end.

140. Have your students make litmus indicators from petals of flowers.

141. Assign themes or problems that require students to predict or hypothesize decision making in a critical incident.

142. Use Polaroid cameras for students to record and immediately share observations.

143. Use cassette-tape recorders to record sounds of the environment. Compare day and night sounds. (This can also be helpful in poetry writing.)

144. If you are a life science teacher, make sure your classroom looks like a place for studying life rather than death.

145. The technique of "show and tell" is an excellent motivator and can be modified to be useful to the secondary school teacher. Do not allow students to "rip off" the environment of such things as flowers or beneficial insects or tide-pool life.

146. Encourage students to hypothesize, then to collect data, using their own environment.

147. Use your imaginations. If you want, for example, to study predator-prey relationships but you are located in an inner-city school, then your class might use landlord-tenant situations for the study.

148. Have your students make their own cosmetics. Share what you are doing with the Home Economics teachers—perhaps you can combine your efforts.

149. Divide your class into groups and ask each group to create an environment for an imaginary animal using discarded items from the environment. By asking questions each group will try and learn about other groups' "mystery" animals.

150. Be aware of relevant programs being shown on local television stations. Perhaps you can let students observe one during class time by pretaping if necessary.

151. If your students have never seen an ocean, a forest, or mountains, and you cannot take them on an appropriate field trip, then do the next best thing and go yourself (perhaps during vacations) and take slides or moving pictures to show them. (Become aware of any income-tax advantages available to you as a teacher.)

152. Become familiar with the many educational games available for teaching science. Refer to Chapter 12 for sources.

153. Have your students make their own useful items as related to science, things such as the following:
    a. Library paste: one-half cup cornstarch to three-fourths cup cold water, stir to paste, then add six cups of boiling water and stir until translucent, then cool to room temperature.
    b. Baby oil: two tablespoons of almond oil, eight tablespoons of olive oil, and a few drops of perfume, stir all ingredients together—keep out of reach of children.
    c. Concrete cleaner: dry mix these—sodium metasilicate, three and one-quarter cups; trisodium phosphate, three-quarters cup; soda ash, one-half cup.

    Build a collection of "home recipes." Perhaps that would be a good class project; a special bulletin board could be arranged to display the collection.

Social Science:

154. Establish a special "people and things" bulletin board.
155. Have your class play charades to learn geography.
156. Set up a classroom broadcast studio where students prepare and present news broadcasts.
157. Take your class on an imaginary trip around the world. Students can role-play countries.
158. Let your class plan how they would improve their living environment, beginning with the classroom, then moving out to the school, home, and community.
159. Become familiar with the many games available for teaching social studies. Refer to Chapter 12 for sources.
160. Start a pictorial essay of the development and/or changes of a given area in your community, e.g., a major corner or block adjacent to the school. This is a study that would continue for years and has many social, political, and economic implications.
161. Start a folk hero study. Each year ask "What prominent human being who has lived during the twentieth century do you most admire?" Collect individual responses to the question, tally, and discuss. After you have done this for several years you may wish to share with your class for discussion purposes the results of your surveys of previous years.
162. Play the "Redwood Controversy" game. (See Chapter 12.) Perhaps you and your class can design a simulation game on a controversial social issue.
163. Role-play a simulated family movement West in the 1800s. What items would they take? What would they throw out of the wagon to lighten the load?
164. Have students collect music, art, or athletic records from a particular period of history. Compare with today. Predict the future.
165. Using play money, establish a capitalistic economic system within your classroom. Salaries may be paid for attendance, bonus income for work well done, taxes collected for poor work, and a welfare section established in a corner of the room.
166. Divide your class into small groups and ask that each group make predictions as to what world governments, world geography, world social issues, or some other related topic, will be like some time in the future. Let each group give its report, followed by debate and discussion.

With the preceding suggestions we have only scratched the surface in providing ideas. The total possibilities are limited only by the courage and imagination of the teacher.

A source of valuable information, including ideas for motivation, can be the professional journal(s) for your field. We provide here a list for many fields. Check for their availability in your school library.

PROFESSIONAL PERIODICALS USEFUL TO SECONDARY TEACHERS

Art

Art Education
School Arts
Studies in Art Education
The Art Teacher

Bilingual Education

Bilingual Review

Business Education

American Business Education
Business Education Forum
Business Education World
Business Teacher
Journal of Business Education

English and Reading

English
English Journal
English Language Teaching Journal
Educational Theatre Journal
Journal of Reading
Research in the Teaching of English

Foreign Languages

Classic Journal
Hispania
Language Learning
Modern Language Forum
Modern Language Journal
The French Review
The German Quarterly

Home Economics

Forecast for Home Economics
Journal of Home Economics

Industrial Arts

Industrial Arts and Vocational Education
Industrial Arts Teacher
Industrial Education
School Shop

Mathematics

Arithmetic Teacher
Mathematics Teacher
School Science and Mathematics

Music

The American Music Teacher
Educational Music Magazine
Journal of Research in Music Education
Music Educators Journal
The School Musician

Physical Education

Athletic Journal
Journal of Physical Education
Journal of Physical Education and Recreation
Physical Education

Science

Journal of Chemistry Education
Journal of Geological Education
School Science and Mathematics
Science and Children
Science Education
The American Biology Teacher
The Chemistry Teacher
The Physics Teacher
The Science Teacher

Social Studies

Social Education
Social Studies
Integrated Education

TESOL (Teaching English for Speakers of Other Languages) Quarterly

EXERCISE 10.1 DEVELOPING YOUR OWN INVENTORY OF MOTIVATIONAL TECHNIQUES

We leave this exercise somewhat open and to be designed by your class, but what we do suggest is that you build—perhaps by a card file—your own inventory of ideas you might sometime use as motivational strategies. Share your ideas with other members of your class. You might start by completing the following task: List four ideas on motivation that you might try and that are not included in the 166 suggestions in this chapter.

_____

_____

_____

_____

11

What Kinds of Teaching Methods and Techniques Are Available? Specifics for Building A Strategy Repertoire

The competent teacher has a large repertoire from which to choose his specific strategy. In this book we have supplied a large section on methods of instruction, to enable you to develop your own repertoire.

It is important that the teacher know why he has chosen a particular strategy. The novice teacher is likely to be inclined to use the strategy that was most common in his college classes—the lecture. The lecture method, unless it is a 15-minute minilecture, is seldom an effective strategy for the instruction of secondary school students.

Our experiences indicate that competent teachers in secondary schools are skillful strategists with questioning. They are aware of the significance of teacher response strategies and are capable in the fitting of questioning and response strategies into the larger strategy concept of inquiry teaching. Much of this chapter is devoted to the development of these competencies.

SOME INSTRUCTIONAL STRATEGIES

Audiovisual
Committee activity
Computerized instruction
Debate
Demonstration
Discovery
Discussion (large group/small group)
Dramatization
Drill
Field trip
Games
Group therapy/encounter experiences/sensitivity
    awareness

Guest speaker
Independent study
Individualized instruction
Inquiry
Laboratory
Learning activity packets
Lecture
Library/resource center/media center
Panel
Problem solving (problem analysis)
Question and answer
Review and practice
Role playing

Roundtable
Self-instructional packages
Study guides
Supervised study
Symposium

Teaching machine
Team learning
Team teaching
Textbook
Unipac

A. THE LECTURE[1]

In spite of the fact that secondary school teachers are constantly admonished not to lecture to their students, the technique is widely used. This method of teaching has been grossly abused by many teachers and their students have suffered; but, correctly used, it is functional.

At the outset it should be pointed out that there is a difference between formal lecturing and informal lecturing or "teacher talks." The short informal lecture can be used to good advantage in introducing a unit, summarizing a problem for study, providing information difficult for students to find, supplying motivation, or sharing one's cultural experiences with the class.

How to Make the Lecture Effective

The teacher talk or informal lecture can be made more effective by giving attention to the following suggestions:

1. Lectures for secondary school students should usually be short. One of 15 or 20 minutes is possibly the maximum; in most cases five or ten minutes may be better. Teachers must recognize that attention spans are relatively short. Although instruction by television depends briefly on lecture, it is also highly spread with demonstration and visual cuing. Time intervals tend to be longer, but variety is the key. Straight lecturing must still be for short periods.
2. The approach to the lecture should be informal. The language should be clear and simple, not stilted. The purpose is to inform, to enrich, to motivate.
3. Lectures should be tailored to people, and in the high school the teachers must not forget that the audience is one of adolescent boys and girls. Lecturing teachers are inclined to use words beyond the students' backgrounds, knowledge, and skills.
4. Lectures should be related to students' backgrounds, knowledge, skills, and interests. If they are not, the students are soon "lost."
5. Lectures should not rehash textbooks or other material the students have read or should read for themselves. The lecture should present new and fresh ideas not readily available to the students.
6. Lecturers should avoid reminiscences or discourses on trivial personal incidents.
7. Lectures should be planned and organized so that they do not digress. In the main the teacher should announce his purpose at the beginning of the lecture. Its development should then stick to the theme. The exact purpose of the talk must not be forgotten as it develops. Some lectures are like the classic report on Columbus and his discovery of America: "He didn't know where he was going when he started, he didn't know where he was when he got there, and when he returned he didn't know where he had been."
8. Talks should be replete with verbal illustrations. Illustrations can accent abstract ideas.
9. Frequently lectures are improved if supplemented by simple visual aids such as specimens, flat pictures, or chalkboard sketches.

[1] Marvin Alcorn, James S. Kinder, and Jim R. Schunert, *Better Teaching in Secondary Schools* (New York: Holt, Rinehart and Winston, 1970), pp. 154–155. Reprinted by permission.

10. The relatively long lecture should include a summarization at its close.
11. The teacher should give the class instruction in taking simple notes and in organizing verbal material.

B. QUESTIONING[2]

Questioning is a useful art or tool and, in the hands of a skillful teacher, serves numerous useful learning purposes. Good questions stimulate thought and encourage students to question themselves, other students, and the teacher; they act as a sounding board against which the correctness or acceptability of ideas may be tested; they promote the aims of the lesson in a concise manner; and they encourage discussion.

The Nature of Questions

Good questions will have some of these characteristics:

1. They should be worded in clear, concise, and suitable terms to fit the abilities and ages of the pupils.
2. They should avoid vague, general queries. As far as ambiguity is concerned, the most common type of faulty question begins with "What about . . .?" Such a vague query as "Are there any questions?" also fails to elicit a response. Make the question specific, as in this example: "What causes the earth to rotate on its axis?"
3. Questions should be asked in a quiet, encouraging manner. Avoid firing questions like pistol shots or conducting a third degree. Students need to be at ease and free from tension.
4. Key questions should be well worded and thought out in advance. However, there should be flexibility to deviate from preplanned discussion to allow for unexpected and timely questions by students.
5. Questions should elicit complete responses (except in unison drill), not just "yes" or "no." Ask a few significant questions during a discussion period rather than innumerable minute ones that capitalize on the memorization of isolated facts. This is why it was suggested in the chapter on lesson planning that a few key questions be included in daily plans.
6. Questions should be varied in type. Questions may be asked to elicit simple recall, comparison and contrast, choice of alternatives, classification, illustration or example, or to present a relationship. Other types may ask the students to describe, explain, outline, or organize ideas in any of several ways. We recommend that you practice three question types:

   A. *Probing Questions*—probing requires that teachers ask questions that require pupils to go beyond superficial "first-answer" responses.
      (1) Ask the pupil for more information and meaning.
      (2) Require the pupil to rationally justify his response.
      (3) Refocus the pupil's or class's attention on a related issue.
      (4) Prompt or give hints.
      (5) Bring other students into the discussion by getting them to respond to the first student's answer.

[2] *Ibid.*, pp. 157–158.

B. *Higher-order Questions*—questions that cannot be answered from memory or simple sensory description. They call upon the student to draw his own conclusions. A good higher-order question prompts students to use ideas rather than just to remember them. Although some teachers intuitively ask such questions, far too many overemphasize questions that require only the simplest intellectual activity on the part of their students.

C. *Divergent Questions*—these are usually open-ended and have no single correct answers. They require the student to think creatively; to leave the comfortable confines of the known and reach out into the unknown.

Recognizing Levels of Classroom Questions[3]
(The Three Main Types)

What is expected in the use of a competent questioning strategy is to move the students from simple cognitive levels of recall to higher levels of application. The material that follows will identify these levels of questioning and provide some exercises designed to assist you in recognizing and developing your questioning skills.

1. The *Recall* question is designed to draw out of the student the information, feelings, or experiences which he has acquired in the past. It is intended to bring forth data from the student which he can then process at the next higher level. Some examples of cognitive processes which students use at this level are:

Enumerating	Recalling	Describing	Counting
Listing	Matching	Completing	Identifying
Observing	Reciting	Defining	Selecting

Some examples of teachers' questions are:

"How many states are there that bound California?"
"How did it feel when you touched the battery?"
"Tell us how the picture looks to you."
"What word does this picture go with?"
"What is the definition of 'haggard'?"
"What did you see the man doing in the film?"
"What were the names of the children in the family?"
"What did they do when it rained?"
"How many of you are buying milk today?"

2. The *Processing* question is designed to have the student draw some relationships or cause and effect, to synthesize, analyze, compare, or classify the data which he has acquired. Some examples of cognitive processes that students use at this level are:

Inferring	Comparing	Sequencing	Making analogies
Explaining	Classifying	Organizing	Experimenting
Analyzing	Contrasting	Grouping	Distinguishing

[3] Arthur Costa, *Basic Teaching Behavior* (San Anselmo, CA: Search Models Unlimited, 1973), pp. 6–7. Copyright by Arthur Costa. Reprinted by permission.

Some examples of teachers' questions are:

"How can we compare the strength of steel to the strength of copper?"
"Why did Columbus believe he could get to the east by sailing west?"
"What (do you think) the author means by the phrase, 'darkling pool'?"
"How did the direction the rivers ran affect the Civil War?"
"Compare the results from the first trial to the results of the second trial?"
"What do these results mean to you?"
"Why wouldn't you keep this acid in a glass bottle?"
"Can you put into groups the things which a magnet will and will not pick up?"

3. The *Application* question is designed to have the student go beyond the data or concept which he has developed and to use it in a new or hypothetical situation. Some examples of the cognitive processes which students use at this level are:

Applying a principle	Theorizing	Extrapolating
Speculating	Predicting	Model building
Imagining	Hypothesizing	Evaluating
Forecasting	Finding examples	Modifying
Inventing	Judging	Generalizing

Some examples of teachers' questions are:

"What (do you think) would happen if the nomads of the desert had all the water they could use?"
"What are some of the things which might happen if the Sierra Nevada Range were to disappear?"
"What do you think Mary is going to do to solve her problem?"
"Can you tell us how you think the story is going to end?"
"Give some examples of Romantic period music."
"Can you think of some way to use this bimetal strip to make a fire alarm?"
"Which of these pictures best describes the way you feel?"
"What can you say about countries which are dependent upon one crop?"
"What will happen to our weather if a high pressure area moves in?"
"If our population continues to grow as it does, what will life be like in the twenty-first century?"

EXERCISE 11.1 DEVELOPING YOUR QUESTIONING STRATEGIES

The chart that follows illustrates the differences in the level of questioning and the ways in which students and teachers respond to given questions. Study the chart carefully and check your recognition by doing Exercise 11.2. Test your answers against those of other members of your class. Exercises that follow will further develop your questioning skills.

QUESTIONING STRATEGIES

Level of Questioning	Teacher Initiates with:	Student Responds by:	Teacher Responds to Student with:
Recall	Questions or instructions that cue the student to respond with a descriptive statement, to recall, to recite, to list, or to enumerate. *Example:* "Who invented the telegraph?" "What is the capitol of California?"	Recalling facts or previously learned information. *Example:* "Marconi." Or "I don't know."	Cues that maintain or reinforce the level of student's thinking. *Example:* "Good," "That's right," "O.K."; OR Instructions or follow-up questions. *Example:* "Do you remember where that was?" "Would you look that up for us?"
Processing	Questions or instructions that cue the student to use data to show relationships or cause and effect; to synthesize, classify, analyze, or compare data. *Example:* "How do the rhythmic strengths of these two melodies compare?" "Why shouldn't you keep this liquid in a metal container?"	Explaining, inferring, analyzing, or showing relationships between the data.	Acceptance, elaboration, or classification responses that maintain the inference level. OR Follows with another processing question.
Application	Question that causes the student to predict, theorize, or apply a principle in a new situation; to do divergent thinking. *Example:* "What do you think would happen if Americans were no longer dependent upon outside sources of oil?"	Predicting, hypothesizing, or applying the principle he has learned previously to a new situation.	Acceptance, elaboration, clarification that maintain this cognitive level.

EXERCISE 11.2   IDENTIFYING COGNITIVE LEVELS OF CLASSROOM QUESTIONS

Mark each statement with:

1 if it asks the student to recall, identify, or enumerate.
2 if it asks the student to process data.
3 if it asks the student to apply, predict, or theorize.

_____   1. Who was the author of the poem we read yesterday?
_____   2. How is the poem we read yesterday like the poem we are reading today?

_____ 3. Why do you think the author of this poem repeated the last line of every verse?

_____ 4. What do you think would happen if the Sierra Mountains were to disappear?

_____ 5. How many states border California?

_____ 6. When did Columbus arrive in America?

_____ 7. In what year was Hawaii granted statehood?

_____ 8. Can you summarize some of the things we learned about the Spanish settlers of California?

_____ 9. In what ways did they differ from other early settlers?

_____ 10. How do you think the lives of early settlers would have been different if California had not been under the government of Mexico?

_____ 11. Why did people have to fight each other for the land?

_____ 12. How could we change it to the Dorian mode? (Music students will explain.)

_____ 13. From what you have read, what are the three laws that both governments have in common?

_____ 14. What are some similarities between the Republican party today and when it was first organized?

_____ 15. What would life be like if there were no laws?

_____ 16. What are the three branches of American government?

_____ 17. How does Guilford's structure of the intellect compare with Bloom's taxonomy?

_____ 18. What would happen to a dialogue if every student wrote his answer on paper before the teacher called for him to respond?

_____ 19. In what ways are spoken and written questions similar and different?

_____ 20. How would classroom dialogue be affected if students understood the questioning strategy the teacher was using?

_____ 21. What are some of the examples of cooperation as found in "competitive" sports?

_____ 22. In which ways does girls' basketball differ from boys'?

_____ 23. How would batiks differ if you were to use differing kinds of wax?

_____ 24. How would music be today had the piano never been invented?

_____ 25. How many Romance languages exist today?

Check your responses to this exercise with those of other members of your class and discuss until you concur and understand. Now go to Exercise 11.3 and practice writing some examples of processing and application questions.

EXERCISE 11.3   RAISING QUESTIONS TO HIGHER LEVELS

Recall	*Processing*	*Application*
1. How many new cars are being sold today?	Why are Americans buying new cars? Are there more new cars being sold this year than last?	What do you think would happen if Americans stopped buying new cars?
2. What was the theme of last week's major news event?	How does the news today differ from the news of a year ago? 100 years ago? Why is it different? What similarities are there?	What do you think the major news items will be a year from now? 100 years from now?
3. What are the names of the countries that make up the oil monopoly?	Complete these blanks and share your responses with members of the class.	

4. What are the primary colors?

_____

5. Name three Spanish cognates.

_____

Check your responses of Exercise 11.3 with other members of your class. After reaching agreement and understanding now move on to Exercises 11.4-5, in the same manner as the preceding parts of Exercise 11.

EXERCISE 11.4   CREATING COGNITIVE QUESTIONS

After you have read "The New Catechism" in Chapter Two of this text, compose *three* questions that cause the students to identify, list, or recall; *three* questions that cause the students to analyze, compare, or explain; and *three* questions that cause the students to predict, apply, or hypothesize.

Recall Questions: 1. _____

_____

_____

2. _____

_____

_____

3. _____

_____

_____

Processing Questions: 1. _____

_____

_____

_____

2. _____

_____

_____

3. _____
_____
_____

Application Questions: 1. _____
_____
_____

2. _____
_____
_____

3. _____
_____
_____

EXERCISE 11.5   ANALYZING TEXTBOOK QUESTIONS

Examine secondary school student textbooks and workbooks from your teaching field. (Complete the following on separate paper.)

1. List examples of recall questions you found.
2. Rewrite an example of a recall question you found into a processing and into an application question.
3. List examples of process questions you found.
4. List examples of application questions you found.
5. Locate a series of questions in the text and describe the sequence of questions as to types.
6. Identify the book(s) you examined by title, publisher, and year.
7. Locate an older (or newer) textbook for the same subject and examine the types of questions found as you did for the first book. Similarities or differences?

EXERCISE 11.6   MINI LESSON FOR PRACTICING QUESTIONING STRATEGIES

Before class each member should plan a five-minute mini-lesson for the purpose of posing different types of questions and teaching a brief lesson via this questioning.
Form groups of four, comprised of:

1. Sender.
2. Receiver.
3. Judge.
4. Recorder.

Your tasks:

1. The Sender: pose recall, processing, or application questions.
2. The Receiver: respond to the questions of the sender.
3. The Judge: After the sender has asked a question and the receiver has responded, identify the level of question used by the sender and the level of response given by the receiver.
4. The Recorder: (a) Tally the number of each level of question used by the sender on the tally sheet, and (b) record any "hang-ups" or problems that your group encounters or identifies.

Each member of the group will function in each role for about five minutes, then switch roles so that each member has an opportunity to serve in each role.

The Types of Problems the Teacher May Encounter in Questioning.[4]

Several situations will arise with all teachers, but especially with beginning teachers. Among them are the following:

1. *Student questions for which the teacher doesn't know the answer.* In such situations you can:
   a. Toss the question to the class.
   b. Ask a student to look up the answer, or ask the class to look in their books to make sure of the answer.
   c. Admit you don't know the answer but will look it up.

Don't guess or bluff about questions on which you are not sure. You are very likely to be trapped in a hole from which you cannot extricate yourself!

Students need to find out that no one can know everything. But they also need to learn that you and they can go to the right places for answers.

2. *Student questions that do not relate to the topic.* Your decision at this point will be determined by how important the question is, whether this student needs to have an immediate reply, and whether it will take too long to answer. Here are some of the possible ways to handle such a situation:
   a. Answer it quickly and return to the topic.
   b. Postpone the question until later. In that case you may want to write a word or phrase on the board to remind you of this question.
   c. State that it is a good question but that you will answer it after class or the next day.
   d. Decide to depart from the lesson you had planned in order to clarify the question that has been raised. It may be very germane to the lesson and you may not be able to proceed until it is answered.

Perhaps this example will help you. If you are planning to go to Chicago from New York City and must reach that point in a limited amount of time, don't tarry on the way. If you have lots of time, take a detour. You may discover something interesting en route. If you have still more time and really don't have to go to Chicago anyway, take the road that leads to Boston!

[4] Leonard S. Kenworthy, *Guide to Social Studies Teaching in Secondary Schools*, 4th ed., pp. 141–142. ©1973 by Wadsworth Publishing Company, Inc. Reprinted by permission of Wadsworth Publishing Company, Belmont, California 94002.

C. INQUIRY[5]

In an increasing number of classrooms, the students, instead of remembering isolated facts, are learning how to learn. Their teachers, instead of acting as dispensers of ready-made conclusions, are teaching them to think for themselves and to use the methods of disciplined inquiry to explore concepts in the various domains of knowledge and to study the world about them.

Teaching through inquiry is the process of formulating and testing ideas and implies an open classroom climate that encourages wide student participation and the expression of divergent points of view.

Mystery Island: A Lesson in Inquiry[6]

One of the most effective ways of stimulating inquiry is to use materials that provoke the students' interest. These materials should be presented in a nonthreatening context, such as a game or puzzle, in which students can think and hypothesize freely. The teacher's role is to encourage the students to form as many hypotheses as possible and to be able to back up these hypotheses with reasons. After the students suggest several ideas, the teacher should begin to move on to higher-order, more abstract questions that involve the development of generalizations and evaluations.

Inquiry lessons, such as the Mystery Island geography problem presented here, have a special advantage because they can be used with almost any group of students, regardless of ability. Members of each group approach the problem as an adventure in thinking and apply to it whatever background they can muster. Background experience may enrich a student's approach to the problem but is not crucial to his use or understanding of the evidence presented to him.

Mystery Island is presented as it is given to students. They receive information about the island in sequence. Map 1 includes data about rivers, lakes, and size (scale). This map is followed by information about landforms (Map 2), vegetation (Map 3), and climate (Map 4). Other data maps, one showing mineral deposits or transportation networks, for example, could easily be added to this series.

All students are asked to solve the same problem after getting each new piece of information. The key problem is to locate "the biggest city." Students are asked, in effect, to accumulate geographic evidence about a place, to form hypotheses, to review these hypotheses in the light of new evidence, and to refine their notions about the reasons underlying the location of cities.

After introducing each new element of Mystery Island, the instructor could ask: "Now that you have this information about Mystery Island, what additional information would be most important to you in understanding the Island? Explain why." Other questions could include: "Where would most people live?" "Where would the least number of people live?" and "What would people do for a living on Mystery Island?"

All student hypotheses or predictions about the location of cities, population distribution, or the economy of Mystery Island should be backed by reasons. These hypotheses can then be analyzed, discussed, and evaluated by the class as a whole.

In addition to analytical problems concerning Mystery Island, value issues may also be proposed for solution. One such issue could center on the clash that occurs when a technologically advanced culture and a technologically undeveloped culture meet on the island. For example, what would happen

[5] Byron G. Massialas, *Today's Education* (NEA Journal, May 1969), p. 40. Reprinted by permission.
[6] Jack Zevin, *Today's Education* (NEA Journal, May 1969), pp. 42–43. Reprinted by permission.

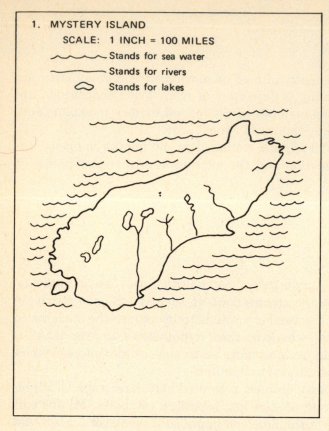

1. MYSTERY ISLAND
   SCALE: 1 INCH = 100 MILES
   ～～～ Stands for sea water
   ——— Stands for rivers
   ⌒ Stands for lakes

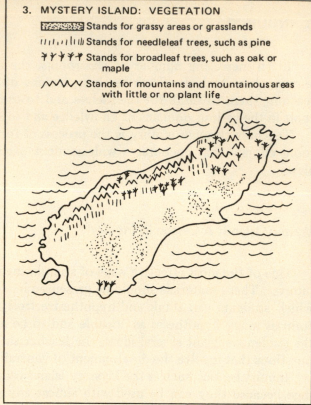

3. MYSTERY ISLAND: VEGETATION
   ▨ Stands for grassy areas or grasslands
   ιιιιιιι Stands for needleleaf trees, such as pine
   ⋎⋎⋎⋎ Stands for broadleaf trees, such as oak or maple
   ∧∧∧∧ Stands for mountains and mountainous areas with little or no plant life

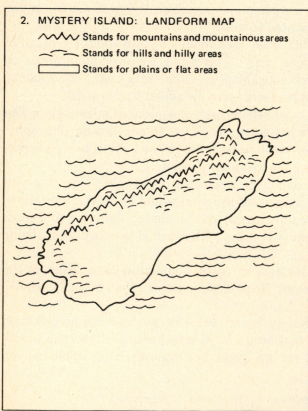

2. MYSTERY ISLAND: LANDFORM MAP
   ∧∧∧ Stands for mountains and mountainous areas
   ～⌒～ Stands for hills and hilly areas
   ▭ Stands for plains or flat areas

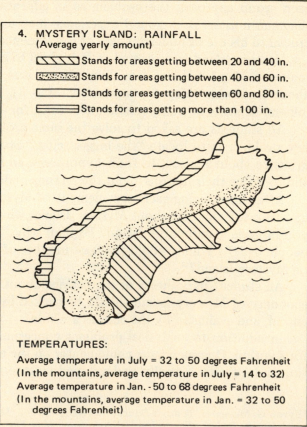

4. MYSTERY ISLAND: RAINFALL
   (Average yearly amount)
   ◨ Stands for areas getting between 20 and 40 in.
   ▨ Stands for areas getting between 40 and 60 in.
   ▭ Stands for areas getting between 60 and 80 in.
   ▤ Stands for areas getting more than 100 in.

TEMPERATURES:

Average temperature in July = 32 to 50 degrees Fahrenheit
(In the mountains, average temperature in July = 14 to 32)
Average temperature in Jan. - 50 to 68 degrees Fahrenheit
(In the mountains, average temperature in Jan. = 32 to 50 degrees Fahrenheit)

if Mystery Island were inhabited by a group of hunters and gatherers and was then invaded by people of a different racial or ethnic origin who possessed superior skills?

Students could be asked such questions as: Should the original population be allowed to mix with the new people? What problems will each group face if they live separately? If they live together? What would be best for all concerned parties? Why?

The reader is invited to look at Mystery Island and try to solve the problem posed to the students—locating the biggest city on the island. Take into account all the evidence provided here and make a list of reasons to back up your decision.

D. DISCUSSION[7]

This is a job that really calls for some expertise. The leader must be able to draw from the members of the group their ideas, responses, and information. He must facilitate talk. He is the parliamentarian, as it is he who, by a nod, a word, or some transitional phrase, skillfully passes the verbal ball from person to person. It is the discussion leader who keeps the group "in the groove," when there is the potential for a heated exchange, or the group is getting sidetracked over some irrelevant point. He must know what to do and how to do it.

What to Do	*How to Do It*
Elicit responses.	Be accepting and nonjudgmental.
Encourage presentation of different points of view.	Get to know the members of the group through pre-discussion conversations.
Act as parliamentarian.	Know and observe the rules of order without being inflexible or rigid.
Prevent domination by any member or small group.	Set time limits per speaker and for summary time.
Keep the discussion relevant.	Elicit several statements of the central ideas presented.
Summarize the outcomes of the discussion.	Present the final summary.

The discussion leader cannot be partisan, particularly if the topic considered is such that members of the group could become sharply polarized. He must prevent domination by a minority or a majority. In the prediscussion warm-up or preparation session, he should try to identify those who try to talk too much and those who do not want to offend by talking. The leader himself must never dominate the discussion, for this will "turn off" all members of panel and audience who feel frustrated in trying to express their ideas. The leader must be alert to the signals for recognition. He can direct the discussion by using comments such as, "What do you want to add to George's statement, Frank?"

An effective discussion leader should have some idea of the maturity of the members of the group to be sure that he is eliciting maximum participation in quality as well as quantity. A student may be reluctant to handle controversial aspects of an issue. This reluctance may stem from his lack of experience, lack of maturity, or the fear that he will "get in bad" with the teacher or the other students if he says what is on his mind. Such inhibitions to discussion can only be removed by a long-range program in which you have emphasized.

1. Respect for the ideas and opinions of others
2. Protect the right of everyone to say what he is thinking even if it is not popular
3. Discuss as a means of seeking truth, not a forum for forcing one idea upon all

[7] Joan M. Leonard, John J. Fallon, and Harold von Arx, *General Methods of Effective Teaching: A Practical Approach* (New York: Crowell, 1972), pp. 231–232. Reprinted by permission.

From this consideration of the role of the discussion leader, it might appear that only a mature, experienced teacher could fill this post. Even though you may be the best equipped person available to lead a discussion, education involves the giving of responsibility to the learner. Therefore, you must use student discussion leaders and let them learn by doing. You will have to work closely with those students selected for this sensitive position in order to introduce them to the demands of the role they are to play. As students learn to assume this responsibility, they will better understand the delicate balance that any leader must strike to ensure the maximum benefit in a learning situation.

What is Your Role in Discussions?

In small-group discussions you will assist the group in setting up the presentation, prepare the audience for active listening and participation in questioning, and help to create an atmosphere in which the learning experience can be put to use. Your maturity, your greater knowledge of content, and the special insights you have developed about your students will be of great value in this preparation for a meaningful discussion.

During a large-group discussion, you may be a member of the panel, you may be the discussion leader, or you may be a member of the audience. Whatever your role in a particular discussion, stick to it. It is important to let students assume responsible positions and undertake the leadership and planning of some discussions. Your role will then be that of a consultant. You assist them in learning to express their ideas and opinions and set up guidelines and operating rules. As the students gain experience in this kind of activity, you will find that they are more willing to assume responsibility in other types of learning activities. They will be able to work more independently in laboratory or workshop sessions; they will assume more responsibility for doing their homework assignments, summarizing, reviewing, and studying. They are then really learning how to learn.

E. COMMITTEE ACTIVITY

Contrary to what some teachers think, committee types of activities for small-group discussions, projects, and so on, require a great deal of preparation on the part of the teacher. It is not "students do all the work" and "teacher just watches" or "rests." The following guidelines will help you in using the committee method successfully:

1. Explain to the students the purposes and the functions of each committee.
2. Be specific in instructing the students about the tasks to be accomplished. You can plan the tasks together with the students.
3. If appropriate, have students form the committee; let them select the chairman, recorder, and so on, as flexibly and as voluntarily as possible. Sometimes it is necessary for the teacher to assign committee members to balance the academic and socioemotional climate of the group.
4. Remind students that committee activity is a socialized team-learning situation, the success of which depends on the cooperation and the orderliness of the committee members.
5. Please don't give up when the first trial-run fails, especially when the students are not used to this method. Try again.

F. THE DEMONSTRATION

Whenever you plan to use demonstration as a method in your class, the success of your lesson will largely depend on how well you prepare for the demonstration.

GUIDELINES FOR A SUCCESSFUL DEMONSTRATION

1. Identify for yourself the purpose of your demonstration. The purpose might be one of the following:
   a. To illustrate a particular concept.
   b. To set up a discrepancy or to establish problem recognition.
   c. To assist in the recognition of a solution to an existing problem.
   d. As a means of review.
   e. To serve as an unusual lesson closure.

2. Familiarize yourself with the advantages and disadvantages of the demonstration as a teaching strategy. Incorporate this awareness in your planning for the demonstration lesson. A potential disadvantage is a result of the fact that the students are not learning by doing but rather by watching, but this may be necessary because of time pressures, lack of sufficient materials, or potential hazards involved. A good demonstration, however, can stimulate thinking and productive discussion. Use the following guidelines in planning your demonstration:
   a. Decide the best way to conduct the demonstration, i.e., talk or be silent; student or teacher; entire class or small groups.
   b. Insure that the demonstration is visible to all students. The installation of overhead mirrors is sometimes worth the expenditure in classrooms where demonstrations are frequent.
   c. Be sure to familiarize your class with materials and procedures being used in demonstration.
   d. Carefully plan your pacing in the demonstration, allowing time for wait-see events.
   e. Take time to insure the understanding of events.
   f. Keep your demonstration as simple as possible and working toward its stated purpose.
   g. And, finally, plan for what could go wrong during the demonstration. Make a dry-run demonstration.

3. If you want to create some special effects during your demonstration, you can spotlight it by turning off classroom lights and using a slide projector as the spotlight. Special prerecorded music can add an even greater dramatic effect.

G. TEXTBOOK TEACHING

Experience tells us that the majority of teachers do not like the textbook that they are currently using. Our feeling is that secondary school students need a textbook in their hands regardless of the merits of the book. We would suggest that the teacher who does not like the book make this clear to the students with such a statement as "this is the best we have, let's make the most out of it." Several very effective teachers we have known have had their classes put together their own textbooks during the course of the year or have modified the existing text.

Levels of Textbook Teaching[8]

Since the textbook lends itself readily to a variety of procedures of varying merits, it is perhaps well to indicate some of them in the approximate order of ascending merit:

[8] Edgar B. Wesley and Stanley P. Wronski, *Teaching Social Studies in High School*, 5th ed. (Lexington, Mass.: Heath, 1964), pp. 362–363. Copyright by Stanley P. Wronski. Reprinted by permission.

1. Perhaps the most unworthy level on which the textbook can be used is that of memorizing recitations. This procedure, as originally practiced, has almost passed from the scene, but remnants of it are still evident in the requirement that pupils repeat the phrases of the textbook and give the events in the order of the textbook account.

2. The second level of the textbook method is that on which the teacher assigns designated pages and then devotes the class period to ingenious questions designed to see how literally and faithfully the pupils remember what the author said. The exact words of the textbook are not required, but the faithful paraphrasing of them is called for. Within a very narrow interpretation, students on this level may be said to master given passages of the textbook even though they secure only a dim view of the whole book.

3. On the third level of the textbook method, the students read the designated pages and prepare outlines, summaries, or parallel accounts. This procedure involves a considerable degree of insight and originality and the ability to read critically. The teacher or a designated student presents his contribution, orally or on the chalkboard. The class discusses its merits and defects, modifies and amends it, and agrees upon a final authorized version, which becomes the basis of future reviews and syntheses. Although work on this level can easily become formalized, it has great possibilities for teaching skills and qualities as well as for imparting information.

4. On the fourth level the teacher utilizes the class period to teach the pupils how to read, to analyze, to outline, to summarize; in brief, how to study. Instead of the textbook being the principal objective, it becomes the means toward the achievement of information, worthy skills, attitudes, and qualities. The textbook is still important, but it is recognized as a means rather than the standard of achievement, as the repository of raw materials rather than the pattern for pupil imitation. This level might be described as the open textbook method. It means that emphasis is placed upon directed learning rather than upon inspectional quizzing.

5. On the fifth level, the teacher, with the aid of the class, superimposes upon the textbook an independent organization. This organization is fundamentally similar to that of the textbook, but it contains additional parts and points in order to force departures from the textbook. Relying largely upon the text, but to some extent upon other texts and references, the class fills in the outline of the independent organization. This process involves the synthesizing of two organizations and the wider use of materials. It is a high level of teaching.

6. On the sixth level of textbook teaching, the book is utilized, but it determines none of the fundamentals, such as content, organization, or method. It is used, but merely because it is a convenient aid. It is useful as a supplement, as a basis for common understanding, as a point of departure, but it does not mark the limits of content or procedure. In fact, this level, to a considerable extent, is no longer in the categories of the textbook method, and is here described to show that the textbook can be useful in a great variety of procedures; for no matter what project, activity, or problem the class proposes to follow, its members will still gain by having a statement of the basic information and procedures. The textbook becomes, not a restricting force, but the actual means of liberation. When it is so used, the class is free to pursue discussions, work problems, engage in projects, or perform any kind of activity that the teacher thinks is profitable.

H. ASSIGNMENT TEACHING

Guidelines for Developing Assignments

1. Plan early in the course the types of assignment you would give (daily assignments, long-range assignments, minor or major assignments) and prepare assignment specifications.
2. Provide differentiated assignments (different assignments according to the interests and abilities of students) rather than uniform assignments (everyone doing the same assignment).

3. Present as many choices of assignments for the students as possible.
4. Find out in advance what resources would be required for the completion of assignments (resource materials they can use at home or in the school or library; materials they need to purchase; and so on).
5. Do not use assignments as punishment.
6. Do not use assignments purely as a busy work. The teacher must have a clear and educational objective behind each assignment.
7. You need to follow up assignments methodically. When the majority of your students are not responsible for the assignments (especially reading assignments), you should use part or whole of your class time on the assignment.
8. Help your students with the assignments individually. Explain the work in detail so that the students will not say, "I don't understand what you want" or "This assignment doesn't tell me what to do and how to go about it."
9. When the students choose an assignment of a controversial nature (for example, a survey of racial attitude, drugs, or sex) or an assignment that poses a safety hazard (for example, science experiments or using power machinery), have the students obtain permission for it from their parents.
10. *It is best not to give assignments orally.* Daily or minor assignments should be written on the board and long-range or major assignments should be prepared in printed form. Never give the assignment by shouting at the end of the period after the bell has rung.

I. INDIVIDUALIZING INSTRUCTION

After you become more familiar with the needs, interests, and abilities of your students, you can make concrete attempts to individualize your teaching in many different ways. You may find some of the guidelines below useful:

Slow Learners

1. Emphasize effective communication skills (speaking, listening, reading, and writing).
2. Help them to improve their reading skills (pronunciation, word meaning, and comprehension). Reading is a *skill* that every teacher must teach no matter what subject he teaches.
3. Teach subject-matter content in small sequential steps, with provision for lesson options.
4. Use a wide variety of audiovisual and game materials, as they tend to appeal to more than one sense at a time.
5. Through constructive discipline, teach positive attitudes of self.
6. Do not depend on a single textbook. Use interesting supplementary materials of different reading levels.
7. Minimize homework assignments. Let them work in class with your assistance and under your supervision.
8. Review and reinforce the materials as frequently and as meaningfully as possible.
9. Compliment and reward for work well done.
10. Whenever and wherever appropriate, subdivide the class into several small groups of similar ability and interest.
11. Learn as much about each of your students as you can.
12. Cover the material *slowly* and methodically.
13. Help the students in the development of their reading skills.
14. Prepare self-instructional packets for individual students (See Chapter 8).

More Capable Learners

1. Find out as accurately as possible the present level of achievement of the student.
2. Enrich the student's reading skills (speed reading or enrichment reading program).
3. Provide self-instructional, independent learning opportunities. Try programmed texts, teaching machines, learning activity packets, self-instructional packages, or time waiver assignments.
4. Emphasize skills in critical thinking, problem solving, and research.
5. Provide as many alternatives as possible for projects, experiments, investigations, or assignment options.
6. Let the student plan and carry out with responsibility his own activities for learning.
7. Provide seminar situations for the students to discuss topics or problems under study.
8. Stress the quality of the process and product of learning rather than the quantity and duration of various activities.
9. Encourage your department to adopt "enrichment" classes and to pursue the development of an "alternative" curriculum.
10. Encourage your department to pursue a flexible or modular schedule.
11. Bring in effective guest speakers with whom the students can identify and relate.
12. Plan field trips.

J. INDEPENDENT STUDY

Of the numerous innovative programs in secondary education today, independent study has gained increasing recognition from secondary school teachers. Independent study, as the term connotes, is a means of learning activity whereby the student can independently or with teacher assistance pursue his own course of action for the investigation, experimentation, and application of concepts, problems, or skills of his choice.

It must be stated clearly, however, that the student engaged in an independent study must demonstrate strong commitment for the responsibility and the freedom he can exercise during his independent study activities. Consider the following programs for your application.

Some Possible Activities for Independent Study in Secondary Schools[9]

1. Some released time given from a regular class so that some students may work independently on individually planned studies *in addition* to class assignments.
2. Some released time given from a regular class so that some students may work independently on individually planned studies *in lieu of* class assignments.
3. Seminar groups that are smaller than ordinary classes in which students work independently, at least part of the time, on common or individual topics, units, or problems.
4. Individually planned program of *curricular* study with regularly scheduled time to study independently, in or out of school, with a minimum of teacher direction and supervision.
5. Independent study as part of a program of instruction organized around large- and small-group instruction.

[9] James D. Wells, from unpublished doctoral dissertation at the University of Florida, Gainesville, FLA: "Independent Study Students in Secondary Schools and Their Expectations and Satisfactions in Independent Study." Reprinted in William Alexander and Vynce Hines, *Independent Study in Secondary Schools* (New York: Holt, Rinehart and Winston, 1970), p. 182.

6. Individual *extracurricular* enrichment study with students working independently before or after school or on weekends (school facilities open mornings, nights, or weekends).
7. Vocational or work experience programs of instruction in which students work independently, in or out of school, so that they will develop salable skills.
8. A curricular program that emphasizes the development of student responsibility in regard to the individual's use of regularly offered independent study time. Subsequently, one of the objectives of the school's instructional program is developing the independent, self-directed learner.
9. A regularly scheduled class in the school's instructional program which *normally* requires that students work independently (for example, school publications, advanced courses in art, industrial arts, music) as individual members of a regular class.

Some Ideas for Independent Study in Various Subject Fields

Art and Music

1. Study history and appreciation; collect slides and make narrations.
2. Student show or concert.
3. Visiting or conversations with local artists and performers.
4. Performance of original works.
5. Participation in local festivals.
6. Participation in beautification of campus.
7. Differentiated contract assignments.

English

1. Individualized reading for remedial or enrichment.
2. Selected reading in area of one's own interest about an author, a period, or a current best seller.
3. Interview or correspondence with prominent authors, journalists, or theatre performers.
4. Cross-age tutoring in reading and language arts.
5. Projects in creative writing, drama production, filming.
6. Differentiated contract assignments.

Foreign Language

1. Individualized reading for remedial or enrichment.
2. Use of audio equipment for dialogue.
3. Visiting compact communities where a foreign language is used extensively.
4. Pen pal or exchange student.
5. Special reports on foreign country visits.
6. Special credit for foreign travel.
7. Differentiated contract assignments.

Mathematics

1. Cross-age tutoring.
2. Advanced placement study.
3. Special studies on history of mathematical topics.
4. Building math models.
5. Differentiated contract assignments.

Physical Education

1. Independent study in skill preferences.
2. Differentiated contract assignments.
3. Use of video-tape equipment for special skill development study.

Science

1. Observation and participation in community laboratories.
2. Participation in science fairs.
3. Participation in local "clean-up" drives.
4. Communication with scientists, engineers, and technicians.
5. Differentiated contract assignments.

Social Studies

1. Interviews and opinion polling for local and national issues.
2. Attendance and reporting on local governance agency meetings.
3. Establishment of student court.
4. Participation in student government.
5. Intensive study in specific areas of interest.
6. Differentiated contract assignments.

Whatever the agreement for independent study, there should be systematic monitoring of student progress and organized procedures for reporting and evaluation of completed studies.

EXERCISE 11.7   ANALYSIS OF A TEACHING EPISODE

Instructions: The following scenario describes an actual teaching episode. Read it carefully, then answer the questions that follow and prepare to discuss in class.

Background Information: A high school government class
30 students present on this day
A Monday in March
Period 1, 8:30–9:20 a.m.

The Episode:

8:25–8:30—The students are arriving, teacher is in room chatting with some of the early arriving students.

8:30   —Bell rings, all stand for Pledge of Allegiance.

8:31   —Teacher: "Open your books to p. 49 and read for about 10 minutes the background material for today's lesson, to p. 55."

8:31–8:41—Students read quietly, one or two arrive (tardy) during this time; teacher takes attendance, places attendance slip on door hook; teacher writes on board a list of words to remember and the word "SAVE."

8:41   —A quiet buzz session involving three students begins in one area of room, teacher moves there and quietly asks if they are finished reading, students answer "yes"—the three students quiet now, teacher moves and stands in rear of room.

8:45   —Teacher: "Is everybody finished?" No response tells teacher it is time to begin lecture.
        Teacher: "From the reading, what problems faced the organization of labor?" (pause) "Anyone?"
       1st Student: "Leadership!"
         Teacher writes "leadership" on board.
       2nd Student: "Money!"
         Teacher writes "financial" on board.
       3rd Student: "Time!"
         Teacher writes "time" on board.
       1st Student again: "Criminal infiltration!"
         Teacher writes "criminal infiltration" on board.

8:58   —Teacher lectures for next 20 minutes on "problems of organizing," mentioning the problems the Indians of South Dakota must be facing today in organization.
       Although no student response was solicited, one boy says, "Yeh! Let's go on strike against the school."
       Another says, "Yeh, man, let's go sit in the Principal's office."
       Another student adds, "Let's get the Principal!"
       A fourth student comments, "Right on, man. Teachers strike!"
       The teacher does not respond to these comments, other than with an occasional smile.

9:18   —Teacher completes the lecture and adds, "Tomorrow we will look at the way in which labor solved these problems."

9:19   —Students begin to meander toward exit in anticipation of class change bell.

end of scenario

Questions to answer for Exercise 11.7:

1. *Identify* the teaching strategies used by this teacher. Consider specifically set induction, closure, methods and materials used, and specific teacher behaviors such as acceptance, silence, etc.
2. How effective was each strategy during this lesson?
3. What were the good points of the instruction?
4. How might the instruction have been improved?

QUESTIONS FOR DISCUSSION

1. Would you like to teach by inquiry? Compare what you now know about inquiry teaching with the descriptions of two teaching styles as found in Chapter 3.
2. Did you as a high school student experience independent study?
3. What new strategies have you learned about that you are now anxious to try in your teaching?
4. What are the limitations of "linear teaching?"
5. What is your opinion regarding homogeneous grouping in the subjects you intend to teach?
6. Items 1 through 5 call for your subjective opinions on various issues related to teaching strategies. Take one of your opinions that evolved from the discussions and see if you can research evidence to support that opinion.
7. In Exercise 11.7 did you consider carefully the Background Information? Does it have any significance for this scenario?

12

What Are Some Game Techniques and Devices for Teaching?
Educational Games and Communication Exercises

It used to be believed that teaching and learning must be all work and no play. With this conviction, teachers traditionally based their teaching on rote memory, reasoning, and problem solving, theorizing, that (1) the learning occurs only when the learner is confronted with difficult tasks, and (2) the student's mind must be rigorously disciplined (mental discipline theory).

We are convinced that the game elements in teaching can play important and valuable roles at all levels of education. Judiciously and intelligently used, game activities can serve as:

1. motivational devices.
2. media for instructional variety.
3. simulated learning experiences.
4. devices to evaluate the students' progress.

WHAT ARE "EDUCATIONAL GAMES?"

Games are devices intended to promote fun and laughter. Contests, on the other hand, stimulate competition. A game-contest includes both characteristics, fun and competition. A third device is a simulation, which is intended to model reality. A simulation-game would then be a device that is fun and that models reality, but for which there is no competition, that is, no winner and losers. As you can see, there are seven potential combinations of devices loosely referred to as "educational games." These are:

1. pure games.
2. pure contests.
3. pure simulation.
4. contest-games.

5. simulation-games.
6. contest-simulations.
7. simulation-game-contests.

It is beyond the scope of this text to analyze the advantages and disadvantages of each of these types for classroom use. Games within each type can have benefits to classroom teaching and we would encourage the reader who is interested to explore further the references cited in this chapter.

Microlab communication exercises (also called self-awareness, group encounter, and communication workshop exercises) can be educationally sound and psychologically constructive when they are used prudently, with the objectives and directions clearly communicated to the students. Microlab exercises in secondary school teaching often contribute to greater understanding of the communication problems involving oneself, interaction in the classroom, and the group dynamics of the learning environment. We suggest that you examine the games and microlab exercises introduced in this chapter and use them when appropriate.

A. GAMES FOR TEACHING—EXAMPLES

Game 1: Name Anagrams[1]

1. Write your full name at the top of a sheet of paper.
2. See how many words can be found in your first name.
3. See how many words can be found in your middle name.
4. See how many words can be found in your last name.
5. Now, see how many words can be found in your entire name.
6. Try to use all the letters in either your first, middle, or last name in one word; for example, Mary—Army.

Game 2: Sentence Scrummy[2]

Card Sample Directions:

---

[1] Mary E. Webb, original games, unpublished, 1972. Reprinted by permission.
[2] *Ibid.*

1. Shuffle the cards word side down.
2. Deal each player five cards.
3. Place the rest of the cards face down on the table.
4. The dealer then draws one card from the deck; he discards either the new card or one of the five cards he was dealt. He may never have more than five cards in his hand.
5. The discard pile should be reshuffled if the deck runs out.
6. Each player adds and discards until one player has five cards which make a complete meaningful sentence.
7. Articles, prepositions, and conjunctions may be inserted into the sentence as they are needed.
8. Any form of the verbs may be used.
9. Adjectives may be changed to adverbs.

Calling for specific sentence patterns, such as noun, verb-intransitive, adverb, adds variety to the game.

The first player to form a meaningful five-word complete sentence wins the hand for a count of ten points.

One hundred points constitutes a game.

Game 3: Living Tic Tac Toe[3]

Place nine chairs in the center of the room to represent "tic tac toe" diagram. Divide class into two sides. Teacher asks side 1 a question; if a student gets the right answer, he takes his position as desired to represent an "X." If he gets the wrong answer, the teacher asks side 2 a new question. Alternate sides until one side has made three in a row.

Game 4: Musical Bingo (Adaptable to Any Subject)

Five categories are chosen. In the sample music game, the categories are: rock groups; solo artists; songs; solo or band artists from the 1950s; and, instruments.

The bingo caller will draw a category with a corresponding column on it and the student will cover the subject which relates to the particular category. For example: the caller would say "G song" and if the student has a song title in the "G" column he/she will cover it with his/her marker. The game continues until there is a winner.

Different varieties of bingo may be played, e.g., blackout, four corners, across, up and down, and diagonal.

Blank bingo cards are given to the students before the game begins and the students fill in the squares with subjects pertaining to the five categories chosen.

---

[3] Games No. 3–6, materials obtained through various in-service workshops for teachers, unpublished. Original sources unknown.

B I N G O

B	I	N	G	O
Eagles	piano	tambourine	trumpet	The Four Seasons
Chuck Berry	Fats Domino	America	Cher	guitar
Drums	Paul Simon	Free Spot	Rhinestone Cowboy	Neil Sedaka
Elton John	Let Your Love Flow	Barry Manilow	Chicago	Oh What A Night
Silly Love Song	Spinners	Elvis Presley	Platters	Bill Haley

Game 5:   Descriptive Writing

Bring into the class objects of different textures: velvet, sandpaper, peeled grapes, soapstone, and so on. Students feel the objects and describe them in written form.

Game 6:   Tasting Party

Break the class into five or six groups. Each group should have things to taste, such as canned chips, onion rings, banana chips, boiled eggs, cold soup, brown mustard, and so on; each tests, tastes and independently writes a description. The group corrects for accuracy and detail.

Game 7: Equivalent Fractions Game[4]

1. *The Cards:* The deck is made up of 42 cards, each card bearing one fraction. Make two cards of each of the following: 1/2, 1/4, 2/3, 3/2, 3/5, 5/4, and 1/5. Make one card each of: 6/12, 3/6, 4/8, 8/16, 4/16, 3/12, 2/8, 6/24, 8/12, 10/15, 6/9, 4/6, 18/12, 9/6, 12/8, 24/16, 6/10, 12/20, 9/15, 15/25, 10/8, 15/12, 20/16, 30/24, 3/15, 4/20, 2/10, 5/25.
2. *Objective:* To be the first to get two "books." Each person (four players) deals six cards. A "book" is composed of three cards: one card with a fraction reduced to lowest terms, two cards with fractions equivalent to the fraction reduced to lowest terms.
3. *Play:* After being dealt six cards, the players look at them to see if they have any equivalent fractions. If they do, put them together. The players take turns drawing and discarding cards until one person gets two books. As a player completes a book, he must lay it on the table, face up. Play continues until one person collects two books. The winner is the person who first collects two books.

Alternative Version (Similar to "Concentration"):

All cards are placed face down on the table. The two players take turns turning over two cards until one gets a pair of equivalent fractions. The player getting the pair then collects the pair, gaining a free turn. Play continues until all cards have been collected. The winner is the player with the most cards.

Game 8. Cooperation Square Game: An Experiment in Cooperation[5]:

Before class, prepare a set of squares and an instruction sheet for each five students. A set consists of five envelopes containing pieces of stiff paper cut into patterns that will form five 6- by 6-inch squares, as shown in the diagram. Several individual combinations will be possible but only one total combination. Cut each square into parts a through j and lightly pencil in the letters. Then mark the envelopes A through E and distribute the pieces thus: Envelope A, pieces i, h, e; B, pieces a, a, a, c; C, pieces a, j; D, pieces d, f; and E, pieces g, b, f, c.

Erase the small letters from the pieces and write instead the envelope letters A through E, so that the pieces can be easily returned for reuse.

Divide the class into groups of five and seat each group at a table equipped with a set of envelopes and an instruction sheet. Ask that the envelopes be opened only on signal.

Begin the exercise by asking what *cooperation* means. List on the board the behaviors required in cooperation. For example: Everyone has to understand the problem. Everyone needs to believe that he can help. Instructions have to be clear. Everyone needs to think of the other person as well as himself.

Describe the experiment as a puzzle that requires cooperation. Read the instructions aloud, point out that each table has a reference copy of them, then give the signal to open the envelopes.

The instructions are as follows: Each person should have an envelope containing pieces for forming squares. At the signal, the task of the group is to form five squares of equal size. The task is not completed until everyone has before him a perfect square and all the squares are of the same size.

---

[4] Patricia Skinner, an original game, unpublished, 1973. Reprinted by permission.
[5] *Today's Education* (NEA Journal, Oct. 1969), p. 57. Reprinted by permission.

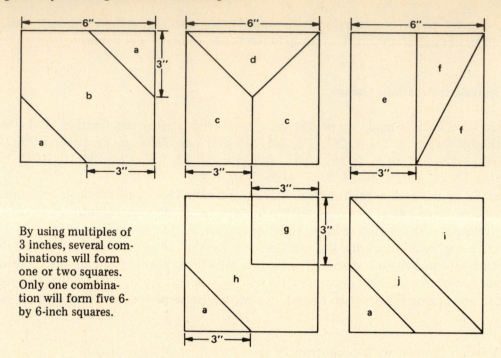

By using multiples of 3 inches, several combinations will form one or two squares. Only one combination will form five 6-by 6-inch squares.

These are the rules: No member may speak. No member may ask for a card or in any way signal that he wants one. Members may give cards to others.

When all or most of the groups have finished, call time and discuss the experience. Ask such questions as: How did you feel when someone held a piece and did not see the solution? What was your reaction when someone finished his square and then sat back without seeing whether his solution prevented others from solving the problem? What were your feelings if you finished your square and then began to realize that you would have to break it up and give away a piece? How did you feel about the person who was slow at seeing the solution? If you were that person, how did you feel? Was there a climate that helped or hindered?

If students have helped to monitor, they may have observations to share.

In summarizing the discussion, the teacher may wish to review behaviors listed at the beginning. He may also want to ask whether the game relates to the way the class works from day to day.

Game 9.   Lunar Survival Game: Lost on the Moon—Problem Sheet[6]:

You are in a space crew originally scheduled to rendezvous with a mother ship on the lighted surface of the moon. Mechanical difficulties, however, have forced your ship to crash-land at a spot some 200 miles from the rendezvous point. The rough landing damaged much of the equipment aboard. Since survival depends on reaching the mother ship, the most critical items available must be chosen for the 200-mile trip. Below are listed the fifteen items left intact after landing. Your task is to rank them in terms of their importance to your crew in its attempt to reach the rendezvous point. Place number 1 by the most important item, number 2 by the second most important, and so on through number 15, the least important.

____ Box of matches

____ 50 feet of nylon rope

[6] Original source unknown.

____ Two .45-calibre pistols

____ Life raft

____ Portable heating unit

____ Two .45-calibre pistols

____ One case of dehydrated milk

____ Two 100-pound tanks of oxygen

____ Stellar map of the moon's constellation

____ Life raft

____ Magnetic compass

____ 5 gallons of water

____ Signal flares

____ First-aid kit containing injection needles

____ Solar-powered FM receiver-transmitter

Lost on the Moon—Scoring Key

Listed below are the correct rankings for the "Lost on the Moon" items, along with the reasons for the rankings.

_15_ Box of matches (little or no use on the moon).

_4_ Food concentrate (supplies daily food).

_6_ 50 feet of nylon rope (useful in tying the injured, helps when climbing).

_8_ Parachute silk (shelter against sun's rays).

_13_ Portable heating unit (useful only if party landed on dark side).

_11_ Two .45-calibre pistols (self-propulsion devices could be made from them).

_12_ One case of dehydrated milk (food; mixed with water for drinking).

_1_ Two 100-pound tanks of oxygen (filled respiration requirement).

_3_ Stellar map of the moon's constellation (one of the principle means of finding directions).

_9_ Life raft (its carbon dioxide bottles could assist in self-propulsion across chasms and the like).

_14_ Magnetic compass (probably no magnetized poles, thus useless).

_2_ 5 gallons of water (replenishes water loss, e.g., from sweating).

_10_ Signal flares (distress call within line of sight).

__7__ First aid kit containing injection needles (oral pills or injection medicine valuable).

__5__ Solar-powered FM receiver-transmitter (distress signal transmitter, possible communication with mother ship).

COMMERCIALLY PRODUCED EDUCATION GAMES

This is a sample of the many educational games that are available and that can be used to teach, in a fun-filled and interesting way, the understanding of various concepts. This list is by no means exhaustive. Please add to this list successful games that you have used.

All games listed here are suitable for use with persons of junior high school through adult age. The game titles sometimes imply that the game is worthwhile only in a specific subject field, but this is not always the case, as the list will indicate. The games are listed alphabetically according to their titles.

Subject Area	Title	Approximate Cost	Publisher	Address
Biology	*Biology Bingo*	$ 12.75	Nova Scientific	5
	Dirty Water	10.00	Urban Systems	10
	Circulation	20.00	Nova Scientific	5
	Ecology	10.00	Nova Scientific	5
	Endangered Species	9.95	Nova Scientific	5
	Extinction	12.00	Sinauer	7
	Evolution: Geologic Time Chart	17.50	Nova Scientific	5
	Food Chains	20.00	Nova Scientific	5
	Food Web	15.00	Nova Scientific	5
	Metric Bingo	12.75	Nova Scientific	5
	Mouse in the Maze	6.00	Houghton Mifflin	1
	Monarch: Game of B & M	5.75	Nova Scientific	5
	Pollution	9.00	Houghton Mifflin	1
	Population	10.00	Urban Systems	10
	Predator-Prey Ecology Kit	6.00	Urban Systems	10
	Predator: The Food Chain Game	5.20	Nova Scientific	5
	Redwood Controversy	7.50	Houghton Mifflin	1
	Smog	10.00	Urban Systems	10
	The Pollination Game	6.60	Nova Scientific	5
	110 Animals	9.00	Nova Scientific	5
Business	*Ecology*	10.00	Urban Systems	10
Chemistry	*Elements*	5.60	Union Printing Company	11
	Metric Bingo	12.75	Nova Scientific	5
Civics	(see Government)			
Computer Programming	(see Mathematics)			
Consumer Education	(see Home Economics)			
Earth Science	(see Science)			
Ecology	(see Environmental Education)			
Economics	*Inflation*	23.00	Social Studies School Service	8
	Planet Management	12.00	Houghton Mifflin	1
	Pollution	9.00	Houghton Mifflin	1
	Star Power	3.00	Social Studies School Service	8
	(see also Social Studies)			

Subject Area	Title	Approximate Cost	Publisher	Address
Energy Education	*Energy Bingo*	12.75	Nova Scientific	5
	Energy Management	38.50	Nova Scientific	5
English	*Modern Logic*	13.00	Wiff'n Proof	12
	Phlounder	7.95	3M Company	4
	Propaganda Game	11.00	Wiff'n Proof	12
	Redwood Controversy	7.50	Houghton Mifflin	1
	Science & Language	13.00	Wiff'n Proof	12
	Word Structures	10.00	Wiff'n Proof	12
Environmental Education	*Anyone Can*	29.50	Nova Scientific	5
	Blacks & Whites	6.95	Psychology Today	6
	The Cities Game	6.95	Psychology Today	6
	Commercial Land Use Game	75.00	IHERS	2
	Dirty Water	10.00	Urban Systems	10
	Ecology	10.00	Urban Systems	10
	Energy Management	38.50	Nova Scientific	5
	Environmental Planning	12.60	Nova Scientific	5
	Endangered Species	9.95	Nova Scientific	5
	Food Chains	20.00	Nova Scientific	5
	Food Web	15.00	Nova Scientific	5
	Predator: Food Chain Game	5.20	Nova Scientific	5
	The Dead River	15.00	Nova Scientific	5
Health Science	*Health Science Bingo*	12.75	Nova Scientific	5
	Super Sandwich	14.95	Nova Scientific	5
General Science	*110 Animals*	9.00	Nova Scientific	5
	AC/DC: The Electric Circuit Game	5.75	Nova Scientific	5
	Constellation: Card Game of the Stars	3.50	Nova Scientific	5
	Elements	5.60	Union Printing	11
	General Science Bingo	12.75	Nova Scientific	5
	Metric Bingo	12.75	Nova Scientific	5
	Mouse in the Maze	6.00	Houghton Mifflin	1
	Nautilus: Game of Seashells	5.95	Nova Scientific	5
	Science and Language	13.00	Wiff'n Proof	12
	Space Hop	13.95	Nova Scientific	5
Government	*Acquire*	7.95	3M Company	4
	Election U.S.A.	16.95	Social Studies School Service	8
	Metropolis	3.00	Social Studies School Service	8
	Redwood Controversy	7.50	Houghton Mifflin	1
	Smog	10.00	Urban Systems	10
	(see also Environmental Education)			
History	*American History Game*	210.00	Science Research Associates	9
	North vs. South	10.00	Social Studies School Service	8
	Redwood Controversy	7.50	Houghton Mifflin	1
Home Economics	*Cost of Living Game*	3.00	Social Studies School Service	8
	Decimeter	14.00	Nova Scientific	5
	Go and Grow	26.00	Nova Scientific	5
	Inflation	23.00	Social Studies School Service	8
	Metric Bingo	12.75	Nova Scientific	5
	Super Sandwich	14.95	Nova Scientific	5
Industrial Arts	*AC/DC: The Electric Circuit Game*	5.75	Nova Scientific	5
Mathematics	*Creative Mathematics*	10.00	Wiff'n Proof	12

Subject Area	Title	Approximate Cost	Publisher	Address
	Decimeter	14.00	Nova Scientific	5
	Metric Bingo	12.75	Nova Scientific	5
	Set Theory	10.00	Wiff'n Proof	12
Psychology	Ghetto	24.00	Social Studies School Service	8
	Propaganda Game	6.00	Social Studies School Service	8
	Society Today	7.95	Psychology Today	6
Social Studies	Acquire	7.95	3M Company	4
	Blacks & Whites	6.95	Psychology Today	6
	The Cities Game	6.95	Psychology Today	6
	Community Land Use Game	75.00	IHERS	2
	Cost of Living Game	3.00	Social Studies School Service	8
	Dirty Water	10.00	Urban Systems	10
	Ecology	10.00	Urban Systems	10
	Extinction	12.00	Sinauer	7
	Ghetto	24.00	Social Studies School Service	8
	Indian Reservation Life	12.00	IHERS	2
	Mouse in the Maze	6.00	Houghton Mifflin	1
	Planet Management	12.00	Houghton Mifflin	1
	Pollution	9.00	Urban Systems	10
	Population	10.00	Urban Systems	10
	Propaganda Game	11.00	Wiff'n Proof	12
	Redwood Controversy	7.50	Houghton Mifflin	1
	Science and Language	13.00	Wiff'n Proof	12
	SIMSOC	20.00	MacMillan	3
	Slave Auction	12.95	Social Studies School Service	8
	Society Today	7.95	Psychology Today	6
	Star Power	3.00	Social Studies School Service	8
	The End of the Line	75.00	IHERS	2
	The Union Divider	10.00	Social Studies School Service	8
	They Shoot Marbles Don't They	45.00	IHERS	2
	Urban Dynamics	75.00	IHERS	2

PUBLISHER ADDRESSES

1. Houghton Mifflin Company, 110 Tremont Street, Boston, MA 02107
2. Institute of Higher Education Research and Services, P.O. Box 6293, University, ALA 35486
3. Macmillan Publishing Co., Inc., 866 Third Avenue, New York, NY 10022
4. 3M Company, (Minnesota Mining and Manufacturing Company), St. Paul, MN 55119
5. Nova Scientific Corporation, 111 Tucker Street, P.O. Box 500, Burlington, NC, 27215
6. Psychology Today, P.O. Box 4523, Des Moines, IA 50336
7. Sinauer Associates, 20 Second Street, Stanford, CT 06905
8. Social Studies School Service, 10,000 Culver Blvd., Culver City, CA 90230
9. Science Research Associates, Inc., 259 East Erie Street, Chicago, IL 60611
10. Urban Systems, 1033 Massachusetts Avenue, Cambridge, MA 02138
11. Union Printing Co., 17 W. Washington Street, Athens, OH 45701
12. Wiff'n Proof Games, 1490-Yx South Blvd., Ann Arbor, MI 48104

ADDITIONAL SOURCES OF GAME IDEAS AND MATERIALS

Allied Educational Council, P.O. Box 78, Galien, MI 49113.

A.R. Davis & Co., P.O. Box 24424, San Jose, CA 95154.

Brain Teaser Games, Crestline Manufacturing Co., 1502 Santa Fe St., Santa Ana, CA

Charles and Stadsklev, *Learning with Games*, Boulder, Social Science Education Consortium, Inc., 1973.

Drew, Arthur M., *The Cokesbury Game Book*, New York: Abingdow Press, 1960. See Chapters 2, 3, 5, and 6.

Games and Simulations for School Use. Board of Cooperative Educational Services, June 1974.

Gaming: An Annotated Catalogue of Law-Related Games and Simulations. Special Committee on Youth Education for Citizenship. American Bar Association, 1155 East 60th Street, Chicago, IL 60637.

Game Materials, Creative Publications, Inc., P.O. Box 10328, Palo Alto, CA

Game Catalog, Educational Activities Inc., 164 E. Dane St., Mountain View, CA 94040.

Gordon, Alice K., *Games for Growth*, Science Research Associates, College Division, Palo Alto, CA

Guide to Simulation/Games for Education and Training. Hicksville, New York: Research Media, 1973.

Hounshell, P.B., and I.R. Trollinger. *Games for the Science Classroom: An Annotated Bibliography*. Washington, D.C.: NSTA, 1977.

Lewis, Darrel R., and Donald Wentworth. *Games and Simulations for Teaching Economics*. New York: Joint Council on Economic Education, 1971.

Marie's Educational Materials, Inc., 193 S. Murphy Avenue, Sunnyvale, CA 94086.

Math and Science Games, Damon Educational Division, 80 Wilson Way, Westwood, MA 02090.

Nesbitt, William. *Simulation Games for the Social Studies Classroom*. Foreign Policy Association, 345 E. 46th Street, New York, NY 10017 ($1.00).

Warren's Educational Supplies, 980 W. San Bernadino Road, Covina, CA 91722.

B. COMMUNICATION EXERCISES

EXERCISE 12.1   BLIND WALK

One student is assigned to be a "blind" person and another is assigned to be a guide. The sighted person leads the other inside, outside, up, down, running, touching—all silently. Write objective and subjective paragraphs of objects encountered and feelings experienced. This is also an experience in trust or lack of it.

FOLLOW-UP EVALUATION ON BLIND WALK

1. Did you follow the rules; that is, no talking; introduction of blind partner to world?

    poorly   somewhat   well

2. Did your partner follow the rules?

                    poorly   somewhat   well

3. Were you trusting?

                    poorly   somewhat   well

4. Was your partner trusting?

                    poorly   somewhat   well

5. Were you trustworthy?

                    poorly   somewhat   well

6. Was your partner trustworthy?

                    poorly   somewhat   well

7. Were you open to this experience?

                    poorly   somewhat   well

8. Was your partner open to this experience?

                    poorly   somewhat   well

9. Did you learn anything about your partner?

                    poorly   somewhat   well

10. Did your partner learn anything about you?

                    poorly   somewhat   well

EXERCISE 12.2   ORAL COMMUNICATION

Have all students pair off and stand shoulder to shoulder but facing opposite directions. Student 1 is to talk for two minutes *without looking* at student 2. Student 2 is not to interrupt. Then student 2 talks for two minutes under the same rules. (All the class does this together.) Then ask the students to write their reactions to the exercise. Collect and discuss these orally. In addition to saying that the exercise is stupid and dumb, students of all ages will usually discover for themselves the need for eye contact, the pleasure of talking uninterrupted, the need for feedback, and so on.

Have each student write a sentence of ten words or so containing an abstract idea, such as, "Love is the most important thing in the world to me." The student then tries to get his idea across to others, without words. This exercise helps students discover why we study words and methods of verbal expression. (They have to know and feel comfortable with each other before they will do this one.)

EXERCISE 12.3 LISTENING[7]

Divide into groups of from five to ten persons, depending on how many groups can operate in your room and still hear. The smaller the space, the smaller the groups have to be in order for conversation to be heard. This exercise may be carried out with the total group; however, the larger the group, the fewer opportunities there will be to participate.

Select any topic for discussion which is controversial and in which participants are interested. A current political or education issue or a class or college issue is suitable.

Anyone may begin the discussion and say whatever he wishes to say on the topic. The second person to speak must repeat the essence of what the person has said—that is, he doesn't have to give a verbatim repetition, just the main idea or ideas. Then he must check with the first speaker to be sure he has repeated correctly. A nod from the first speaker or an "OK" will be enough of a sign to indicate that the message has been correctly interpreted. The second speaker may then go on and state his own point of view.

When the second speaker finishes, the third speaker must repeat what the second speaker has said and check out with him before he can go on to have his say. Each speaker repeats only the message of the person immediately preceding him, and anyone may speak—do not take set turns around the circle. If a person cannot repeat what was said before, he is not permitted to offer his own point of view.

EXERCISE 12.4 SELF-DISCOVERY[8]

The activities in this part are included to help in the creation of more open and caring environments. In addition, they were designed to help you and your pupils focus upon personal and interpersonal feelings and recognize the important part that feelings play in all our lives.

1. Talk with each other, with no set agenda, for 10 minutes.
   Try to avoid "cocktail party chatter"; express your feelings and be open and honest with one another. (10 minutes)
2. Complete the following sentences, using paper and pencil:
   a. Sometimes I think I'm _____

   b. People don't like me when I _____

   c. People like me when I _____

   d. I feel hurt when _____

   e. I feel happy when _____

   f. The thing about me that I'd like to change is _____

   _____

---

[7] Elizabeth Hunter, *Encounter in the Classroom: New Ways of Teaching* (New York: Holt, Rinehart and Winston, 1972), p. 52. Reprinted by permission.
[8] *Ibid*, p. 28.

    g. The best thing about me is _____

    h. I really am _____
3. Share the results with each other. (12 minutes)
4. What are some problems you have in your life now? (7 minutes)
5. What are some satisfactions you have in your life now? (7 minutes)

EXERCISE 12.5 SECRETS[9]

Each person writes a secret he has, anonymously, on a piece of paper. All papers are placed in a pile, and everyone draws one out, reads it aloud, and tells how he thinks it might feel to have this particular secret. Secrets may be "owned" or not, depending on personal wishes.

[9] *Ibid*, p. 33.

13

What Kinds of Instructional Aids and Resources Are Available to Teachers and How to Use Them?

If you look back to your learning experiences in elementary, secondary, and collegiate education, you will recall that education in the early grades tended to be lively and active, whereas in secondary school and college, education tended to be more passive and text-lecture oriented. One explanation for this is that teaching and learning by means of sensory experiences was gradually reduced and students were conditioned from one type of symbolism to another on a primarily abstract basis.

APPLYING THE LEARNING EXPERIENCE STEPS TO TEACHING

The schematic ladder illustrates that each experience represented has a unique place for a specific learning outcome utilizing various sensory-motor or audiovisual devices.

Note that low on the ladder the learning experience is realistic and concrete, thus making the learning tasks easier and more enjoyable; high on the ladder the learning experience is difficult, sophisticated, and abstract. Teachers working with slower students should try to use lower ladder experiences, because the practical experience makes their learning more concrete. Even for the high-ability students, it is best not to use the visualized or verbalized symbolic experiences all the time.

Careful planning on the part of the teacher to combine the various experiences will afford good variety from teaching/learning, thus avoiding boredom.

What, then, are some of the aids and materials that make the teaching more effective and thus make the student's learning more meaningful and concrete through the use of his sensory experiences? Page 156 lists various representative examples of instructional aids and resources that can be used to enrich your teaching.

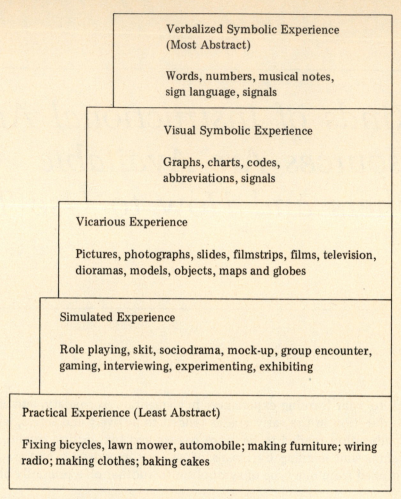

THE LEARNING EXPERIENCE STEPS

VARIOUS KINDS OF AIDS AND RESOURCES FOR TEACHING—A LIST

1. *Printed Aids:* mimeographed or dittoed materials, textbooks, workbooks or laboratory manuals (regular and programmed), reference or library materials (encyclopedias, dictionaries, etc.), magazines, and newspapers.
2. *Audiovisual Aids:* pictures, photographs, slides, films (8-mm loop or single-concept films and 16-mm films), opaque and overhead projection, tape recorder (cassette and regular), chalkboard, magnet board, felt board, bulletin board, videotapes, phonographs, earphones, maps, charts, globes, teaching machines, models, objects, mobiles.
3. *Community Resources:* resource persons in the various trades and professions; local libraries; clinics and hospitals; museums and art galleries; radio and television stations; newspaper plants; post office; local, state, and federal organizations; banks; military installations; major business and industry firms.

EXERCISE 13.1 SURVEY OF TEACHING AIDS AND RESOURCES

1. What are some of the commonly used aids and resources in teaching your subject(s)? Identify a few. Check if your school has any of these. (Novice teachers may find a variety of teaching materials through observations and visitations of secondary schools.)

_____

_____

_____

_____

GUIDELINES FOR EFFECTIVE USE OF CONVENTIONAL TEACHING AIDS

The Chalkboard

1. Erase the old chalkboard writing before you begin your teaching.
2. Use chalkboard extensively for visual cues, especially for slow learners; headline the subtopics; names of persons, places, and terminologies.
3. Avoid long and crowded writing; you need to plan the layout of the materials written on the chalkboard.
4. Write or print legibly, large enough to be seen by all students. Either write or print, but be con-

sistent. Check whether the students in the back can see the last two or three lines of your writing. Keep the lines of writing reasonably straight.

5. Refrain from talking when you face the chalkboard. Stand on one side of the material when talking, facing the students.
6. Practice writing on the chalkboard. Use transparencies for overhead projection if you can write better on them.
7. When you have quite a bit to write on the chalkboard, economize the chalkboard space by starting from your far left, as shown below. Do not erase the writing too quickly.
8. Write information or materials on chalkboard before students arrive. It can be covered with screen, map or paper.
9. A teacher can use the chalkboard to record responses of students. This can make students feel that their contributions are heard. Use the chalkboard well. Organize what is going to be written, and write so all can read. Don't write on the board with your back to the class.
10. If you are going to give a lecture, you might put a lecture outline on the board prior to class. This helps students to organize their notetaking.

Films, Filmstrips, and Slides

1. When to Use:
   a. When the class has very little knowledge or experience about a topic, skill, or activity.
   b. When the class is lacking interest or motivation in the subject or topic.
   c. Never to "kill" class time.

2. What to Do:
   a. Examine the audiovisual catalog carefully. Do not depend completely on the catalog description.
   b. Check the projectors before use. Learn how to fix minor troubles (film flickering, replacing bulbs, etc.) Do not rely too heavily on assistants. Learn to do it yourself.
   c. Do the 3 V's—preview, view (with the students), and review (for follow-up and summary).
   d. Asking students to take notes during viewing or to prepare for a test is not generally advisable.
   e. Use loop films (8-mm single-concept films) wherever appropriate.

Carefully selected films can help students *see* concepts, events, and issues in a more concrete way. Preview your choice before showing and have the projector set up ahead of time. Plan ahead! Check the bibliography at the end of this chapter for the many free films and filmstrips available.

Pictures and Charts

1. If you want to show several pictures or charts effectively to the entire class, use an *opaque* projector.
2. You may walk slowly around the students with the picture.
3. Put the picture on the bulletin board for viewing later.
4. Passing a picture is not generally advisable *unless* you allow the students to just look at the picture. Do not lecture or have discussion while the picture is being passed around.

Pictures are worth more than a thousand words, as the age-old saying goes. Don't forget it as you prepare your lessons. *Examples:* In studying music history, it is important that the students under-

stand the period in which the music was written. Pictures of architecture, art, costumes, and people are helpful to the student in reaching this understanding.

Pictures can be helpful for the writing of poetry or short stories. Students can try to translate visual images into word images.

Overhead Projection

Overhead projection in teaching can be very useful for many purposes; for any writing you would normally do on the chalkboard, as well as to prepare lecture outlines, discussion questions, charts or drawings in advance, thus avoiding misspellings and messy drawings and showing neater and organized preparations. Overhead projection, when effectively used, shows dynamic images and appeals to students.

What to Use or Do:

1. Use good transparency pencil or transparency pen (not ordinary felt pen).
2. Check the best position in the classroom for projection, so that all students can see the projection clearly.
3. Face students when speaking to them (you don't have to turn around everytime as you would do when using chalkboard.
4. Any transparent models or objects such as plastic ruler, protractor, ripple tanks, and test tubes can be projected vividly.
5. Tracing charts or drawings on construction paper or on chalkboard can be easily done by simply projecting the original transparency.
6. When you do not want to show the entire transparency, cover up the portion of the contents with paper (masking technique).

7. When you want to add or correlate the contents simultaneously, simply add on another transparency (overlay technique).

Maps and Globes

1. Use maps or globes when referring to places and locations. Do not say, for example, "somewhere over there."
2. Choose an appropriate map or globe in terms of kind and size.
3. Use a pointer when pointing to certain places or areas.
4. Use maps and globes interchangeably. For small-group studies use globes instead of maps.

Charts and Graphs

These help students to visualize important points and to facilitate learning. A visual chart showing the effects of smoking from one-half pack to more than two packs of cigarettes a day, for instance, can really drive home the concept of the effects of nicotine upon the human body.

Library/Media Resource Center

1. Consult the librarian/media specialist about the materials and resources available before you assign students to the library.
2. Tell students what should be accomplished for the library activity.
3. Stay with and supervise students when they are engaged in library activity.
4. Utilize resource center facility (or library) for an individualized or independent learning through audiovisual media.

Audio and Video Tapes

If you can remember the first time you ever heard yourself on tape, you will appreciate the usefulness of these devices in teaching. Perhaps you will learn from the exercise in Chapter 17 the self-teaching power of videotape. Review Chapter 10 on motivation techniques for specific ideas on use.

Printed Materials (*mostly dittoed handouts*)

When you do not have a clerical staff to prepare reproductions, you need to:

1. Prepare yourself as much in advance as you can and avoid the last-minute rush.
2. Organize the contents in a concise and well-spaced form.
3. Be sure to proofread your final draft.
4. Write or type the material legibly.
5. Learn to operate the ditto machine, and be sure to get the printed materials neat and clear.

Perhaps the dittoed materials are overused by teachers, and therefore have lost some effectiveness because of frequent usage. And we even suspect that there is a hidden lesson being taught by the overuse of dittoed material, and that is "schools have an endless supply of paper"—which they do not. In any case, dittoed material is useful when textbooks do not supply necessary exercises or worksheets, and students will respond well to dittos that are well prepared. Various colors can highlight a well-constructed dittoed test or worksheet. Your course instructor should be prodded to instruct you in the preparation of a multicolored ditto, if you have not already been so instructed.

The Community

This can be one of your most valuable sources of resource material. A useful resource here is the *Yellow Pages of Learning Resources* book,[1] which includes government agencies, military organizations, hospitals, business and industry, banks. Some of these organizations are especially hospitable to secondary students.

Art Galleries and Craft Fairs

Field trips to these places can be exciting and educational for students in art, music, industrial arts, home economics, and social studies. Plan ahead and give students some specific directives pertaining to what they should look for.

Guest Speakers

Choose them carefully. Talk with them prior to class, to avoid being surprised or embarassed. Inform the speaker about your students in terms of their interest and ability. Introduce the speaker in the most courteous manner and express your thanks with the students by rounds of applause. Either before or after the speaker has left, summarize what the speaker has said. If the topic has not been treated fairly or has reflected biased views, another speaker should be considered to balance it out. This is especially true when a controversial topic is presented: a racial, religious or political topic.

For a class in Fantasy or Folktale (English Department offering) one teacher obtained a professional folksinger to talk and sing with the class. An architect can give a history class a new perspective on how changes in our culture are reflected in our homes and buildings.

SOURCES OF TRANSPARENCY MATERIALS

AeVac Educational Publishers, 1604 Park Ave., South Plainsfield, N.J. 07060. All subjects for secondary school teaching.
Encyclopedia Britannica Film Inc., 425 Michigan Ave., Chicago, Ill. 60611. English and World History, Series of 10–12 transparencies (Approx. $140).

[1] The *Yellow Pages of Learning Resources* book can be obtained for approximately $1.95 from: The MIT Press, 28 Carleton St., Cambridge, Massachusetts 02142.

A BIBLIOGRAPHY OF FREE AND INEXPENSIVE RESOURCE MATERIALS FOR SECONDARY SCHOOL TEACHING

An Annotated Bibliography of Audiovisual Materials Related to Understanding and Teaching the Culturally Disadvantaged. Washington, D.C.: National Education Association.

Educational Film Guide. New York: H. W. Wilson Co.

Educator's Guide to Free Films. Randolph, WI: Educators Progress Service.

Educator's Guide to Free Film-Strips. Randolph, WI: Educators Progress Service.

Educator's Guide to Free and Inexpensive Teaching Materials. Randolph, WI: Educators Progress Service.

Educator's Guide to Free Science Materials. Randolph, WI: Educators Progress Service.

Educator's Guide to Free Social Studies Materials. Randolph, WI: Educators Progress Service.

EXERCISE 13.2   BEGINNING A RESOURCE FILE

Begin your own aids and resources file on 3 × 5 cards listing (a) the name, (b) how and when available, (c) how to use, and (d) some evaluative comments. This file can build throughout your career.

14

Summarizing Modes and Behaviors for Effective, Self-Satisfying Teaching

A. EFFECTIVE, SELF-SATISFYING MODES OF TEACHING[1]

A basic philosophical concept states that human needs exist in a hierarchy—that certain needs are basic and must be met before other needs can be developed, pursued, and satisfied. Enough evidence has accumulated to show that the human needs for love, nurture, belonging, and security are basic, and the need to grow up, to learn, and to master new skills is built upon that foundation. It follows, then, that we as teachers cannot expect that with students the need to learn will arise until we have attended adequately to the basic needs.

An evaluation of the historical evidence from the focus of education, subject matter versus personal needs, would be likely to lead to the conclusion that we are just moving in a circle with little or no progress being made. As stated by Carmical:

> The early historical approach to teaching tended to deemphasize the significance of the needs of the individual students. Progressive techniques moved to the other end of the continuum in an effort to meet all needs of all children.[2]

Occasionally there can be found in current literature the thought that direct attention should be given to the basic needs and interests of students. There is a question as to the appropriate methodology. Should we focus on the subject-matter needs or on the personal needs of the learner? It has been stated:

> If perceptions become the focus, and the development of self-actualizing people our goal

[1] Richard D. Kellough, in *Science Education*, 55(4):457–463 (1971). Reprinted by permission of John Wiley & Sons, Inc.
[2] LaVerne Carmical, "Five Basic Responsibilities of the Classroom Teacher," *The Clearing House*, 38:307–308 (1964).

in education, then the students will learn the subject matter he/she feels it important to learn.[3]

So, if it is necessary to make a choice, then that choice must be to focus on the learner's immediate perceptions of his needs for the purpose of improving his concept of self. Only then will he learn that subject matter which seems important to him. This basic concept of learning behavior must be equally valid for the training of teachers.

However, we do not need to make a choice. We need, though, to learn how to apply the concept of complementarity to utilize the full potential of both focal approaches. In order to bring this concept to fruition, we must become better familiar with the reference points from which we start, and to develop a conceptual model suited to this end. The model is The Developmental Tasks of the Teacher and should be the focal point for the design of all teacher training programs. And only when each of these tasks is completed will we be producing truly effective teachers.

The teacher needs:

1. To know the subject matter.
2. Skills in imparting the subject matter.
3. Skills in evaluation of his work.
4. Skills in working with young people.
5. Skills in working with adults.
6. To develop the philosophy that manhood, not scholarship, is the first aim of education.

These are the problem areas—the needs of the teacher. Helping the future teacher first as a person will ultimately result in a far more mature product upon whose shoulders the fate of our world largely lies.

An appropriate classroom atmosphere should enable students to discover that they are acceptable persons. This does not imply a "permissive" atmosphere if this means permission to do whatever one wishes. It does require that the classroom atmosphere be concerned with personal reference. The idea conveyed is that people rather than things are important.[4]

It takes time in the classroom to develop this kind of an atmosphere. It may take several weeks for students to become convinced that this really is their class, that they can do and say whatever they please as long as the rights of others are not infringed upon.

For awhile there will be minor problems concerning discipline, but, if the convictions of the teacher are strong enough, the students will in time become convinced that there really is something of value and of personal importance going on. Eventually the students begin to realize an understanding of the meanings of frankness, openness, and freedom with responsibility. They feel more free to analyze, criticize, propose, and test their ideas.

Success in this mode of teaching relies upon students being able to make real decisions—decisions as to what they will study, whether they are to be evaluated and graded, whether they want tests, homework, and a textbook. The students are presented with new experiences in freedom. As the teacher illustrates trust and faith in the students, they begin to trust themselves. The students will make occasional mistakes, but these are not handled by force, threat, ridicule, or humiliation. Any other way you can think of to handle mistakes is probably all right. The authority really rests in the situation. The students gain new perceptions about their mistakes and learn about alternatives to their behavior. The teacher's role is one of helping students see alternatives.

The students are provided opportunities to practice skills of cooperative procedures, through the

[3] Richard D. Kellough, "Perceptions and Self-actualization: A Goal for Education and a Theory for Teacher Training," *Science Education*, 52:47–55 (1968).
[4] Association for Supervision and Curriculum Development. *Perceiving, Behaving, Becoming: A New Focus for Education* (1962 Yearbook) (Washington, D.C.: The Association, 1962).

defining of goals, planning of class activities, and the interaction of deliberately planned discussions, in both small and large groups. The students are provided freedom to raise and discuss questions about any topic. There is interplay among all members of the class. Evaluation is a cooperative student–teacher effort. Individual student–teacher conferences are frequent, a planned technique not resulting merely from a classroom incident and a teacher-felt need for disciplining the student.

The deliberately planned discussion is a frequently used technique. Advantages of the discussion technique are those of: (1) reducing threat by the establishment of pleasant interpersonal relations (2) distribution of leadership within the class by involving students, (3) increasing group we-feeling and individual student sense of belonging, and (4) establishment of the importance and sense of personal worth of each member of the class.

The insight period or introductory period of the first several days of class meeting affords an opportunity for the teacher and students to become acquainted and to reach levels of informality and reduction of defenses.[5] Traditionally, the first day of school is devoted to formal activities—roll taking, distribution of textbooks, and explaining the procedures and requirements of the course. But "devoting the first hour to desk work is a mistake."[6] And, along the same lines, throughout the year devoting the first ten minutes or so of class time to housekeeping chores is equally a mistake. Small wonder that students of the "system" get the idea things rather than people are important.

THE MULTIACTIVITY APPROACH

In the most effective classrooms there are typically two types of activities: those which involve the entire class and those where members are simultaneously involved in a variety of activities.

DISCUSSION CENTERED ABOUT PROBLEMS OF CONCERN TO THE STUDENTS

Teacher planning for each day's class is, of course, important, but also important is that the program remain flexible and ready to give to apparent student interest of the day. Effective teachers have developed an uncanny ability to "read" a class at the beginning of each period, to foresee just when the students will be receptive to certain types of activities. The orderliness with which students come into the room and the expressions on their faces seem apparent keys. An entire class is like an individual, having a personality for the day.

The nondirective (open-ended) interview technique has significance and importance that cannot be overemphasized, although I am certain the technique is infrequently used by teachers. The procedure goes as follows: during the first few weeks of school, out-of-class time is set aside and each student meets privately with the teacher. All students are eventually interviewed, although some will fail to keep their original appointments.

The interviews are private and confidential. The students are encouraged to discuss freely their experiences, feelings, attitudes, goals, values, and home and social lives. There is no difficulty in getting most students to open up to this type of discussion. They will be eager and gratified to find a teacher having a personal interest in their lives, and personal communication through private interviews can encourage development of adequacy.[7]

---

[5] J.R. Gibb, Grace N. Platts, and Lorraine F. Miller, *Dynamics of Participative Groups*, (St. Louis: John Swift, 1956).
[6] Rudolf Dreikurs, *Psychology in the Classroom* (New York: Harper 1957).
[7] Richard D. Kellough, "The Humanistic Approach: An Experiment in the Teaching of Biology to Slow Learners in High School—An Experiment in Classroom Experimentation," *Science Education*, 54:253–262 (1970).

Certain rules are established for this technique. These are as follows:

1. Take a friendly attitude, conveying to the student the idea that you like him and enjoy talking with him.
2. Encourage him to talk freely and, so far as is possible, without interruption.
3. Keep him on the track with a question that comes back to the heart of the problem if he strays too far.
4. Resist the impulse to tell him a long story of what you did in a similar situation.
5. Occasionally offer a tentative or alternative suggestion in question form; for example, "Could it be that . . .?" or "Had you thought of . . .?"
6. Allow the student to do most of the talking.
7. Ask questions for which he can see purpose.
8. Try to see through the student's eyes and remember that his attitudes are not necessarily identical with yours.
9. Accept what he tells, understanding why he feels as he does, neither criticizing nor yet giving approval.
10. Give direct attention to the student, not taking notes or tape recordings during the interview.
11. Look the student in the eye most of the time, if not all the time.
12. Do not be afraid of moments of silence during the session.
13. Bring the interview to an end tactfully but definitely, allowing the student to leave feeling satisfied.
14. Keep all confidences.

Student writing in class is a technique used primarily for the purpose of providing a source of understanding of each student's progress and perceptions—"for spotting and assessing problems, personal makeup, his life style."[8]

Information provided by students on sensitive topics is kept confidential. Most often the information provides background for interesting group and private discussions.

There is constant student evaluation of their own activity as well as that of others in the class. This is another aspect of the in-class writing. They are asked to write statements on such topics as:

What have you learned thus far in this course?
How has your behavior changed as a result of this class?
Give a brief evaluation of your oral report.
What was the aim of the film shown today?
In whom do you have faith?

For most of these questions there are no right or wrong answers. Attention is focused on big ideas, change of perceptions, the value of helping the student test and extend his own cognitions by creating opportunities for him to clarify his current needs, to develop immediate purposes for learning, and to set more realistic individual standards.

The individual student project study technique is observed frequently. Class time is given for project work. Emphasis upon competition, upon what they ought to do (pressure), and general demands by the teacher are kept minimal. Some students become frustrated after obtaining a little knowledge about their chosen topic and discovering how encompassing it really was. The teacher then assists these students in redefining their goals in terms more meaningful and readily obtainable. It is important here to reiterate what Dreikurs[9] has stated:

[8] Dreikurs, *op. cit.*
[9] *Ibid.*

Frustrated overambition is perhaps the most frequent cause for giving up. Children who are trained to believe that it is important to be ahead of others will shy away from any activity which does not provide them with the opportunity to prove their superiority. . . . thwarted overambition is often at the core of juvenile delinquency.

The spontaneous reaction of the teacher to classroom incidents is another technique important and significant to effective teaching. The teacher's fear of making "wrong" responses is probably perceived by students and creates an unrest. The effective teacher is aware of the importance of the feelings and attitudes he communicates to the students by both verbal and nonverbal action. He is sensitive to the impact of his own actions in facilitating and encouraging the growth of students. Consequently he evaluates his behavior as it appears to him, in terms of its effect upon the self concepts of his students. The effective teacher appears to respond slowly, thoughtfully, and cool headedly. He tries to discover the true meaning of each situation and the purposes for which the student is behaving in the manner he is.

Evaluation is characteristically a continuous ongoing process in the effective learning setting. Learning behavior, as seen in the conventional setting, is a matter of forces exerted upon the student, and teaching is simply a matter of controlling these forces, but from my observations of effective teachers in action, learning behavior seems more a function of personal meanings, and perceptions are the center of the teaching–learning situation. Evaluation of student progress then takes on this new meaning of helping the student to clarify his current needs, to develop immediate purposes for learning, and to set realistic standards. Consequently, students in this setting are always aware of where they are. The effective teacher seems aware of the learner's readiness and capable of guiding the student to an understanding of the structure of the subject matter.

Finally, the effective teacher is obviously optimistic about his students' capacities to learn, and is constantly changing and improving techniques with an awareness that there are ways of helping students to learn. Furthermore, he is unafraid of including his own human feeling and emotions, of showing his own ethical and moral values, because when he looks at himself, he likes what he sees, at least well enough for it to be operational. He sees himself as cast in a creative role, as a part of a world on the move. He lives a "zoom-zap" life style. Some days he is zooming up, is totally effective, and positively involved with people. Like everyone else, he experiences his bad days, gets zapped, flounders, runs down cul-de-sacs, and makes mistakes, but he handles these experiences courageously with all the hope, dignity, and artistic talent he can muster.

B. SEVEN TEACHER BEHAVIORS FOR COMPETENT TEACHING[10]

The following seven teacher behaviors appear to create the basic conditions that enable students to learn anything, whether it be the acquisition of concepts and generalizations, the internalization of attitudes and values, or the development of cognitive processes:

Behavior 1: Structuring

Every teacher in every classroom structures that total classroom environment for students, consciously and unconsciously, directly and indirectly. Even the nonstructured classroom imposes a

[10] Arthur Costa et al., in *Journal of Teacher Education,* XXII(3):342–347 (Fall 1971), pp. 342–347. Reprinted by permission.

structure to and within which the students act and react. The structuring behaviors are conscious and deliberate and derived from a teacher commitment (1) to develop autonomous learners, students who become increasingly responsible for directing their own learning energies; and (2) to create an environment that is socially and psychologically safe for learners to take risks and to learn by successes as well as failures.

With this commitment, the teacher may define roles and tasks, establish ground rules, provide directions, identify the limitations of time and circumstances under which any learning activity will be performed. He does this structuring with the notion of facilitating—not directing—the student's personal meaning. Some examples follow:

1. We're going to see a film today, and afterward I'll ask you to list what you have observed.
2. It is important for us to hear all the ideas you want to share, so if you'll raise your hands, I will know when to call on you.
3. That kind of question is the kind *you* must answer. You will have to decide for yourself why it started to boil again.
4. While I'm reading the story, think what you would do in this situation. For a while we will form into couples in which one expresses a feeling and the other receives. After a while, we'll reverse roles.
5. Today, let's follow up with our role-playing problem from yesterday. Mary, will you take the role of mother, and Sammy, will you take the role of father?

Behavior 2: Focusing on a Problem

This teacher behavior calls attention to a problem situation to which the student is invited to respond. Frequently it poses a dilemma, discrepancy, or conflict that needs resolution. Many times it is a call for data, for an expression of feeling, or for an application of a principle; it is always conceived with multiple objectives in mind.

In setting problem focuses, the teacher is aware of the kinds of expected learnings and presents the verbal stimulus in carefully, consciously stated ways. He is conscious not only of the content being taught but also of the kind of learning being sought. If he desires data from students, he will formulate a recall question that solicits a variety of appropriate recall responses. If the desired student behavior is to perform more complex mental tasks, the focusing will be to seek higher levels of thinking; if to decide from a variety of alternatives, then a focus will expose many alternatives along with their possible consequences. In the focusing behavior, the teacher attends to both the content and the process objectives of the learning activity. Since all four strategies have the goal of helping students become better able to identify and solve their own problems, this problem-focusing behavior of the teacher gradually shifts to become more and more a student behavior:

1. How do you think we can handle this problem so that you won't feel the way you do and I won't have to worry about it?
2. Why do you think the town was deserted?
3. What is Jackie's dilemma? Why is she upset?
4. Harvey knows who took the money, and the person who took the money knows that Harvey saw him. The person told Harvey not to tell anyone and he'd share the money with him. What should he do now?

Behavior 3: Accepting

Basically, the teacher is nonevaluative and nonjudgmental. He gives no clues through posture, gesture, or word as to what is right or wrong, good or bad, better or worse. The intent is to provide a psychologically safe climate where a student can take risks, where he is entrusted with the responsibility of deciding for himself where he can collect data that will allow him to decide for himself, and where he is encouraged to examine and compare his own data, values, ideas, criteria, and feelings with those of others rather than with the teacher's.

The acceptance behavior encourages the learner to develop his own motivation and reinforcement patterns through such behaviors as (a) recasting or restating the student's ideas, (b) restating or recasting the feelings expressed by those ideas, (c) recognizing and nonjudgmentally expressing the nonverbal clues of the student, and (d) empathically stating and sharing student's feelings. Using these behaviors, the teacher indicates his acceptance of the student—his ideas, feelings, and behaviors—which, although they may differ from the teacher's, can still be accepted by him, for he knows that only the student is able to modify them and make them more consistent with reality.

Some examples of accepting behaviors are offered below in a sequence that is intended to convey increasing empathy:

1. OK.
2. I understand your idea.
3. That is one possible outcome.
4. Let's write your idea on the board along with the others.
5. That sounds like another way of playing the role that could be checked out.
6. It seems to me you must be very happy with those results. I think I can understand why.
7. When you tore up Jane's report, I perceived that you were very upset. I can understand that feeling. I feel the same way at times; I get angry and want to break something.

Behavior 4: Clarifying

Clarifying behaviors are related to accepting behaviors in that they reflect the teacher's interest in listening to what the student is saying or trying to say. They extend that acceptance because they enable the teacher to understand more fully the student's concepts, behaviors, and feelings. Clarifying shows the student that his ideas are worthy of exploration and consideration.

Clarifying behavior ensures that the teacher provides the appropriate information or direction the student is seeking. It also gives the teacher some diagnostic information as to how the student is perceiving a problem, developing a concept, or reacting to a situation. Regardless of whether it is a probe for the student to be more specific or a request for further interpretation, its major intent is to help the teacher to understand better what the student is doing, saying, thinking, or feeling; it is not a dubious way of changing or redirecting the student. Some examples:

1. What does it mean, "It makes you mad?"
2. Are you saying that when you finished the book, you felt there were too many questions to answer?
3. Could you explain to me what you mean by "expansion"?
4. What I hear you saying is that you can do this by yourself rather than in a group. Is that correct?
5. Help me understand what you mean.
6. Are you trying to find out what would happen if we turned it upside down?

7. You'll have to be more specific and tell me just how many drops to add to the mixture.
8. Are you suggesting that we add more color to the painting? Which colors do you mean?

Behavior 5:   Facilitating the Acquisition of Data

Since these strategies are intended to develop decision-making processes and problem-solving abilities in others, the teacher must make data accessible to the student as input that he can process. The teacher creates the environment that is responsive to the student's quest for information. He may do this by serving as a resource himself or by making it possible for students to experiment with ways of working with equipment and with various behaviors; he may elicit information or feelings for the group to consider; he sees that primary and secondary sources of information are available; he facilitates data by supplying raw materials from which ideas and data can be generated.

The teacher facilitates the generation of data while the student processes and acquires them. More often than not, the teacher becomes the responder, not the initiator; the student becomes the programmer instead of the programmed:

1. Mary, tell us how you felt when the gang approached you.
2. Here are several thermometers if you would like to try them.
3. Howard, I'd like you to know that every time you hit someone, I become very nervous.
4. The red liquid would not go up in the tube if it were not heated.
5. Mary, here's an almanac. On page 34, it tells what the average rainfall is for Hawaii.
6. On this chart we have a list of all the things we saw in the film. We can keep this chart in front of us so that we can use it again and again.
7. We can see the film again if you want to verify that.
8. Water boils at 212° Fahrenheit at sea level.
9. We have looked at the consequences of several solutions to Andy's problem. Are there any other ways you'd like to explore it?

Behavior 6:   Silence

Another behavior is one we have called "teacher silence." In each strategy, the teacher is asked to tolerate periods of what could be lengthy silence. He says nothing, and he says nothing nonjudgmentally. Teacher silence is not a classroom control weapon; instead, it is a time for students to do their own thinking, reflecting, and generalizing. This behavior helps maintain the appropriate role patterns for autonomous learning. When the teacher poses a problem focus and then remains silent, it helps the student further realize that the responsibility for the problem solution is his—not the teacher's.

Behavior 7:   Modeling

A final category that is significant is the teacher's modeling of the types of behaviors desired as student behaviors. The value of teacher behaviors as models is seen, not for the purpose of having students imitate certain types of desired behaviors but rather for having teacher behaviors consistently reflect desired educational outcomes as positive mediating influences.

Modeling tends to improve students' perceptions regarding the value of stated goals; for example, the way the teacher behaves when solving a classroom problem influences the way the student will approach his own problems. If listening is a valued outcome of instruction, then teachers who listen to students will do much to reduce feelings of confusion, frustration, and hostility on their part. This may result from the fact that the student senses a discrepancy between what he is taught and what he perceives in the teacher's behavior that does not match a stated value. In other words, the student sometimes develops a credibility gap between what he senses is important and what he sees in the teacher's classroom behaviors; a congruence between teacher behavior and what is being taught as desirable behavior helps lessen this gap. It is essential that the teacher be aware of the learning behavior he is modeling so that it may reinforce the student's behavior when it is performed. If there is an inconsistency in the learning behavior modeled and that which is reinforced, confusion and anxiety are probable.

EXERCISE 14.1   AN ESSAY ON MODES AND BEHAVIORS

We suggest that you take this "test" at home, type your responses and then bring to class for peer or instructor discussion and evaluation.

1. Early discussion in Chapter 14 talks of the needs of the individual. Compare this discussion with what you can research in the library on the "progressive Education Era."
2. It sometimes seems that much of what happens in public education conveys that individuals and their learning form the least important activity going on in the school. Find evidence to support or reject this notion.
3. Define in your own words the meaning of the "concept of complimentarity" as discussed early in this chapter.
4. Practice empathic acceptance behaviors for one week and write a paragraph on the experience.
5. For one week practice periods of controlled silence, i.e., pausing longer than normal, in all of your verbal communications. Write a paragraph on this experience.

Selected References

Beach, Don M. *Reaching Teenagers: Learning Centers for the Secondary Classroom.* Santa Monica, CA: Goodyear Publishing Co., 1977.

Calder, Clarence R., Jr., and Eleanor M. Antan. *Techniques and Activities to Stimulate Verbal Learning.* New York: Macmillan Publishing Co., Inc., 1970.

Carin, A., and R. Sund. *Developing Questioning Techniques—A Concept Approach.* Columbus, Ohio: Charles E. Merrill, 1971.

Castillo, Gloria A. *Left-Handed Teaching: Lessons in Affective Education.* New York: Praeger Publishers Inc., 1974.

Clark, Leonard H., and Irving S. Starr. *Secondary School Teaching Methods.* New York: Macmillan Publishing Co., Inc., 1976.

Dell, Helen Davis. *Individualizing Instruction.* Chicago: Science Research Associates, Inc., 1972.

Erickson, Carlton W.H., and David H. Curl. *Fundamentals of Teaching with Audiovisual Technology.* New York: Macmillan Publishing Co., Inc., 1972.

Howley, Robert C. *Value Exploration Through Role Playing: Practical Strategies for Use in the Classroom.* New York: Hart Publishing Co., Inc., 1975.

Heitzmann, William Ray. *Educational Games and Simulations.* Washington, D.C.: National Education Association, 1974.

Henson, Kenneth T. *Secondary Teaching Methods.* D.C. Heath and Co., Lexington, Mass., 1981.

Horton, Lowell. *Mastery Learning.* Bloomington, Indiana: Phi Delta Kappa, 1981.

Howes, Virgil M. *Informal Teaching in the Open Classroom.* New York: Macmillan Publishing Co., Inc., 1974.

Hunkins, Francis. Questioning: *Strategies and Techniques.* Boston: Allyn & Bacon, Inc., 1972.

Hyman, Ronald T. *Strategic Questioning.* Prentice Hall, Englewood Cliffs, N.J., 1979.

Judy, Stephen N., and Susan J. Judy. *The Teaching of Writing.* New York: John Wiley and Sons, 1981.

Kemp, Jerrold E. *Planning and Producing Audio-Visual Materials.* Fourth Edition. New York: Thomas Crowell Publishing Co., 1980.

Krupar, Karen R. *Communication Games.* New York: Free Press, 1972.

Livingston, Samuel, and Clarice S. Stoll. *Simulation Games.* New York: Free Press, 1972.

McNergney, Robert F. *Teacher Development.* Macmillan Publishing Co., 1981.

Miller, John P. *Humanizing the Classroom: Models of Teaching in Affective Education.* New York: Praeger Publishers, Inc., 1976.

Minor, Edward O. *Handbook for Preparing Visual Media.* Second Edition. New York: McGraw-Hill Book Co., 1978.

Orlich, Donald C., et al. *Teaching Strategies: A Guide to Better Instruction.* Lexington, Mass., D.C. Heath and Co., 1980.

Raths, Louis, Merril Harmin, and Sidney B. Simmon. *Values and Teaching: Working with Values in the Classroom.* Second Edition. Columbus, Ohio: Charles E. Merrill Publishing Co., 1978.

Silberman, Melvin L., et al. (ed.) *The Psychology of Open Teaching and Learning.* Boston: Little, Brown and Co., 1972.

Woodbury, Marda. *A Guide to Sources of Educational Information.* Washington, D.C.: Information Resources Press, 1976.

Zuckerman, David W., and Robert E. Horn. *The Guide to Simulation/Games for Education and Training.* Lexington, Mass.: Information Resources, Inc., 1973.

Part IV

Classroom Management, Interaction, Discipline, and Legal Guidelines

A Short Course in Human Relations

The SIX most important words:
"I admit I made a mistake."
The FIVE most important words:
"You did a good job."
The FOUR most important words:
"What is your opinion?"
The THREE most important words:
"If you please."
The TWO most important words:
"Thank you."
The ONE most important word:
"We"
The LEAST important word:
"I"

—Unknown

15

What Are Some Guidelines for Classroom Management, Routine Housekeeping Chores, and Legal Responsibilities?

In this chapter we share with you experiences, concerns, and guidelines related to classroom management and efficient procedures for the conduction of routine "housekeeping" chores. Since it is paramount that a teacher be knowledgeable about legal responsibilities we conclude the chapter with information regarding the legal status of the classroom teacher.

A. ABOUT CLASSROOM INTERRUPTIONS

It is dismaying to think of the number of classroom interruptions that occur from sources outside the classroom. Absolutely no one would interrupt a surgeon when he is in the middle of an operation or a lawyer when he is in the courtroom presenting his case summation. But the classroom teacher is very often interrupted when he is doing the creative act for which he has prepared so long. A classroom teacher can have his students right in the palm of his hand as he is bringing closure to what has been a most exciting and well-received series of lessons and—what happens?—the intercom comes on requesting Johnnie Jones be sent to the office at the end of the period or a student knocks on the door with a note from the counseling office. Or, you arrive at school on a given morning to find that third period has been canceled for a pep rally.

With all of these thoughtless and unscheduled classroom interruptions it is no wonder public school students today get the idea that the *least* important activity of school is that which is occurring in the classrooms. That is what we seem to be teaching students, then we wonder why they come to our classes uninterested and unmotivated. An alternative we suggest for the improvement of the situation is that you lobby in your faculty to eliminate needless classroom interruptions, with such changes as these:

1. All classroom interruptions are to be allowed only during the first five or the last five minutes of each 50–60-minute class period.

2. No classes are to be canceled for assemblies and other school activities without at least three days' notification.
3. For ADA (average daily attendance) purposes, attendance is taken during the second period of the morning and again the second period of the afternoon. The reports are collected for those two periods. For the remaining periods of the school day teachers may take attendance (for their own records) at any time of the periods.

Schools must teach students that what is happening in the teacher's classroom has top priority. Teachers must see that this remains the focus, otherwise maintenance can become the focus of the school's existence. Giving highest priority to academic instruction can perhaps alleviate much of the cause for the large number of "on-campus dropouts."

B. SUGGESTIONS FOR MAINTAINING PROPER PHYSICAL CONDITIONS OF YOUR CLASSROOM

The appearance, tidiness, and physical conditions of the classroom reflect the personality of the teacher. The observer (parents, colleagues, administrators) can readily tell what kind of "housekeeper" he is. Check your classroom regularly with regard to the following:

1. Physical condition of the room: Room temperature, room ventilation, shades to control light and glare.

2. Tidiness of the room: Bulletin board appearance and arrangement, decorations, storage spaces, shelves, bookcases, equipment.

3. Seating arrangements: Arrangements of desks, chairs, tables (semicircle, roundtable, or hollow square), rearrangements of seats for small-group work, team-learning or project activities; rearrangement of seats for individual needs (for poor hearing, poor vision, or for isolating uncooperative students).

4. Handling of materials and supplies (especially in fine arts, industrial arts, home economics, and science classes).
   a. Preparation of materials and supplies, in advance.
   b. Orderly distribution of materials and supplies.
   c. Orderly collection of materials, equipment, and tools.

C. SUGGESTIONS FOR HANDLING CLERICAL AND ROUTINE MAINTENANCE TASKS

Maintenance tasks such as taking attendance and distributing papers can consume much of the teacher's time if not planned carefully. Here are some suggestions that might increase your efficiency and reduce the potential "fooling around" time.

1. Completing forms and questionnaires: read them carefully making sure you understand the purpose and directions.
2. Maintenance of classroom inventory: keep a running inventory of furniture, materials, and supplies.

3. Taking attendance: this is, of course, required by law. Choose a procedure that is quick and accurate. Seating charts can be very helpful here.

4. Completing tardy slips: again, choose a procedure that is quick, accurate, and appropriate.

 Regarding attendance and tardy reporting, we strongly urge you to begin the lesson first rather than letting the class sit idly while you complete these clerical tasks. Perhaps you can lobby or solicit for help to accomplish clerical tasks. In many schools these tasks are performed by teacher aides and assistants.

5. Distribution and collection of materials: these are maintenance tasks that should be performed quickly and accurately and that can be done with the help of aides and assistants. Students sometimes need instruction in the importance and necessity of proper care and handling of textbooks and supplies. Here are some specific hints:

 a. Enforce school policy when textbooks and equipment are damaged.

 b. Maintain accurate records when material is loaned.

 c. Streamline your procedure for distributing and collecting student papers—protect student individual score recognition when returning scored papers.

6. Homework and other assignments: maintain due dates except for very special reasons; read and/or evaluate all assignments; return graded work promptly.

7. End of grading period examinations: schedule them a week prior to the end of your grading period in order to give yourself ample time for reading. You might end your grading period one week before the official school term is ended.

8. Students exchanging papers in class for checking and grading: Not recommended!

9. Reading of school bulletin: we have seen many times classes in which the daily or weekly bulletin is read by a student volunteer in the class and have consistently found the procedure less than satisfactory. Items of the bulletin should be heard and understood. As the teacher your reading of the bulletin can be an opportunity to show your own interest in the total school program.

10. Preparing deficiency notices for students having difficulty in your class: prepare these with extra care, checking carefully for spelling errors. After initial writing, read the notice as if you were the recipient parent to see if the proper meaning is being conveyed. We strongly urge teachers to consider the writing of *efficiency* notices and sending them to parents also.

11. Phoning parents: a phone call to a parent of a student who is having difficulty in your class can be very beneficial. We recommend an occasional call to a parent of a student who is showing improvement also. In either case think over carefully what it is you wish to convey prior to calling.

12. Your gradebook: This is a legal document, and like a checkbook it should be complete and accurate. It should be a clearly understood record of each student's attendance and progress in your class. The records of an individual student should be private and not available for other students to see, so we do not recommend leaving your gradebook open on the desk for all to read.

EXERCISE 15.1 LEGAL GUIDELINES FOR THE TEACHER

Obtain copies of your state Education Code and of local district guidelines, or the faculty and student handbook of a secondary school in your area. You will find such topics as:

1. What is the legal status of the classroom teacher?
2. What is the legal status of the secondary school student?
3. What is the legal status of the teacher's contract?
4. What are your state's teacher dismissal and tenure laws?

5. What are your state's teacher retirement laws?
6. Identify your state and local positions on teacher collective bargaining.
7. What is the position regarding teaching the course of study?
8. What are the legal requirements regarding punishment and discipline?
9. What are the legal requirements regarding teacher liability and negligence?
10. What is the legal status of the student teacher?

THE TEACHER AND THE LAW

While it would take another volume to treat fully the questions outlined above, it is to the advantage of the teacher to keep the following essence in mind:[1]

Teachers have certain constitutional rights which cannot be disregarded and it is the responsibility of administration to protect these rights. Specifically, *the teachers have the RIGHT to:*

1. Receive support from the school administration assisting them to carry out their role as teachers.
2. Expect their classrooms will be free from disruption by students, parents, and others.
3. Use reasonable physical restraint to protect themselves, other students, or to maintain safe conditions in the performance of their duties.
4. Suspend a student within the limits of the Education Code.
5. Exclude from their extracurricular activity any student who does not meet the minimal standards established by the teacher of the activity for which the teacher is responsible, provided the rights of students are not violated.
6. Expect the student to come to class prepared and with the materials needed to carry out the activities for the day.
7. Request from appropriate authority that a student be considered for transfer, for specific reasons, out of their classroom.
8. Receive all available pertinent information regarding students placed in their classes.

Students have the RIGHT to:

1. Due process, which includes:
   a. a hearing within the school;
   b. explicit knowledge of charges brought against them;
   c. the opportunity to be heard in their own defense.
2. Know the behavior expected of them and the consequences of not obeying rules.
3. Be treated with courtesy and respect by staff and other students and have their constitutional rights protected.
4. Participate in school activities, provided they meet the qualifications of the sponsoring organizations.

Student Conduct and Behavior Standards

Disciplinary action for violation of school and state rules and regulations are based on the student and his/her deliberate defiance of the law. Some forms of action may be: calling in the parents for a conference, detention, suspension, transfer to another school, or expulsion. The school staff and

[1] Excerpted from the *Sacramento City Unified School District Faculty, Parents and Student Handbook*, 1981, Sacramento, California. (not copyrighted)

administration shall at all times try to consider what forms of disciplinary action will be best for the student.

By penal code in most states, assaulting, attacking, or menacing another individual is an unlawful act. A student who either assaults, attacks, or menaces another student or school employee is guilty of violating the penal code and may be subjected to arrest as well as school disciplinary procedures.

Definitions:

Assault: An assault is an unlawful attempt to commit injury on the person of another.
Attack: An attack is any willful and unlawful use of force or violence upon the person of another.
Menace: A show of intent to inflict harm; a threatening gesture, statement, or act.

Extortion: It is a criminal act to ask another person for money or other valuables and at the same time threaten to harm the person or his property in any way. If a student is approached by another student or students in this manner, he should report it to the office immediately. Any student who takes or attempts to take money or valuables from another by force or intimidation is subject to school disciplinary penalties as well as arrest.

Removal of Students from School

Students may be removed *involuntarily* from school for these reasons:

A. *Suspension*
  1. *Definition:* Suspension is a temporary removal from school attendance and school activities for misconduct. Generally, a student may be suspended for behavior harmful to the welfare of other students or behavior that adversely affects school discipline.
  2. *Types:* There are two types of suspension:
     a. *Teacher suspension:* A teacher may suspend, for good cause, any student for the remainder of the class period the day of the suspension and the class period on the following day. Note that the student does not leave school (but only the teacher's class) under this type of suspension.
     b. *Principal suspension:* The principal, or his designee, is given the right to suspend for a period not to exceed 5 days at one given time and not to exceed more than 20 days in a school year except that the student shall first be transferred to and enrolled in either one other regular school for adjustment purposes, an opportunity school, or a continuation high school.

B. *Expulsion*
  1. *Definition:* Expulsion is the most serious action that can be taken against a student. It is a disciplinary measure that removes a student from school for a specified period of time and that, after that time, allows the student to return to school only if he has met the conditions imposed by the Board of Education.
  2. *Reasons:* A student may be expelled for behavior that harms or threatens to harm other students or for behavior that seriously disrupts school discipline, whether such behavior takes place on or off the school grounds.
  3. *Procedure:* Because expulsion is such a serious action, the procedure is explicit and such as to give a student full protection of due process and of a fair hearing. Generally, the procedure is that the initial action is a recommendation by the principal, this being done on the Suspension

Notice form, supplemented with case documentation. The next action is a hearing before an administrative panel which the student and his parent attend and give testimony and in which all testimony is recorded. If the panel recommends expulsion, the next step is for the superintendent to present the case to the Board of Education for approval or disapproval.

Teacher Liability

As indicated in the *Code of Ethics of the Teaching Profession*, the teacher must "protect the health and safety of students." With this in mind, the teacher is looked upon as "in loco parentis" (in the place of parents) in the classroom or as "substitute parents" at school. While the teacher can be dismissed for various reasons such as incompetence, immorality, unprofessional conduct and/or negligence, the last category is by far the most frequent cause for legal disputes resulting in teacher dismissal. The central question here is whether or not the school and/or the teacher has exercised adequate supervision and whether there is evidence for negligence of duty on the part of the school and the teacher in the execution of their assigned duties. Some liabilities are likely to arise when the teacher is either unaware of or being imprudent in situations such as these:

1. Some states and Boards of Education allow teachers to administer corporal punishment. However, when there are some evidences that this is done in anger, unreasonably, or has caused some degree of permanent injury, the teacher is liable.
2. Teachers in special courses and activities should be especially well aware of safety precautions to prevent accidents or injuries. These would include science demonstrations/experiments, and handling tools and equipment in arts and crafts, home economics, or industrial arts classes. Extra care should be exercised by the physical education instructors and coaches about checking apparatus and equipment. Any teachers who take the students to fieldtrips or sponsor any extra curricular activities, either on campus or outside the campus, must also be prudent in this matter.

Teacher Contracts and the Tenure Laws

Legally speaking, teaching contracts are binding agreements between the school board and the teacher being employed. This means that the hiring institution (the Board of Education in this case, not any one individual, such as a superintendent or a high school principal) ensures the teacher of employment with specific assignment, compensation, length of service, etc. At the same time, the teacher is legally bound to perform the assigned duty as specified in the contract, whether it is an annual or a continuing contract. In most states, there are tenure laws that provide a continuing contractual agreement after the teacher has served a probationary period of three to four years. While the interpretation and the actual implementation of the tenure laws vary from state to state and from school district to school district, it must be remembered that *the tenure law guarantees the teacher due process against unjust change of assignment, transfer, demotion, change or reduction in salary, etc. The tenure law does not warrant the teacher the continuance of his teaching position no matter what.*

EXERCISE 15.2   WHAT DO YOU KNOW ABOUT LEGAL GUIDELINES FOR THE PUBLIC SCHOOL TEACHER?

We have prepared the following 25-item true-false quiz merely as a focus for your class discussion. In no way is the quiz comprehensive, but it may serve well its purpose as stated. The items and their "answers" originate from California law and should be compared with the legal guidelines of your own state. We recommend that you first read and answer the statements and check your answers first against those of other members of your class, then against existing laws of your state.

True—False

1. Classroom teachers may not be assigned supervision duties outside of their classroom teaching assignments. ____
2. A student was struck in the eye by a student-thrown object. The incident occurred during class while the teacher was present. Because the teacher was present he cannot be held for negligence. ____
3. A teacher has the responsibility to break up even a friendly "slap fight." ____
4. Teachers have the responsibility to see to it that disciplinary offenses are met with disciplinary punishments. ____
5. If a teacher is attacked, assaulted, or menaced by a student, and the teacher's supervisor does not report the incident to law enforcement authorities, the supervisor is then guilty of a misdemeanor and is subject to a fine of up to $200. ____
6. If a student has assaulted your teacher colleague and you have advised your teacher friend to not report the incident, then you are guilty of a misdemeanor. ____
7. The California Education Code forbids corporal punishment. ____
8. Recently (July 1974), teacher tenure in California was abolished. ____
9. If a student pulls down the pants of another student in public, then the offender is subject to a penalty of up to 6 months in jail and a fine of $50 to $500. ____
10. If a student taunts and challenges another to fight, this could be a disturbance of the peace and the student could be arrested by a witnessing teacher. ____
11. Extortion is a felony. ____
12. If a student is asked to stand and salute the flag and he refuses, he may be punished for "disobedience." ____
13. Suspension may be imposed by a teacher, a principal, or a governing body. However, a teacher may suspend the student only from his class for that day and the day following and must immediately report the suspension to the school principal. ____
14. A student threatens a teacher with, "I'll get you one day after school." The student could be punished with a fine up to $5,000 and sentenced to state prison for up to 5 years. ____
15. If a student throws a "stink bomb" into your room, he is guilty of a misdemeanor. ____
16. A teacher may arrest a student; a student may arrest another student. ____
17. If a student uses force to resist an arrest, this itself is cause for a charge of assault and battery. ____
18. Teachers and/or administrators may search students or lockers at random. ____
19. It is illegal to administer a test, questionnaire, or a survey, concerning a student's beliefs or practices in sex or family life unless the parent or guardian gives consent in writing. ____
20. It is permissible for you to request that your students purchase a weekly news supplement as long as you provide free copies to those students who cannot afford it. ____
21. A teacher may not receive royalties for a textbook he has written. ____
22. Teachers must maintain attendance records. ____
23. A teacher may be dismissed for not following the course of study. ____
24. Substitute teaching, summer school teaching, and adult teaching are not included in computation for permanent teaching status. ____
25. State law permits giving women teachers less compensation than men teachers for like services when holding the same credentials. ____

Answers to Quiz as related to California Education Code.

1. False Ed. Code 13557	4. True Ed. Code 13357
2. False Biggers v. Sac City USD	5. True Ed. Code 12916
25 Cal App 3d 269	6. True Ed. Code 12912
3. True Daily v. Los Ang USD	7. False Ed. Code 10853-54
2 Cal ed 741, 747	8. False

17. True		9. True	Ed. Code 10852
18. False		10. True	Penal Code 415
19. True	Ed. Code 10901	11. True	Penal Code 520
20. False	Ed. Code 9552, 9851	12. False	West Va v. State Bd. of Ed.
21. False	Ed. Code 9256		319 U.S. 624
22. True	Ed. Code 10951	13. True	Ed. Code 10601
23. True	Ed. Code 13556	14. True	Penal Code Sec. 71
24. True	Ed. Code 13332, 13333	15. True	Penal Code Sec. 403
25. False	Ed. Code 13501	16. True	Penal Code 837

16

What Are Some Guidelines for Constructive Group Morale and Discipline?

It is an aphorism in teaching that prevention of problems is easier than resolving them. From that standpoint we will begin this important chapter with suggestions as to how problems can be prevented.

We begin with this list called "If I do Any of These, Please Let Me Know," which we share with our own students at beginning of each semester. (We hope that the original author of this document will contact us for recognition). The list provides an exhaustive number of things we as teachers like not to do. Of course, none of us is perfect and at times certain "violations" are unavoidable, but still the list provides an important set of goals that, when followed, should aid in our efforts toward attaining the ideal.

A. "IF I DO ANY OF THESE, PLEASE LET ME KNOW"[1]

RUGGED BEGINNING

Rushes in late to class.
Gives a ridiculous excuse for being late.
Asks, "What are we supposed to do today?"
Flips pages in the book looking for suitable material.
Has no chalk and goes out hunting for it, blaming the janitors.

LACK OF PREPARATION AND PLANNING

States definitions and content incorrectly.
Has no examples planned in advance.

[1] Original source unknown.

Attempts to make up examples on the spot, which turn out to be overly complicated, very difficult, trivial, or inappropriate to the idea at hand.

Loses line of reasoning and has to keep referring to the book.

Assigns homework thoughtlessly (e.g., to solve the odd-numbered problems from 1 to 200).

INEFFECTIVE STYLE OF PRESENTATION

Proceeds with maddening slowness.

Speaks in a monotonous, dull, pedantic, or inarticulate manner.

Rushes through the material, talking much too fast.

Does not write down enough of what is said.

Does not bother writing down definitions.

Uses terms without defining them.

Indicate diagrams only by handwaving.

Presents no overview, summary, or relationships among ideas.

Does not attempt to motivate students to study the material.

Assumes that students already know the basic material and humiliates them when they do not.

Goes off on tangents involving overly advanced material.

Simply reads the book to the students.

Makes numerous errors in computations, logic, and grammar.

LACK OF RAPPORT WITH STUDENTS

Makes no eye contact with the class; talks to the board, walls, floor or ceiling.

Loses everyone's attention and goes on anyway.

Makes disparaging comments about the low level of the course material.

Insults the students: tells them they are stupid or unprepared.

Keeps saying "trivial" or "obvious."

Shows no enthusiasm.

Keeps looking at the time.

Displays irritating mannerisms.

Does not know students' names.

Has no positive comments for anyone.

POOR HANDLING OF QUESTIONS

Does not permit questions or embarrasses students who ask them.

Does not answer questions adequately.

Tells students to look up the answers to their questions in the book.

Misunderstands the student and answers a question that has not been asked.

Spends excessive class time answering questions of little general interest.

Asks almost no questions of the students.

Ask questions that are vague, confusing, impossible, or extremely simple.

Calls on the first person to raise a hand, without giving others time to think.

Harshly criticizes student responses to teacher questions.

POOR BLACKBOARD TECHNIQUE

Makes messy, indistinct drawings.

Labels diagrams unclearly or inadequately.

Reverses coordinates.

Places figures too high or too low so that key portions run off the board.

Crowds items together.

Mixes distinct problem solutions together on the board.

Leaves insufficient space for important items.

Writes illegibly (too small, too large, or on a slant).

Blocks students' vision by standing in front of the board work.

Skips steps or combines too many steps at once.

Keeps changing the same statement by erasure or addition, rather than rewriting it on another line.

Erases too quickly, thereby preventing comprehension or questions.

B. MAINTAINING A POSITIVE STUDENT MORALE[2]

Regarding Students

1. Know your students. Learn their names immediately.
2. Analyze the class periodically as to proper rest, diet, and general health.
3. Be aware of students' feelings. Pay attention to attitudes revealed in writing and discussion. Respect the personality of the pupil. Don't talk down to the class.
4. Pupil participation is necessary for good pupil morale. Help the student become a member of the group. Never set him apart from his classmates.
5. Emphasize the strengths of each student. Always look for the good points in a student. Build up the confidence of each student—help him feel important to the group. All people, young and old, like praise. Use it.

Regarding the Teacher

1. If you make a promise, keep it. Students expect and should receive fairness on the part of their teacher. If you make a mistake, apologize. Share with the students the fact that everyone makes mistakes.
2. Be willing to try out ideas. A teacher must be flexible. Be as creative and innovative as you know how to be.
3. Employ a procedure that is friendly and informal but businesslike and consistent. Treat all pupils with the same degree of fairness, impartiality, and consideration. Don't let the last teacher's report bias you, or punish the whole class for the actions of a few, or hear and see absolutely everything.
4. The teacher should possess a good sense of humor. If any professional needs a sense of humor, it's the educator.
5. Establish a good rapport with students so that they feel confident in approaching you with problems or questions. Be as courteous as you expect them to be with you. Never act in anger or use threats as a deterrent.
6. Teacher example will set the stage for many things. Be well groomed and speak and act like a lady or gentleman.

[2] Leslie J. Chamberlin, *Effective Instruction Through Dynamic Discipline* (Columbus, Ohio: Merrill, 1971), p. 225. Reprinted by permission.

Regarding the Learning Atmosphere

1. A busy class is usually a happy class. Provide activities that stretch the students' abilities and afford sufficient work to keep them busy. Develop a sense of timing—know when to speed up, slow down, or change the activity, but avoid creating pressure.
2. Rules for behavior should grow out of the purposes of the group and should be developed jointly by class and teacher.
3. Try to make the class environment meaningful in terms of the feelings of the students. Be enthusiastic—it's contagious. Create an atmosphere to make each individual feel important. Maintain an orderly environment in terms of bulletin boards, displays, exhibits, and classroom demonstrations and presentations.
4. Easily recognizable rewards should follow approved behavior without delay. Give recognition whenever possible for superior work or behavior. Try to overcome poor work with encouragement rather than scolding.

Regarding Learning Activities

Teach each day as if the superintendent were scheduled to visit. Teach like an intelligent person. Be prepared in terms of routines, materials, equipment, and activities. Start and end on time.

C. PREVENTION OF DISCIPLINE DIFFICULTIES[3]

1. Don't react to classroom misbehavior personally.
2. Don't threaten to do things. Take the needed action without the threat.
3. Don't use sarcasm, ridicule, or embarrassment. It usually causes bitter feelings toward the teacher, alienates the whole class, and humiliates individual members. Also, these techniques can easily backfire.
4. Don't punish in anger. Try to keep your composure regardless of the situation. Keep hands off the student while angry.
5. Don't, *as a general practice*, send students out of the room for misbehavior.
6. Don't use penalties that are personally or publicly humiliating to a pupil. Therefore, don't correct a student publicly; don't use a scolding attitude; don't prolong an incident.
7. Don't argue with students.
8. Don't reward students for improper behavior. Students should not receive certain jobs in order to gain their favor.
9. Don't use assignments as a punishment for misbehavior. This helps destroy the real value of schoolwork in the learning process.
10. Don't punish the whole class for individual infractions. This will cause resentment among the other students toward the teacher.
11. Don't use or threaten to use corporal punishment.
12. Don't make threats of any sort. Act!
13. Don't publicize offenses and their treatment before the other students.
14. Don't force a student to apologize to you. If an apology is freely given, accept it. A forced apology is usually a humiliation to both student and teacher.
15. Don't allow chain-reaction situations to develop. Some things spread through a class-

---

[3] Some borrowed with permission from Chamberlin, *op. cit.*, p. 312.

room and the most recent violator is often the one punished. Learn to recognize this type of situation and stop it without saying much.

16. Don't try to provide a final solution for every disciplinary situation immediately. Poor timing is a common error made by teachers in dealing with disciplinary situations.
17. Don't try to talk over student-to-student talk.
18. Don't use subject matter as punishment, e.g., don't assign homework as punishment.
19. Don't plead with them, e.g., "Would you please be quiet?"
20. Don't challenge every minor disturbance. While such disturbances often irritate only the teacher, they may be easily magnified out of proportion so they affect the entire class.

D. MAINTAINING ORDER IN THE CLASSROOM[4]

The position must be taken that true democratic classroom control is the only desirable method of those just described. Application of the following suggestions will aid in securing and maintaining desirable group control.

1. Be sincere. Be convinced that you can help all students. Demonstrate the fact that you like all your students. Attempts to disguise negative feelings toward some will be detected, with the result that student faith in you will be lost.
2. Be cheerful and have a sense of humor. At the same time do not try to win a teacher popularity contest. Winning cheap popularity at the expense of genuine student respect may lead to a teacher's undoing.
3. Avoid the use of vindictive punishment, especially mass punishment for misdeeds done by a few individuals. Punishment for the sake of proving that the teacher is the "boss" is of little consequence in correcting the cause of behavior problems.
4. Begin the class activities immediately at the start of the period. Don't delay by checking attendance or doing other tasks. Do these at a more appropriate time or let students perform them while you begin the important job of teaching. Refer to Chapter 15A and 15C.
5. Work to improve your teaching techniques. By planning challenging experiences with your students and by using a wealth of instructional materials, there will be fewer opportunities for behavior problems.

Each teacher will add suggestions to this list as he experiences success with various ideas. It is well to remember that all students will not respond in exactly the same manner to any one technique of classroom control.

Checklist for Group Morale and Discipline Problems

If you are troubled with difficulty in your working relationship with students, check yourself against the following to see if there are techniques or approaches you have not yet tried.

1. Have you talked to the student privately about the problem?
2. Have you talked with the parents about the problem?

[4] H. Orville Nordberg, James M. Bradfield, and William C. Odell, *Secondary School Teaching* (New York: Macmillan, 1962), p. 216. Reprinted by permission.

3. Have you talked with your cooperating teacher about the problem? (student teaching situation)
4. Have you talked with other teachers who also have this student?
5. Have you talked with a counselor or the vice-principal?
6. Have you found something your problem student can do for himself without disrupting the class?
7. Have you done something students want to do for a change when they are very cooperative? (skip a quiz, free reading, etc.)
8. Have you tried new seating arrangements? For the entire class.
9. Have you tried "giving up the lesson planned" and doing something different with the class?
10. Have you raised your voice, changed your facial expression and told them with a stern voice, "Be quiet!" or "too much noise" instead of pleading for personal favor by saying, "Please be quiet!" "Keep it down, please" or "Shush—?"

E. WHAT TO DO ABOUT UNRULY CLASSES

There is no one magic solution for all discipline cases. Some of the general guidelines are:

1. Be businesslike. Make clear to the students what is to be done for the day. Begin on time and close on time.
2. Learn the names of the students as quickly as possible and identify them by their names. Do not use a nickname or some tag (such as "you there, in the brown sweater").
3. *Say what you mean and mean what you say.* Do not be punitive-minded; develop a *preventive* and *remedial* approach.
4. Emphasize "do" rather than "don't." A positive approach is often more successful than a negative approach in unruly situations. For example, "We need to be quiet to work together better," rather than "Don't talk too loud."
5. Watch the entire class at all times. Be extra firm in requesting cooperation of the students and avoid making false accusations of misconduct. Do not ignore misconduct when the act is repeated.
6. Strive to remain calm and confident. You need calm nerves and a clear mind for teaching. Don't get irritated or argue with the student. Make it known to the students that you enjoy being with them but do not intend to put up with any nonsense.
7. Develop a wholesome and cooperative attitude among the students by being sincere in expressing your concern about unruly situations. Don't be frantic to teach your subject matter. Good class control is a prerequisite to good teaching.
8. Promote a give-and-take spirit. Do a favor for students once in a while (such as granting a free study period or buzz session or skipping a quiz).
9. When your authority is challenged, be calm and collected. Deal with the challenging student(s) individually and not in front of the whole class. If the situation is not too serious, ask the student to see you after the class; if serious, take the student with you to an appropriate office (principal's or counselor's). In that case you need to locate someone to take your place in the classroom.
10. Punish, if necessary, as a last resort, with prudence. Find out from the school authorities what types of punishment are permissible.
11. Let the students know early in the year just exactly what your tolerance level and "ouch lines" are. Here is a form used by one teacher to distribute at the beginning of the school year.

THINGS TO REMEMBER

1. Attendance will be taken daily at the beginning of the class. All absences and tardies are recorded. It is the responsibility of the student to bring a readmit. Any absence not

cleared by a readmit after three days becomes a truancy. Attendance is related to your grade. Students are responsible for making up missed homework and tests. No work accepted from truants.

2. Each student is to bring a pencil or pen, paper, and a notebook to class everyday. You should keep all handouts and assignments given in class in your binder. A GOOD IDEA: Keep all papers that pertain to your grade in case of any question about the final grade in this class.

3. My desk and rollbook are off-limits to all students.

4. No eating, drinking, or gum disturbances in class.

5. Students are asked to use the bathroom facilities before class starts except in an emergency. (You are allowed one emergency per semester!!!).

6. Students are expected to take care of their books, furniture, and the facilities. You may cover your book with a purchased book cover or you may use a paper bag, but YOU MUST COVER YOUR BOOK.

7. Students are not to walk around the classroom. Please stay in your seat unless you're coming up to see me for help. You may not leave the classroom without permission in the form of a hallpass. Again! STUDENTS ARE TO BE IN THEIR SEATS AND READY TO WORK WHEN THE BELL RINGS FOR CLASS TO BEGIN AND UNTIL THE BELL RINGS FOR CLASS TO END!! Thank you.

GRADING

Tests

The number of points earned per test will be recorded in my grade book. I will give a letter grade but record the number.

Homework

All assignments turned in are worth 10 points. They are returned with a $\sqrt{}$, $\sqrt{}+$, or $\sqrt{}-$. Late work is only 5 points.

F. EXAMPLES OF ATTEMPTS TO RESOLVE DISRUPTIVE BEHAVIOR ON CAMPUS[5]

Programs aimed at reeducating and controlling disruptive youth fall into eleven general classifications: alternative programs, behavior modification, communications network, counseling groups, financial incentives, honor passes and awards, minicourses, monitors and safety committees, peer counseling, police liaison programs, and special reports. These programs are usually beyond the domain of an individual teacher but should be of extra interest to teachers as viable alternatives to traditional efforts to resolve problems that extend beyond individual classrooms. The following examples may offer ideas for implementation in your own school. Addresses are given so that you may write for more specific information.

East Baton Rouge Parish School District
Post Office Box 2950, Baton Rouge, Louisiana 70821
Robert J. Aertker, Superintendent

The East Baton Rouge Parish policy on discipline includes the use of a behavior clinic based on the

[5] This information was obtained from *The Practitioner*, vol. 2, no. 2, 1976, p. 6–12, and reprinted with permission from the National Association of Secondary School Principals, 1904 Association Dr., Reston, VA 22091.

concept of positive intervention. Students are assigned to the clinic for minor offenses such as disobedience, class cutting, smoking, gambling, etc. Assignment is made for as many as six clinic sessions for a single offense. Repeated offenders, as well as students committing major offenses, are suspended rather than enrolled in the clinic.

The clinic is conducted after school for a period of approximately one hour and forty-five minutes. Parents are informed of a student's assignment to the clinic. Students may attend clinic for up to four minor offenses. Suspension starts with the fifth offense.

The students assigned to the clinic receive individual and group lessons and counseling. The activities concern personal values, interpersonal relationships, feelings toward family and parents, and a student's feelings about his own worth in the school and community.

Blue Spring R–IV School District
1801 West Vesper, Blue Springs, Missouri 64015
Nelson Hanmann, Educational Center Counselor

Blue Springs operates a program to provide "disordered adolescents" between the ages of sixteen and twenty and who have dropped out of school with programs leading to a high school diploma. Other goals include a reduction of "acting out" behavior and the acceptance of responsibility by these youths.

Each student selected must have dropped out the previous year and must meet the criteria established for "behavior disordered" youth. These criteria are: (1) difficulty in learning that cannot be explained by intellectual, sensory, or other health factors; (2) difficulty in building or maintaining satisfactory interpersonal relationships with peers, parents, and teachers; (3) a general mood of unhappiness or depression; (4) a tendency to develop physical symptoms, pains, or fears associated with personal/social problems. Students are provided with both individual and group counseling designed to give the students a feeling of self-worth and of meaningful personal relationships.

Requirements for the high school diploma are the same as for the mainstream school but approaches to learning differ. Learning is individualized for each student with a particular emphasis on identifying strengths and improving weaknesses. Out-of-class work is twice that of in-class work.

Ponce de Leon Junior High School
5801 Augusto Street, Coral Gables, Florida 33146
Ralph V. Moore, Jr., Principal

Ponce de Leon Junior High School operates a Student Adjustment Center (SAC) for students who are disruptive in school. The rationale for SAC is: (1) to keep students in the "regular" program, (2) prevent disruptive behavior, and (3) provide an alternative to suspension.

Students are assigned to SAC for an unspecified amount of time, although teachers may request a minimum length of time. Release from SAC depends upon student progress. Students work primarily on basic skills in math and reading. Appropriate class assignments can be given by teachers as well. SAC personnel incorporate behavioral tutoring. Students must use facilities such as rest rooms, cafeteria, etc., under the direct supervision of the SAC staff and at times other than regular passing periods.

Key elements of this program include the continuous counseling of students, the cooperation and involvement of the parents, and the involvement of the community. A strong liaison exists with the local vocational rehabilitation services.

Goals of the program include (1) improvement of attitudes about work, school, and society; (2) improvement of personal appearance and hygiene; (3) development of realistic understanding of the connection between work and study; (4) development of personality characteristics of dignity, self-respect, self-reliance, perseverance, initiative, and resourcefulness; (5) the receiving of recognition; and (6) achievement in the school's educational program.

Roanoke City Public Schools
917 South Jefferson Street, Roanoke, Virginia 24012
M.D. Pack, Superintendent

The Roanoke City Public Schools have established an alternative education center to provide a different setting for students experiencing difficulty in the city schools. This center highlights the importance of continuing education regardless of the social and/or academic status of the students. It provides a positive atmosphere that develops intellectual independence, self-esteem, and community awareness; that incorporates realistic evaluation sessions for each student, and that provides individualized instruction to students.

The goals of this program include motivating the students to learn, helping students deal with behavioral problems, helping identify personal responsibilities as members of the community, assisting students in their acquisition of actual job experiences, and helping students to acquire self-confidence and belief in their own ability.

Bound Brook High School
West Union Avenue, Bound Brook, New Jersey 08805
Joseph Donnelly, Principal

Bound Brook High School adopted a cooperative incentive program known as AVIP (Anti-Vandalism Incentive Program) to counter vandalism in the school. The Board of Education holds in escrow a sum of money equal to $1.00 per student. Costs of repairs and replacement of equipment and fixtures damaged by vandalism are taken from this account. The amount left in the account at the end of the year may be spent by the student body for equipment to be used in the school for their pleasure and comfort, such as a tape deck, additional athletic equipment, color television, air conditioner, etc.

To administer this program an AVIP committee, consisting of one student and one alternate from each class, one board member, two teachers, and the principal, was organized for the purpose of reviewing biweekly reports to determine if damage was the result of normal wear and tear or vandalism, or a combination of both. If the review determines that damage was the result of vandalism, the amount of repair or replacement is subtracted from the amount held in escrow. This figure is relayed to the student body to keep them informed and to sustain interest. The committee is also responsible for publicizing the program and uses a thermometer-type graph in the school cafeteria that shows the initial amount in the account and the amount that remains.

Monroe Junior High School
5105 Bedford Avenue, Omaha, Nebraska 68104
Robert A. Bathke, Principal

Monroe uses a program called "Positive Peer Culture," which utilizes techniques learned from juvenile correctional programs.

Student leaders, both "positive" and "negative," are identified by the school. These students then are formed into a unified leadership group through an intensive training program. The focus of this training is upon improving the school for *all* students.

The basic philosophy of PPC is: (a) accept peer influence in a youth subculture as a dominant force; (b) use peer influence in a positive and helping way; (c) no one has the right to harm other people; (d) students must be accountable for their actions; (e) adults alone cannot solve every behavior problem in a school; (f) young people must get involved in helping their peers; (g) staff must care about students, be firm, and set fair limits.

As an outcome of the training program, the positive and negative leaders influence their fellowership to support policies identified by the leadership group as generally beneficial for the student body. Thus, through the influence of peer leadership, a "positive peer culture" emerges.

Spring Valley High School
Sparkleberry Lane, Columbia, South Carolina 29206
John H. Hudgens, Principal

Spring Valley High School in Columbia, South Carolina provides a positive option for problem students with an "alternative to suspension group." A Spring Valley student, at the first or second suspension, has the choice of participating in the group or being suspended from school. Students who elect the group attend sessions for five weeks, one period per week.

Through individual and group counseling, students are helped to understand the reasons their offenses are viewed as offensive and to discover and examine alternatives to unacceptable behavior. In addition, students are encouraged to consider their values, attitudes, and goals. They also are assisted to cope with school adjustment.

Individuals set goals for themselves early in the group process. Goals are revised as clarification and understanding develop. Students are encouraged to discuss honestly and concretely the nature of their troubles. Students also are expected to listen and to assist other group members.

Parkway School District
455 North Woods Mill Road, Chesterfield, Missouri 63017
Murray L. Tiffany, Director of Pupil Personnel Services

Parkway schools, in cooperation with the Law Enforcement Assistance Council, have assigned to the district a St. Louis County police officer and a St. Louis Juvenile Court deputy juvenile officer. The deputy juvenile officer's role includes receiving referrals directly from parents, school, court, or police regarding predelinquent or delinquent juveniles, counseling delinquent juveniles, assisting families in obtaining help for delinquent children, offering alternative programs for juveniles, developing volunteer foster placements, and making community and class presentations on juvenile law and youth problems.

The policeman's role is to provide general police services to the schools in the district, to be used as a resource person for police information, to give presentations to the community and to classes, upon request, on topics such as laws, drugs, safety programs, etc., utilizing films, discussions, role-playing techniques, and other instructional methods. The officer also is to be available for informal contacts with the students regarding laws or police matters. He is not to act as a security guard or be on patrol duties.

Vacaville High School
100 Monte Vista Avenue, Vacaville, California 95688
William H. Cornelison, Principal

Vacaville High School utilizes a Youth Service Bureau (YSB) program. This Bureau, located in the main high school office, is manned by two youth service police officers with bachelor's degrees in sociology, psychology, and criminal justice. The officers teach two regular classes, giving students a new perspective on law enforcement personnel and their work. They participate in extracurricular activities as would a regular teacher.

Other duties include serving as liaison between the schools, home referral agencies, and police department. Juveniles are cited to the Youth Service Bureau with the intent that, through counseling, fewer problems will develop.

The benefits offered by this diversion program are significant. Misbehaving youth may continue to live at home while receiving counseling from the Bureau. The youth, in turn, will not have a court record. The Bureau's aim is to correct factors causing offenses to be committed as well as to reinforce the notion that the offense was wrong. Cooperative efforts are mounted with probation departments, family planning agencies, youth corps, and child protection agencies as well.

Miami Killian Senior High School
10655 S.W. 97th Avenue, Miami, Florida 33156
E.J. Arahill, Principal

Killian Senior High School requires all students to take a minicourse concerning assaults and disruptive behavior. Included in the learning activities package (LAP) for the course are definitions of deviant behavior as well as consequences for the different misbehaviors outlined in the school district's policy. The steps for reporting attacks and assaults are also part of the LAP.

Conard High School
110 Berkshire Road, West Hartford, Connecticut 06107
Douglas G. Christie, Principal

Conard High School employs two adult building monitors to help reduce vandalism and disruption in the school. The monitors were professionally trained by a local security agency. Student acceptance of the role of the monitor is fundamental to the success of the program. To gain acceptance, an advisory committee made up of faculty, students, administrators, and the head custodian was appointed. The committee's responsibility was to interview prospective monitors and discern and formulate their duties. Monitors, after selection, were introduced to the student body and their duties were posted and made known to all.

Some of the duties of the monitors include: (1) patrolling the school building and grounds; (2) checking parking areas and entrances to school; (3) questioning persons on school premises who are not students or staff; (4) checking restrooms, stairwells, hallways, and other areas inside the building; (5) conferring with students regarding improper behavior and attempting to obtain voluntary compliance with school regulations; (6) reporting periodically to principals on problems, incidents, and conditions affecting security.

Neumann Preparatory School
970 Black Oak Ridge Road, Wayne, New Jersey 07470
Reverend John G. Pisarcik, Principal

At Neumann Preparatory School the student council is billed for any deliberate destruction of property by unknown students. The student council is briefed periodically on the school's finances to understand the ways that repair and maintenance reduce funds that could be used for student academics and activities. The council, by exerting peer pressure on the student body, is able to determine responsibility in nearly every case. Students responsible for vandalism are then held accountable and the council is relieved of its fiscal responsibility. The council also can make recommendations about cost cutting.

Hocker Grove Junior High School
10411 Johnson Drive, Shawnee Mission, Kansas 66203
William Vick, Principal

Hocker Grove Junior High School uses an honor pass as a reward for positive student behavior. This program promotes in students a feeling of trust and gives students a desire to control themselves.

Each student at the beginning of the year receives an honor pass signed by the principal or assistant principal. This "card of value" says, in effect, that the student operates on his honor when out of class.

Students who misbehave or become disruptive are penalized by points. When twenty points are reached, the honor pass is suspended for a minimum of two weeks. Parents are notified as is the staff. Continued accumulation of points results in increased pass suspensions. Fifty points will result in permanent loss of the pass.

The program relieves some of the clerical duties, such as filling out passes to the rest room or library. It also is an efficient and accountable program for keeping track of and solving minor disciplinary problems.

The honor pass system is designed for the majority of students who are good citizens. The school believes that too often programs are developed for that small percentage of students who are not capable of behaving well without supervision.

Stevensville Middle School
Stevensville, Maryland 21666
Ronald W. Hill, Principal

Stevensville Middle School established a system of reports among parents, teachers, administrators, and counselors.

When students begin to get in difficulties, a daily report card is instituted. This provides each teacher with the opportunity to "grade" students for a number of days. It also allows teachers to know about student behavior in other classes. The reports are signed by the school bus driver and the parents on a daily basis, as well.

To provide positive reinforcement, an "excellence report" is given as a reward for outstanding work in a class. Students meeting certain positive criteria, such as being prepared, completing assignments, showing interest, etc., receive these reports at such times during a marking period as the teacher deems appropriate. An "improvement report" also may be sent for students needing encouragement to improve their classroom performance.

These forms can represent more work, but the school believes that documented and frequent reports will improve student behavior and keep serious discipline problems to a minimum.

After having read this chapter you might now profit from in-class discussions of the exercises that follow.

EXERCISE 16.1 CASE STUDIES FOR CLASS DISCUSSION

The cases that follow have been provided for analysis and discussion in your class. Study the cases and decide what you would do in similar situations. For your convenience, here is a brief statement of what each case is about:

1. A slow learner in junior high school, a boy who hangs around the teacher.
2. A bully in the tenth grade, an active-destructive type.
3. A lonely, unhappy, disinterested girl in Grade 10, a potentially passive-destructive type.
4,5. Accidents at school.
6. "My students are nice youngsters, but . . . ."
7. "Please stop baiting and harrying me."
8. "Five points deducted for your name!"

We hope that use of these case studies will add depth to your perceptions and insight about the day-by-day events that occur in teaching.

Case 1: The Boy Who Hangs Around

Background

Bill is male, age 13, in general science. He is tall and awkward. He has a poor skin condition. He is considered "crazy" by his classmates. He has minor police offenses and is in apparent conflict with his father. He has taken an apparent liking to the general science teacher and spends many extra hours in the classroom. He is energetic and displays an inquisitive nature. He is quick to get interested in projects, but almost as quick to lose interest. He likes to run the film projector for the teacher, but he does not like to participate in discussions with the rest of the class. He likes personal chats with the teacher but feels that the other students laugh at him.

The Situation

Bill's IQ is 95. The teacher attempted to work with Bill in improving his apparent feelings of inadequacy. The teacher had frank talks with Bill about his gangliness and his acne. What follows is actual material as written by Bill during the course of the first semester of school.

September: "I want to make the best out of the time I am on this earth. I want to be somebody, not just exist either. . . . The members of this class influence me and what I think of doing. . . . They also make me feel real low. Their teasing me has changed me. . . . The teacher of my science class has helped me very much. . . . My greatest problem is in holding my head up and fighting for myself. . . .

October: "I have made a lot of headway in the past weeks. . . . I think I have done a good choice in the subject I am studying. . . . I also thank my teacher's actions toward me, that we may get to be very good friends, and learn a lot to know that teachers are human too, that they also have problems to solve and goals to head for.

November: "I don't have to fear anybody or anything on the idea of getting up and saying what I feel I have accomplished in this class and I have learned to make my own dississions on what I will study or maybe do when I get out of school.

December: "I have learned that I have confidence in others only when I have confidence in myself.

January: "I gave my reaport on the afect of geabriilic acid on plants. . . . I told (the class) about all my failures and they were quite interested. I told them that I had failed four times . . . that my science teacher told me I should not give up at this point and that a seintice (scientist) does not give up. I had no longer stated that fact and they all seemed like they could help in some way. I think the report went over well."

So the student developed courage to stand in front of his peers, holding his head high, and confidently reporting to the class how he kept at his plant experiment, even after four failures. He was proud of what he had learned about the work of the scientist. And he was even more proud that the students no longer teased and laughed at him.

Questions for Class Discussion

1. How did you feel after reading this case?
2. Did Bill learn anything that semester? What?

3. Did he learn science?
4. What did this teacher do to facilitate Bill's learning?
5. What is ahead for Bill in school?

Case 2: The Case of the Bully

Background

Tony is considered by his peers as one of the "tough guys." He is 15 and in the tenth grade at Green High. Tony is prone to bullying, frequently quarreling with his fellow students and teachers; is considered by his parents to be disobedient. He has a record of minor offenses that range from truancy to destructiveness of property to drunkenness and offensive behavior. In general, Tony gets his satisfactions in ways that are damaging and unfair to others.

It is obvious to school officials that Tony is beyond parental control. He is frequently beaten by his father. Tony's mother has no apparent ability to control Tony's behavior.

Tony is not a member of any school organization of an extracurricular nature. His midquarter progress shows that he is failing in three subjects.

The Situation

One of the subjects Tony is failing is tenth-grade English. Tony is a discipline problem in your class and although it makes you feel guilty, you cannot help but be pleased when Tony is absent from class.

Questions for Class Discussion

1. Where is the problem?
2. Where is Tony heading?
3. What can and should be done, if anything? By whom?
4. What is the role for Tony? His teachers? His peers? The school administration? His parents? Society in general?
5. Is it too late for Tony?

Case 3: The Case of Mary

Background

Mary has been characterized by her peers and by her teachers as being lonely, indifferent, and generally unhappy. She avoids both students and teachers. She will lie and cheat to avoid attention. Her "close" friends describe her as thoughtless and unkind. She often uses damaging remarks about members of her class, calling them conceited, teacher's pets, and so on. She considers members of her class as thoughtless, unkind, and uninterested in her.

Mary will do what she has to do in order to achieve average success in her studies. Her association with adults, her parents, and her teachers would be described as one of "merely getting along," doing what "I have to do in order not to get too much attention."

The Situation

One of Mary's friends is another 15-year-girl, Jane. Jane is an above-average student in school, seemingly well adjusted, interested in people, and has gotten to know Mary because they are neighbors and walk together to school. Because of Jane's interest in other people and her closeness to Mary, she has become interested in "trying to bring Mary out of her shell."

Mary has told Jane that she feels her teachers are unreasonably severe. Mary said, "The teachers are only interested in the popular kids." Jane disagreed. Mary said, "You only disagree because you are pretty and popular." At this point, the conversation was broken by a boy running up and saying, "Hey, Jane, you're late for the council meeting."

Questions for Class Discussion

1. Where is the problem?
2. What if you were Mary's teacher?
3. How did you feel after reading this case?

Case Studies 4 and 5: Lawsuits

Case 4: The Case of the Science Class Mishap

A science class experiment that resulted in a fire—burning one student seriously—is the subject of a $250,000 suit filed in the Superior Court against the XXX Unified School District.

The personal injury complaint was filed on behalf of 13-year-old Mary, who suffered facial burns January 12 at XXX Junior High School.

The suit contends that Mary's science teacher, Mr. Brown, failed to give adequate instructions before the experiment started.

The mishap occurred, according to the suit, when alcohol that was being poured into a container on a hot plate spilled and caught fire, burning the girl on the face, neck, and left arm.

Case 5: The Case of the Stabbing Victim

Ron King, 16, who claims he was stabbed in the back during an English class, wants $100,000 in damages from North High School, Central Union High School District, and student Richard Decarlo.

According to the action, filed by King's mother, Lee, of 460 Bowman Avenue, the incident occurred last February. King says he was stabbed by Decarlo and lost his spleen as a result.

The suit says there was no teacher in the classroom when the stabbing took place and that the school was negligent in not providing supervision.

The action also contends that school officials knew that Decarlo secretly carried deadly weapons with him on the school grounds.

Questions for Class Discussion

Cases 4 and 5 represent situations involving personal injury and suit being brought against the teacher. After reading the cases, your class might divide into small groups for discussion of the following points:

1. What are your feelings about the cases?
2. Who (if anyone) was at fault?
3. How could the situations have been avoided?
4. What is the extent of the teacher's responsibility? The school's?
5. What legal guidelines exist in your state that are related to the cases?
6. How can a teacher protect himself against negligence?
7. What potential causes of physical injury exist in the classroom of the English teacher, the art teacher, and so on?

Case 6:   "My Students Are Nice Youngsters, But . . . ."

I have a feeling that my tenth-grade class sees through my youth and inexperience to my hidden fears and insecurity. I often feel that they are giggling silently while my back is turned. I catch glimpses of quickly hidden notes. Little things go on that I sense but do not see. My students are nice youngsters, really, but these minor annoyances are making me a nervous wreck. How can I stop these actions without alienating the children?

Case 7:   "Please Stop Baiting and Harrying me!"

I was fortunate enough to get an appealing and able seventh-grade class as my first teaching assignment. However, one boy is ruining my progress with them and my happiness in my work. He is a constant noise maker and trouble instigator. No special incident or difficulty precipitated his attitude, but he seems to take an actual delight in baiting and harrying me. I don't know how to change his attitude. What would you do?

Case 8:   "Five Points Deducted for Your Name!"

I was having difficulty explaining the solution of a problem because of continual talking among the students. I announced to the class, "I have reminded you students several times about our earlier discussion on courtesy in the classroom. Apparently it hasn't meant much to you, so from now on I shall write on the board the names of anyone talking out of place, and those individuals will have five points subtracted from their next examination grade—yes, five points for each time their names appear on the board."

EXERCISE 16.2   ROLE-PLAYING MANAGEMENT PROBLEMS

Teams of approximately five each will develop and present role-playing skits. A skit will be performed and followed by time given for team formation and implementation. Teams will present skits and each skit will last approximately 10 minutes.

Skits should illustrate that the team has researched the topic. Topics could include such things as: a classroom incident, a private student-teacher confrontation, a campus incident, a faculty room incident, an incident during planning an extracurricular function, teacher-departmental chairman incident, student-teacher-administrator confrontation, student-teacher incident, faculty meeting incident, faculty member-parent confrontation, PTA meeting incident, an incident in which the student makes his first mistake.

Here are some sample skits:

1. Group is half-asleep, dreaming, looking out of window, slumped in seats. Some put their heads down on desks.
2. Group is moderately attentive but one boy gradually slumps, finally falls asleep, snoring peacefully. He persists and group is amused.
3. Teacher is talking to a J.H.S. group. Two girls farthest from teacher continually whisper and giggle and others are distracted, turn around, and get the giggles too.
4. Tardy bell has rung but no one is seated and no one is even thinking about sitting down. Look out window, draw on board, talk, etc.
5. Students are reading quietly. Two boys exchange notes, one says loudly "Oh yeah?" and hits other on upper arm with fist.

Selected References

Allen, Paul, et al. *Teacher Self-Appraisal: A Way of Looking Over Your Own Shoulder.* Worthington, Ohio: Charles A. Jones Publishing Co., 1970.

Bremer, John, and Michael Von Moschzisken. *The School Without Walls, Philadelphia's Parkway Program.* New York: Holt, Rinehart and Winston, Inc., 1971.

Copeland, W.D. "Teaching Learning Behaviors and the Demands of the Classroom Environment," *Elementary School Journal.* Vol. 80, No. 162, March 1980.

Dreikurs, Rudolf and Pearl Cassel. *Discipline Without Tears.* New York: Hawthorne Books, 1972.

Henson, Kenneth T. *Secondary Teaching Methods.* Lexington, Mass.: D.C. Heath and Co., 1981.

Hyman, I.J., et al. "Discipline in American Education, An Overview and Analysis," *Journal of Education.* Vol. 161, No. 51, Spring 1979.

Kern, C.R. "Discipline for the 80's, Techniques for the Rocky Road Ahead," *Bulletin of the National Secondary School Principals.* Vol. 64, No. 121, May 1980.

Krumboltz, J.D., and H.B. Krumboltz. *Changing Children's Behavior.* Englewood Cliffs, N.J.: Prentice-Hall, 1972.

Long, James D., and Virginia H. Frye. *Making It Till Friday.* 2nd ed. New Jersey: Princeton Book Co., 1980.

Lunetta, Vincent N., and Leon J. Zalewski. *Interactive Incidents from Classroom, School, and Community.* Washington, D.C.: National Science Teachers Association, 1974.

Mager, Robert F. and Peter Pipe. *Analyzing Performance Problems or "You Really Oughta Wanna."* Belmont, Calif.: Fearon Publishers, 1970.

Ryan, Kevin (ed.). *Don't Smile Until Christmas.* Chicago: University of Chicago Press, 1970.

Sevich, Kevin J. *Disruptive Student Behavior in the Classroom.* Washington: D.C.: National Education Association, 1980.

Part V

Evaluation of Performance and Achievement

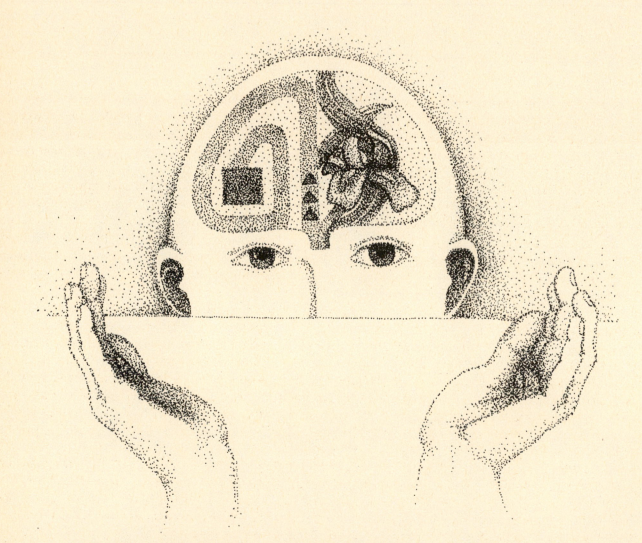

Drawing by Carol Wilson, unpublished material. Reprinted by permission.

*The mediocre teacher tells. The good
teacher explains. The superior teacher
demonstrates. The great teacher inspires.*
–William A. Ward

This section on evaluation is designed to communicate the following points:

1. The teacher needs to know how he is doing.
2. The student needs to know how he is doing.
3. Evidence, feedback, and input for Items 1 and 2 should come from a variety of sources.
4. Evaluation of student progress should be frequent and continuous.
5. If grades are given, the student should at all times know where he stands.
6. Self-evaluation is an important aspect of the total process.
7. Much of the evaluation process should be systematized.
8. The evaluation process should contribute to the improvement of the teacher and to the growth of the student.
9. Evaluation is a reciprocal process; that is, it includes evaluation of teacher performance as well as evaluation of student progress.
10. The teacher's professional responsibility is to teach and to assess his progress, and he will be held accountable for this responsibility.

The first chapter of Part V is concerned with techniques for obtaining evaluations as to how you are doing in implementing teaching plans. A micro-peer teaching exercise is provided for pre-service training. The verbal activity analysis that follows is useful in in-service as well as pre-service training. The Verbal Interaction Category System (VICS) is provided to assist in identifying and improving upon the kinds of interactions that go on in the classroom. As an example, we find that many teachers are unaware that they spend 80–90 per cent of their class time in teacher-directed talking, much of which is aimed at low-level cognitive operation. Frequently, these same teachers have the most trouble with classroom discipline and student motivation. There are teaching strategies to be learned that assist in getting students motivated and operating at higher cognitive levels. Structuring questions and developing an awareness of utilization of teacher response behaviors are important to skill and competence development. The contributions to this book mentioned above should be helpful to the beginning teacher in diagnosing and evaluating his progress.

The authors hope that by the time a teaching credential candidate begins to practice teaching in the classroom (sometimes called "student teaching"), he has already learned some teaching skills and is now ready to practice and to develop these skills. In this case, practice teaching should be a period of clinical diagnosis and therapy rather than a matter of "sink or swim"—pass or fail. He practices and develops his skills not only in working with youngsters but in working with other adults as well. We have included in this section some samples of instruments used by supervisory personnel for more general evaluations of student teaching performances. Also included are forms used by school districts for their evaluation of probationary teachers. These illustrate the criteria by which the beginning teacher is likely to be evaluated.

The remaining chapters of Part V introduce the two types of evaluation of student progress: formal and informal guidelines are provided for obtaining data for evaluating student achievement. The teacher has the professional license, training, and responsibility to teach and to assess student progress. The teacher must know how to do these and to do them well. He must exercise his best professional judgment in the selection and utilization of evaluating instruments and mechanisms. For this the teacher is held accountable, as he should be.

How Can I Become a More Competent Teacher? Techniques for Evaluating Teacher Performance

A. MICRO-PEER TEACHING: AN EXERCISE FOR PRESERVICE SKILL DEVELOPMENT SKILL DEVELOPMENT

Micro-peer teaching (MPT) is a useful skill development strategy used in methods classes. The strategy is that the "teacher" prepares and teaches a brief lesson to a (usually) small number of peers. This is followed by immediate feedback and diagnosis of the presentation.

Micro-peer teaching is a scaled-down teaching experience involving:

1. A limited objective.
2. A brief period of time for teaching the lesson.
3. Usually a few students in the class.

Research indicates that this training can be an excellent predictor of subsequent teacher behavior in the regular classroom. But, more important, the MPT can provide the opportunity to develop and improve specific teaching behaviors.

The use of the videotape recorder can allow the "teacher" to view himself as others saw him, and immediate replay is useful for self-evaluation and diagnosis.

The MPT evaluation should be related to the following criteria:

1. What was the quality of "teacher" preparation and presentation? For example, did the lesson appear well prepared and creative? How were the teacher's voice and mannerisms?
2. What was the quality of "student" involvement?
3. Were the teacher's objectives reached?
4. Was the cognitive level appropriate?

EXERCISE 17.1   THE MPT

In this exercise you will prepare and implement a teaching lesson to a group of your peers. The lesson duration we recommend should be 20 minutes at most. Your instructor will specify the exact time. The form that follows may be used to prepare your lesson. From this form you should then prepare a lesson plan, using one of the suggested forms in Chapter 7.

Note to the Instructor: With the aid of a split-screen generator (approximately $300.00) and two cameras you can record simultaneously on one screen both students and teacher. This affords the "teacher" the opportunity during playback to view student reactions during the teaching without losing the picture of the teacher.

MPT PREPARATION FORM

1. Concept I will teach. _____
   _____
   _____
   _____
   _____

2. Strategies I will use. _____
   _____
   _____
   _____
   _____

3. Student experiences I will provide. _____
   _____
   _____
   _____
   _____

4. Performance objectives. _____
   _____
   _____
   _____
   _____

5. How the lesson is to be evaluated. _____

_____

_____

_____

6. Materials I will use. _____

_____

_____

_____

_____

EXERCISE 17.1

To identify the skills demonstrated in the MPT and to reinforce thoughts with respect to specific skills, the following evaluation forms are prepared. An evaluation of the compilation may be helpful for each of us in identifying areas of strengths and weaknesses.

MPT EVALUATION FORM 1

Teacher: _____ Topic: _____

Rate the following by circling the appropriate number; 1 is very poor, 7 is excellent.

Content: (Was this of help to you? Did it extend your knowledge of the area?)
  1   2   3   4   5   6   7

Comment: _____

_____

_____

_____

_____

Presentation: (Did the presentation hold your interest? Was it clear and logical?)
  1   2   3   4   5   6   7

Comment: _____

_____

_____

_____

_____

Improvement: (How could the presentation have been improved?)

   1   2   3   4   5   6   7

Comment: _____

_____

_____

_____

_____

MPT EVALUATION FORM 2

Teacher _____ Subject _____ Date _____

I. *Organization of Lesson:*

	5	4	3	2	1

A. Lesson preparation	Very evident	Somewhat evident	Not evident
B. Lesson beginning	Effective start	Effectiveness somewhat lacking	Poor start
C. Subject-matter knowledge	Well informed and much to offer	Some knowledge evident and valuable	Needs to be informed more
D. Closure	Effective ending	Effectiveness somewhat lacking	Poor finish

Comments: _____

_____

II. *Lesson Presentation:*

A. Audience contact	Excellent eye contact	Needs to see audience more	Heavily relies on notes, looks above audience
B. Enthusiasm	Intense	Somewhat evident	Lacking (another job to be done)
C. Speech quality and delivery	Very articulate and natural	Clear and appropriate	Monotone and boring
D. Use of language (vocabularies)	Well chosen	Appropriate	Above head (comprehension)
E. Use of aids and materials	Well chosen and effective	Effectiveness doubtful	None evident; could use some

F. Examples and analogies	Excellent and logical	Needs better selection	None evident; could use some
G. Involvement of audience	Excellent and tactful	Somewhat passive	No involvement
H. Responses to audience	Very personal and accepting	Somewhat passive or indifferent	Impersonal or no response
I. Directions and re-focusing	Extremely clear and to the point	Somewhat vague or not too evident	Confusing or vague
J. Transition and closing	Very smooth and clear	Somewhat disjointed and unclear	Abrupt or unclear ending

Comments: _____

_____

EXERCISE 17.1 WHAT TO LOOK FOR IN PLAYBACK SESSION FOR SELF-EVALUATION

1. Effective use of verbal responses.
2. Effective use of nonverbal responses (gestures).
3. Fluency in use of questioning.
4. Use of voice inflection and nonverbal cueing.
5. Use of set induction.
6. Stimulus variation (variety of materials, etc.).
7. Use of time and closure.
8. Examples and analogies.
9. Eye contact.
10. Peripheral awareness.
11. Acceptance.
12. Listening.
13. Use of names.
14. Sense of humor.
15. Pertinence of MPT (non-frivolous).
16. Keeps you relaxed but interested.
17. Overall creativity.
18. Effective use of body, hands.
19. Mobility.
20. Listen to your questions.

OPTIONAL MPT EVALUATION FORM

Note to the Instructor: From previous editions of this text we had many requests for further details of how we use the MPT Exercise. We include here the information as requested. This evaluation form is the one we have used for several years, and although imperfect in some respects, it does emphasize certain characteristics of the exercise that we consider to be important. We list these here:

1. The exercise is intended to provide the preservice teacher opportunity to prepare and implement a mini lesson, and
2. to receive constructive feedback in the form of (a) peer evaluation, (b) self-evaluation, and (c) instructor evaluation, and in that order.
3. We have always wished we could do several of these during the course of a semester but have usually been limited to one because of the size of our own classes (usually close to 40). If several could be done, then each MPT could focus on practice of specific strategies.
4. From the form here it is apparent that we consider there to be three important ingredients of the completed MPT: (a) the preparation and implementation; (b) the packet turned in by each "teacher" upon completion which is in effect a summative peer and self-evaluation (8) and statements of how the "teacher" would change if he would repeat the presentation (9); and, (c) instructor evaluation of the students participation in the three areas other than presentation, i.e., playback, student, and evaluator. We like to emphasize the learning that also takes place as one performs in these other functions.
5. Each student in your class should perform each of the four functions during this exercise: teacher, student, evaluator, and self-evaluation during playback.

FORM FOR FINAL EVALUATION OF MPT

Student _____

Packet Due _____ Rec'd _____

Criterion I: *The Presentation*
Lesson Objective:

1. Preassessment	10	9	8	7	6	5	4	3	2	1	N.A.
2. Materials	10	9	8	7	6	5	4	3	2	1	N.A.
3. Application	10	9	8	7	6	5	4	3	2	1	N.A.
4. Student Involvement	10	9	8	7	6	5	4	3	2	1	N.A.
5. Post Assessment	10	9	8	7	6	5	4	3	2	1	N.A.
6. Cognitive Level	10	9	8	7	6	5	4	3	2	1	N.A.
7. Poise, Voice, etc.	10	9	8	7	6	5	4	3	2	1	N.A.

Subtotal Criterion I _____

Criterion II: *The Packet*

8. Summary Analysis	10	9	8	7	6	5	4	3	2	1	N.A.
9. Selection and Description	10	9	8	7	6	5	4	3	2	1	N.A.

Subtotal Criterion II _____

Criterion III: *Participation in MPT*

10. In Playback Session	10	9	8	7	6	5	4	3	2	1	N.A.
11. As Student	10	9	8	7	6	5	4	3	2	1	N.A.
12. As Evaluator	10	9	8	7	6	5	4	3	2	1	N.A.

Subtotal Criterion III _____

FINAL MPT GRADE ____ ____ reteach: yes no

Comments: _____
_____
_____
_____

B. THE VERBAL INTERACTION CATEGORY SYSTEM

Many teachers spend approximately 80–90 per cent of their class time talking "teacher talk" to students. Have you thought about the kind of talk you exchange with your students and how you respond to your students when they have reacted to your talk?

The Verbal Interaction Category System (VICS), developed by Amidon and Flanders, is designed to analyze and evaluate the verbal interactions between the teacher and the students. A close examination of the VICS offers the teacher a meaningful insight into the pattern of his verbal interactions with students.

EXERCISE 17.2 A VERBAL ACTIVITY ANALYSIS EXERCISE FOR STUDENT TEACHERS AND IN-SERVICE TEACHERS

Use the following format to aid you to observe and analyze your peer's (the teacher's) verbal activity with the students. Identify (mark, circle, tally, or underline) those behaviors you have observed. Share the results and discuss the strengths and weaknesses of verbal interaction. Ask your friends to do the same for you.

VICS CATEGORIES[1]

TEACHER TALK	Teacher-initiated talk	1.	Gives information or opinion: presents content or own ideas, explains, orients, asks rhetorical questions. May be short statements or extended lecture.
		2.	Gives direction: tells pupil to take some specific action; gives orders; commands.
		3.	Asks narrow question: asks drill questions, questions requiring one- or two-word replies or yes-or-no answers; questions to which the specific nature of the response can be predicted.
		4.	Asks broad question: asks relatively open-ended questions which call for unpredictable responses; questions which are thought-provoking. Apt to elicit a longer response than 3.
	Pupil-initiated talk	5.	Accepts: (5a) Ideas: reflects, clarifies, encourages or praises ideas of pupils. Summarizes, or comments without rejection. (5b) Behavior: responds in ways which commend or encourage pupil behavior. (5c) Feeling: responds in ways which reflect or encourage expression of pupil feeling.

[1] Edmund Amidon and Elizabeth Hunter, *Improving Teaching: The Analysis of Classroom Verbal Interaction*, p. 211. Copyright © 1966 by Holt, Rinehart and Winston, Inc. Reprinted by permission of Holt, Rinehart and Winston, Inc.

		6.	Rejects:	(6a) Ideas: criticizes, ignores, or discourages pupil ideas.
				(6b) Behavior: discourages or criticizes pupil behavior. Designed to stop undesirable behavior. May be stated in question form, but differentiated from category 3 or 4, and from category 2. Gives direction, by tone of voice and resultant effect on pupils.
				(6c) Feeling: ignores, discourages, or rejects pupil expression of feeling.

STUDENT TALK

Teacher response

7. Responds to Teacher:
  (7a) Predictably: relatively short replies, usually, which follow category 3. May also follow category 2; e.g., "David, you may read next."
  (7b) Unpredictably: replies which usually follow category 4.

8. Responds to another pupil: replies occurring in conversation between pupils.

Pupil response

9. Initiates talk to teacher: statements which pupils direct to teacher without solicitation from teacher.

10. Initiates talk to another pupil: statements which pupils direct to another pupil which are not unsolicited.

SILENCE OR CONFUSION

11. Silence: pauses or short periods of silence during a time of classroom conversation.

12. Confusion: considerable noise which disrupts planned activities. This category may accompany other categories or may totally preclude the use of other categories.

C. STUDENT TEACHING EVALUATION FORM AND COMPETENCY DESCRIPTIONS

Student Teacher _____   School _____

Supervising Teacher _____   Subject _____

College Supervisor _____   Date _____

SUMMARY EVALUATION

(check one)   Mid-term _____

Final   _____

Directions: Place an X in one of the three categories for each of the 20 evaluative criteria—a student teacher whose performance at the end of the semester indicates that he or she merits an "inadequate" rating in one or more of the criteria might be adjudged as not ready to receive a teaching credential.

	Through Improvement	
From Inadequacy	*and Adequacy*	*Toward Mastery*

1. Demonstrates command of single subject field.

1. _____   _____   _____   _____   _____

	From Inadequacy	*Through Improvement and Adequacy*		*Toward Mastery*

2. Employs standard English usage.

    2. _____ _____ _____ _____ _____

3. Maintains group control.

    3. _____ _____ _____ _____ _____

4. Maintains physical and aesthetic conditions.

    4. _____ _____ _____ _____ _____

5. Uses a variety of teaching techniques.

    5. _____ _____ _____ _____ _____

6. Chooses techniques suitable to occasion.

    6. _____ _____ _____ _____ _____

7. Uses varied and effective motivational techniques.

    7. _____ _____ _____ _____ _____

8. Plans learning experiences both cooperatively and independently.

    8. _____ _____ _____ _____ _____

9. Shows originality or creativity in devising learning experiences.

    9. _____ _____ _____ _____ _____

10. Assesses student learning in relation to stated objectives.

    10. _____ _____ _____ _____ _____

11. Shows increasing skill in measuring, evaluating, and reporting student progress.

    11. _____ _____ _____ _____ _____

12. Demonstrates ability to accept and deal with student differences.

    12. _____ _____ _____ _____ _____

13. Selects and uses a variety of instructional materials.

    13. _____ _____ _____ _____ _____

	From Inadequacy	*Through Improvement and Adequacy*		*Toward Mastery*

14. Gives directions clearly, timely, etc.

    14. _____ _____ _____ _____ _____

15. Applies acquired knowledge regarding psychological principles of learning.

    15. _____ _____ _____ _____ _____

16. Shows wide range of intellectual, social, and cultural interests.

    16. _____ _____ _____ _____ _____

17. Proves lively and growing interest in student activities.

    17. _____ _____ _____ _____ _____

18. Maintains ethical standards in personal and professional relationships.

    18. _____ _____ _____ _____ _____

19. Shows increasing interest in professional responsibilities and opportunities.

    19. _____ _____ _____ _____ _____

20. Evidences positive relationships with colleagues and students.

    20. _____ _____ _____ _____ _____

COMPETENCY DESCRIPTIONS

From Inadequacy	*Through Practice*	*Toward Mastery*

1. *Demonstrates command of subject field.*

From Inadequacy	*Through Practice*	*Toward Mastery*
Indicates shallow knowledge and lack of academic diligence; occasionally makes misleading or erroneous statements; depends entirely upon textbook or course of study for data and ideas; concepts are narrow or provincial.	Usually offers reliable information; may demonstrate awareness of related ideas or data; indicates cursory acquaintance with recent materials and developments in the field; may point out relationships to other disciplines.	Regularly introduces pertinent data and materials from experience and academic preparation beyond that provided students from school sources; clarifies relationships with other fields; is consistently accurate and resourceful without personal earns respect of colleagues and students for subject mastery.

2. *Employs standard English usage.*

From Inadequacy	*Through Practice*	*Toward Mastery*
Commits grammatical errors and reveals limited vocabulary; fails to	Commits few grammatical or other language errors; uses understandable	Employs standard English with vocabulary, sentence structure, and

From Inadequacy	*Through Practice*	*Toward Mastery*
adapt language to student maturity; often makes spelling and mechanical errors; may use profanity, slang, crudities, or other inappropriate vocabulary, and tolerates substandard language usage in regular classwork.	vocabulary; can adapt language to varying conditions but may lapse on occasion; written work is adequate to immediate needs.	usage appropriate to student ability and maturity; provides an exemplary model in written expression including chalkboard work, tests, and other material given students.

3. *Maintains group control.*

Frequently lacks control over group; allows noise and disruptive conditions to inhibit learning; teacher behavior encourages hostility and resentment; students consistently evidence lack of respect toward teacher and classmates; unaware of school policies and procedures regarding pupil control.	Develops group spirit adequate for instruction to continue regularly; demonstrates understanding and acceptance of school policies and practices on pupil control; most pupil rudeness and defiance kept within bounds; relationships with pupils improve during semester.	Classes evidence individual and group respect by working diligently toward accepted goals; teacher accepts individual needs and differences while protecting group against aberrant behavior; friendly and cooperative spirit evident.

4. *Maintains physical and aesthetic conditions.*

Unaware or unconcerned about classroom ventilation, temperature, safety hazards, cleanliness, neatness, or general appearance.	Is aware of physical and aesthetic conditions and makes occasional attempts to clean, brighten, or otherwise maintain and improve the learning environment.	Regularly maintains and improves classroom physical and aesthetic conditions; checks for safety, light, ventilation, etc.; prepares bulletin boards, brings appropriate learning materials, and otherwise endeavors to make environment attractive and stimulation.

5. *Uses a variety of teaching techniques.*

Uses only one or two instructional procedures; seems unaware of others or reluctant to vary techniques or to innovate.	Occasionally tries a variant technique upon urging of a supervisor or colleague; appears hesitant to attempt anything different.	Stimulates learning, heightens student interest, and adapts instruction to changing conditions by diversifying approaches and procedures.

6. *Chooses techniques suitable to occasion.*

Follows the same limited teaching techniques constantly despite differing conditions, subject, or student maturity.	Usually chooses a technique that works adequately for a given time or place; realizes that different techniques facilitate or inhibit teaching effectiveness.	Identifies purposes of each lesson and consistently selects a matching technique that should prove effective for that occasion; relates technique to students; evidences readiness to change procedures quickly to accommodate unusual conditions.

(continued)

From Inadequacy	*Through Practice*	*Toward Mastery*

7. *Uses varied and effective motivational techniques.*

| Ignores or seems unaware of the need to motivate learning for best results. | Recognizes purposes of motivating learning and occasionally makes a serious attempt to arouse interest through initiatory activities. | Assumes responsibility to develop varied and effective motivational techniques appropriate to student ability and maturity and uses them; relates unit or lesson to student experience; works to help every student see purpose in all learning activities; adapts techniques to accommodate individual readiness. |

8. *Plans learning experiences both cooperatively and independently.*

| Indicates disinterest in working with colleagues or students to plan learning but may show awareness of merits in doing so; appears dependent on others for most ideas and directions; tends to think of teaching as doing something to people. | States willingness to work with others and participates readily; demonstrates some ability to develop adequate materials; can plan independently with minimal direction; seems to realize merit in cooperative planning. | Regularly seeks to develop and share materials and effective learning activities; plans with students and respects their wishes; works confidently with groups and contributes full share to group effort; independent work shows maturity and skill; expresses purposes as student behaviors and provides for flexibility and minimal standards. |

9. *Shows originality or creativity in devising learning experiences.*

| Lacks skill or interest in making the learning interesting to students; teaching is humdrum, characterized by endless rambling, recitation, filling in blanks, etc. | Sometimes innovates or develops variations but usually looks to others for ideas; seldom sees the possibilities for vitalizing instruction; may exploit some opportunities when encouraged by supervisor. | Often performs imaginatively and independently but within professional bounds; students look forward to classes; cordial good humor and surprises usually characterize daily instruction. |

10. *Assesses student learning in relation to stated objectives.*

| Lesson plan objectives occasionally slighted or ignored; evaluations are based often on feelings or other extraneous factors. | Usually measures student performance by developing tests related to objectives; seldom permits extraneous factors to enter into evaluation. | Consistently relates student learning to stated objectives by writing behavioral objectives susceptible to measurement and emphasizing mastery of concepts and data; reinforces learning by referral to objectives. |

11. *Shows increasing skill in measuring, evaluating, and reporting student progress.*

| Reveals need to improve skills in developing suitable test items based on stated objectives; proves inadequate in scoring and evaluating | Develops achievement tests that adequately measure student learning although test items may have ambiguities or uneven coverage | Measures and evaluates student work comprehensively and fairly, using varied instruments; demonstrates self-confidence and sincerity |

From Inadequacy	*Through Practice*	*Toward Mastery*
student performance; insecure in dealing with adults.	of material; meets and talks with parents in friendly, respectful manner; examinations improve in succeeding weeks of experience.	in student and parent conferences; uses a variety of formal and informal evaluative techniques; demonstrates confident use of elementary statistical techniques.

12. *Demonstrates ability to accept and deal with student differences.*

Tends to group students into ethnic, ability, occupational, moral, or academic categories; brings prior attitudes or convictions regarding groups into teaching and tends to generalize toward individuals.	Evidences willingness to work with pupils of diverse origins and cultures; has some difficulty in dealing with the range of ability or achievement but does not pre-judge individuals.	Accepts individuals as personalities rather than as stereotypes or symbols; teacher-pupil relationships are friendly and cooperative; dignity of the individual is accepted; identifies students as being different rather than inherently better or worse, good or bad.

13. *Selects and uses a variety of instructional materials.*

Restricts student learning to a single or very limited variety of sources; lectures continuously, shows films constantly, follows a single book, or otherwise limits learning opportunities.	Demonstrates ability to choose materials appropriate to lesson objectives and uses them with increasing skill and confidence; sees merit in varying media and materials but usually stays securely with tried material.	Provides frequent and useful mix of materials appropriate to student ability and maturity; regularly uses materials with skill and poise; seeks out sources beyond those provided by the school to clarify concepts or supplement information.

14. *Gives directions clearly, timely, etc.*

Sometimes forgets to assign outside work or assigns after dismissal bell; directions hasty or not clear; students often vague or confused about assignments or next steps in class activities.	Usually remembers to give timely directions but students are not always clear as to teacher expectations; teacher often asked to repeat or clarify directions.	Anticipates learning sequences, and leads up to next experiences; reinforces directions by repetition; considers student readiness and gives directions slowly and clearly; asks students to rephrase complicated assignments to assure understanding.

15. *Applies acquired knowledge regarding psychological principles of learning.*

Attempts to proceed without constant referral to student readiness; ignores individual differences; uses same procedures for different groups.	Recognizes that learning rates and qualities vary from day to day and adapts techniques to accommodate; often consciously plans to stimulate interest and follow through to reinforce learning.	Regularly plans motivational experiences, exploits student interests, reinforces learning to point of mastery, varies techniques in recognition of student aptitudes and emotional states.

16. *Shows wide range of intellectual, social, and cultural interests.*

Interests fail to reveal varied concerns or depth of scholarship; cul-	Interests are limited but are sufficiently diverse and profound to meet	Wide and ranging interests reflect knowledge and concern with

(*continued*)

From Inadequacy	*Through Practice*	*Toward Mastery*
tural interests limited or parochial; unaware or disinterested in current intellectual conflicts or national and local controversial issues.	daily needs; can converse on varied topics; shows awareness of nature of other disciplines; usually willing to listen, read, or discuss current events and issues.	diverse contemporary issues; is learned in own field and conversant with others; attends recitals, concerts, lectures, plays, shows, eagerly shares ideas and informed opinion.

17. *Proves lively and growing interest in student activities.*

Attends student activities reluctantly to fulfill minimal demands; seldom refers to student activities or makes hostile statements to classes and individuals.	Attends activities regularly and enjoys some; makes occasional remarks to students about an especially rewarding experience; may participate in some events or student organizations.	Attends and participates and may help to direct or sponsor student activities; often makes supportive statements about activities and performances; recognizes importance of activity program in total school enterprise.

18. *Maintains ethical standards in personal and professional relationships.*

Appears unaware or unconcerned with ethical practices and standards; may deviate from the accepted codes of conduct as to decency, honesty, integrity, and respect toward others.	Aware and compliant with recognized ethical standards; conducts self with sufficient propriety to maintain the acceptance and respects of those around him in the school.	Concerned with maintaining ethical standards and serving as an example to youth without being self-righteous; scrupulous in personal and professional relationships. Careful about maintaining security of public property.

19. *Shows increasing interest in professional responsibilities and opportunities.*

Lacks interest in assuming any responsibilities beyond those firmly assigned; interested only with subject field and in performing minimally.	Willing to accept assigned or commonly assumed responsibilities; occasionally seeks further opportunities to serve; reveals a growing awareness of the breadth of responsibilities in teaching.	Accepts and participates willingly in professional obligations; joins or expects to join and be active in appropriate organizations; seeks to improve own competencies by attending conferences and taking advanced courses; evidences concern over status of professional and its improvement.

20. *Evidences positive relationships with colleagues and students.*

Involved in questionable practices or incidents that arouse concern of colleagues; appears unconcerned with others' welfare; may be hostile, irresponsible, apathetic, or uncooperative.	Proves generally cooperative and respectful with people around him or her; shares interests with others and accepts suggestions with courtesy; colleagues and students willing to work cooperatively and to invite further associations.	Evidences consistently cordial, supportive and wholesome relationships; maintains open but reserved professional position with students; colleagues enjoy and seek out company; students greet teacher happily outside class.

EXERCISE 17.3 COMPETENCY CHECK

1. Use the form of Section C and its accompanying description on page 214 to complete your own competency self-evaluation for this stage of your training.
2. After doing (1) above, repeat Exercise 1.1 of Chapter 1, then compare your results with your original completion of Exercise 1.1.

D. SAMPLE FORMS USED BY SCHOOL PERSONNEL TO EVALUATE TEACHERS

Of the many varying forms of teacher evaluation forms, the following may be considered representative.

CERTIFICATED EMPLOYEE EVALUATION REPORT[2]

Name: _____   School: _____

Assignment: _____   Date of Evaluation: _____

	Exceptional	Standard	Needs Improvement	Unacceptable
1. Compliance with Objectives				
a. The degree to which the evaluatee has contributed to expected student progress with respect to stated terminal objectives.	___	___	___	___
b. (First-year employees) The degree to which the evaluatee is contributing to expected student progress.	___	___	___	___
2. Planning (Daily and Long-Range)				
The degree to which both daily and long-range planning are evident in the evaluatee's performance.	___	___	___	___
3. Management and Organization				
The degree to which the evaluatee employs productive educational practices, structures, and methods.	___	___	___	___

(continued)

[2] Grant Joint Union High School District, Sacramento, Calif., unpublished material, 1972. Reprinted by permission.

	Exceptional	Standard	Needs Improvement	Unacceptable

4. Motivation

   The degree to which the evaluatee has attempted to productively motivate his charges. _____ _____ _____ _____

5. Professional Preparation

   The degree to which effort is shown toward needed professional preparation, involvement, and growth. _____ _____ _____ _____

6. Establishment of Suitable Learning Environment

   The degree to which the evaluatee has contributed to acceptable student productivity and an optimum learning environment within working conditions. _____ _____ _____ _____

7. Total School Environment

   The degree to which the evaluatee has contributed to the total operation of the school (includes extracurricular activities). _____ _____ _____ _____

8. Compliance with Adjunct Assignments

   Evidence of fulfillment of adjunct assignments according to job description. _____ _____ _____ _____

Comments: _____

_____

_____

Evaluator discussed report with *Employee:* ( ) Yes ( ) No

Signature of Evaluator
Other Than Principal: _____ Title: _____

Date: _____

Signature of Principal: _____

Date: _____

I would like to discuss this report with the Reviewing Officer: ( ) Yes ( ) No

In signing this report, I do not necessarily agree with the conclusions of the evaluator.

Signature of
Evaluatee: _____ Date: _____

EVALUATOR'S FORM FOR CLASSROOM OBSERVATIONS

Evaluator: _____ Date: _____

Evaluatee: _____

Approximate number

Class: _____ of students: _____

Subject of the Lesson: _____

_____

Activity in Progress (description of interaction between students and teacher; materials and aids used; suitability of material for level of students):

_____

_____

_____

_____

Evidence of Student Participation and Motivation: _____

_____

_____

_____

Evidence of Evaluatee's Planning on a Daily and Sequential Basis: _____

_____

_____

_____

Optional Additional Comments: _____

_____

Suggestions: _____

_____

_____

_____

_____

PROGRESS REPORT OF GOALS AND OBJECTIVES[3]

Evaluatee: _____   Date Submitted: _____

Goal Classification No.: _____   Goal No.: _____

Note: The evaluatee shall be accountable for his stated goals and objectives. He must produce evidence supporting progress that has been made toward the accomplishment of his commitments. This will be signed and submitted to the evaluator for review by April 1. He will follow the order given in item 2.0

I. Goal Classifications:
   A. Student Progress
   B. Control of Educational Environment
   C. Adjunct Duties
   D. Self-Improvement

II. Statement of the Goal:

_____
_____
_____
_____
_____
_____
_____

III. Objectives: Supporting Evidence of Accomplishment of Objectives:

_____   _____
_____   _____
_____   _____
_____   _____
_____   _____
_____   _____
_____   _____
_____   _____
_____   _____
_____   _____
_____   _____

[3] San Juan Unified School District, Carmichael, Calif., unpublished material, 1973. Reprinted by permission.

_____   _____

_____   _____

_____   _____

_____   _____

_____   _____   _____   _____
Evaluatee's Signature   Date   Evaluator's Signature   Date

STATEMENT OF GOALS, OBJECTIVES, AND ASSESSMENT TECHNIQUES[4]

Evaluatee: _____ Date Submitted: _____

Goal Classification No.: _____ Goal No.: _____

Note: The statement of Goals, Objectives and Assessment Techniques is to be submitted by the evaluatee, reviewed by the evaluator, if necessary revised by the evaluatee, agreed upon and signed by both. Due date October 15. With the concurrence of the evaluator, objectives or assessment techniques may be changed during the year.

Goal Classifications:

A. Student Progress
B. Control of Educational Environment
C. Adjunct Duties
D. Self-improvement

Statement of the Goal: _____

_____

_____

_____

Why the Goal Has Been Selected: _____

_____

_____

_____

Objective(s) (Includes Assessment Techniques and Timeline)	*Instructional Strategies (How I Will Go About It)*	*Resources Required*	*Progress to Date*

(continued)

[4] *Ibid.*

_____

_____

_____

_____

_____   _____   _____   _____
Evaluatee's Signature   Date   Evaluator's Signature   Date

EVALUATION CONFIRMATION REPORT TO THE SUPERINTENDENT[5]

Certificated Person: _____ Date: _____ School Year: _____

Location: _____ Position Assignment: _____

Tenured: _____ Nontenured: _____

I. The following are on file at: _____   _____
                                          School   Office (Director, Ass't Supt)

	Yes	No
A. Goals and objectives for student growth	_____	_____
B. Goals and objectives for educational environment	_____	_____
C. Objectives for adjunct duties	_____	_____
D. Objectives for self-improvement	_____	_____
E. Evaluatee's assessment techniques	_____	_____
F. Evaluatee's goals and objectives accomplished	_____	_____
G. Evaluator's review	_____	_____
H. Resources of support services provided	_____	_____

II. Observation instrument has been completed and discussed.   _____   _____

III. I have fulfilled the required responsibilities as specified in the
     five elements of the evaluation of certificated personnel.   _____   _____

Note: Items checked "No" must be supported by attachment of Recommendation for Improvement form.

Recommendation:

[   ]   Recommend tenure

[   ]   Recommend continuation without reservation

[   ]   Recommend continuation with reservations noted on attachment

[   ]   Recommend termination for reasons stated on attachment

[5] *Ibid.*

Evaluatee's Comments: _____

_____

_____

| _____ | _____ | _____ | _____ |
| Evaluatee's Signature | Date | Evaluator's Signature | Date |

Note: Signature of the evaluatee does not imply agreement.

E. STUDENT EVALUATION OF TEACHERS

Some teachers think that teacher evaluation by high school students is ridiculous and absurd because the students are not intelligent and mature enough to evaluate their teachers. This kind of comment is subject to qualifications and exceptions. It is conceivable and possible that the teachers can assess their teaching effectiveness through observation of students' responses, classroom dialogue, and test results. If one wishes to obtain more objective and specific data from the students on an anonymous basis, a form like the following may be considered. We have observed that beginning teachers have used such a form to their advantage, and to their surprise, they have obtained from students very informative and valuable expressions.

STUDENT EVALUATION OF TEACHING

This evaluation is intended to seek opinions from you regarding what I have done so far in this class. Please be frank and straightforward in expressing your feeling in the categories listed below. Be concise and to the point and do *not* give your name.

1. What I have done well/what you enjoyed/valuable: _____

_____

_____

_____

2. What I need to improve/what you did not enjoy/not valuable, not meaningful: _____

_____

_____

_____

_____

3. Other comments: _____

_____

_____

_____

_____

_____

CHECK LIST FORM

I would appreciate your answering the following questions about this class and the teacher. Please answer these questions according to the way you feel at the present time and *do not* give your name.

Any written comments you wish to make on any of the questions or about the class may be put on the bottom of the page.

Place an X under the answer that best fits your feelings:

	Yes	No	Don't Know
1. Do you feel that the lessons are well planned and organized by the teacher?	_____	_____	_____
2. Do you usually understand what the teacher expects from you on assignments, homework, and tests?	_____	_____	_____
3. Do you feel that you can ask the teacher questions when you don't understand something?	_____	_____	_____
4. Is the classroom work varied?	_____	_____	_____
5. Are the lessons and reading material interesting?	_____	_____	_____
6. Do you feel that there is enough classroom discussion on the lessons?	_____	_____	_____
7. Do you feel that you can participate in classroom discussions freely?	_____	_____	_____
8. Is the teacher's speech clear and pleasant?	_____	_____	_____
9. Do you think the teacher's appearance is acceptable?	_____	_____	_____
10. Does the teacher have a pleasing personality?	_____	_____	_____
11. Do you think the teacher uses enough variety of materials?	_____	_____	_____

12. Please check the materials you have enjoyed having in this class or would like to have more of in the class.

_____ Filmstrips   _____ Worksheets   _____ Films

_____ Records   _____ Review study   _____ Bulletin boards
                                      sheets
                                                            _____ Projects/activities

Any other comments you would like to make would be appreciated: _____

_____

_____

F. STUDENT SELF-EVALUATION FOR THE COURSE[6]

Students frequently remark, "My tests didn't show it, but I learned a lot from that course, really, I did." Or they make some other comment indicating that what they learned in a course is different from what the instructor judged their learning to be. Such remarks suggest that the students are capable of rendering judgment about course outcomes, and that these feelings of accomplishment are not considered by the instructor.

STUDENT SELF-EVALUATION

What are your judgments about yourself and the course you are now completing? Rank yourself with check marks in the spaces at the right using *5* as the high rank and *1* as low.

5   4   3   2   1

1. How would you compare the work you have done in the course with that done in comparable courses?

   a. Amount of time spent on the course

   b. Number of resources encountered (e.g., books, journals)

   c. Effectiveness of use of time in accomplishment of assignments

   d. Other (write in)

2. How valuable have your efforts been to you?

   a. Familiarity with reference material in the library and in the classroom

   b. New knowledge gained: facts, principles, general concepts

   c. New attitudes developed regarding yourself, your interests, capacities, potentials, etc.

   d. Developed (or exercised) skills in organizing my thinking, expression, writing, to the extent apparently expected or encouraged in the course

   e. Other (write in)

3. How do you rate yourself on your major assignments?

   a. Knowledge gained

   b. Organization thorough, treated all aspects of the assignment

[6] Modified from an original and unpublished form designed by Fred W. Fox, Department of Science Education, Oregon State University. By permission.

	5	4	3	2	1

c. Extensive research in preparation, didn't just rehash old ideas but added constructively to them. Tried new ideas

d. Class presentations were such that it was evident that I was familiar with the field studied

e. Other (write in)

4. How adequately did you contribute to the progress of the daily class meetings?

   a. My remarks contributed directly to the topic under discussion and were not too often irrelevant

   b. In view of the amount of participation that seemed to be encouraged in the class and in comparison with others in the class, I participated reasonably well

   c. Other (write in)

5. With reference to 2a, cite some references (author and title) below, indicate the important ideas you got from the source, or make a brief comment about the reference.

_____

_____

_____

_____

6. State two or three viewpoints you now hold regarding yourself which are new or differ from what you believed when you first came to this class.

_____

_____

_____

_____

7. Aside from things you have done in this class or as requirements for the class, what examples can you cite of things you have done that exemplify your interest in, or knowledge or application of the concepts of the class, since the quarter (or year) began?

_____

_____

_____

_____

G. TWENTY COMMON MISTAKES MADE BY BEGINNING SECONDARY SCHOOL TEACHERS

The following list was compiled from conversations between the authors and secondary school administrators about the common mistakes made by beginning teachers. Discuss the items with your classmates.

1. Talks too much and too fast.
2. Too much lecture, not enough relevant class discussions.
3. Grades a student's work generously when it is clearly inadequate.
4. Manner of dress is too sloppy and informal.
5. Too often permits students to break rules and department policy.
6. Makes too many rules unilaterally; should negotiate more with others.
7. Moves too quickly through textbook, leaving content before it is well learned.
8. Neglects to efficiently manage routine requirements and reports.
9. Does not make student assignments clear; too much delay in returning student work.
10. Too lenient in control and discipline; too inconsistent.
11. Seems ignorant of the legal requirements established by the local school district and the state.
12. Uses inappropriate language and too many verbal fill-ins, i.e., "Okay" and "you know."
13. Uses poor questioning skills.
14. Chalkboard writing is poor and unorganized.
15. Objectives of lessons unclear to students.
16. Does not seem to understand overall functioning of the comprehensive high school.
17. Spends too much time behind his desk; needs to move around more in classroom.
18. Gives quizzes and tests too often.
19. Teaches more for the testing rather than for true learning.
20. Is not proficient in the use of audiovisual equipment (motion-picture projector, filmstrip projector, e.g.).

What Are Some Guidelines for Evaluating Student Achievement?

A. AVENUES OF EVALUATION[1]

As you prepare each unit of instruction, you should make provision for checking, during the course of that unit, the effectiveness of your teaching and the extent of the students' learning. This is called *evaluation*.

Informal Evaluations

There are many activities that furnish you with information on a student's progress and development. Some, informal in nature, include:

1. The questions he asks during or after class.
2. The responses he makes to questions.
3. The way he explains an idea or process to others.
4. The way he works in a laboratory or workshop situation.
5. The manner in which he listens.
6. The degree of his involvement in class discussions.
7. The kind of challenges he either seeks out or accepts.

Although these activities do not fit into a numerical grading system, they may be more significant than the results of some formal, written exams.

---

[1] Leonard, et al., op. cit., p. 186.

Formal Evaluations

Other avenues of evaluation, more formal in nature, include:

1. Oral reports.
2. Written exams.
3. Practical examinations.
4. Status reports on projects.
5. Prepared materials such as paintings, a batch of cookies, or a finished bookshelf.

In all these more formal types of evaluation, the students should be aware of the criteria for judging their work long before the results of the evaluation are announced.

B. EVALUATION TOOLS FOR STUDENTS' PARTICIPATION, ASSIGNMENT, AND REPORTING

Many secondary school teachers evaluate student's achievement rather superficially by marking Excellent, Good, Average, Poor, . . . or A, B, C, D, F, ... The authors feel that the student's progress should receive more analytical evaluation and personal comment by the teacher whenever possible. The following forms are suggested for these purposes, the selection of which depends on the nature of the student's tasks. You may use this as a supplement to a citizenship grade portion in the regular report card.

Ask your students to evaluate themselves using any of the forms here.

PARTICIPATION IN THE CLASS

	Always	Most of the Time	Seldom
1. Listens carefully			
2. Follows directions			
3. Shows initiative			
4. Finishes what he started			
5. Asks questions			
6. Contributes to discussion			
7. Involved in the class activities			
8. Helps others in group work			
9. Volunteers for group work			
10. Works for the benefit of the group			

Comments: _____

_____

_____

ASSIGNMENTS

	Always	Most of the Time	Seldom
1. Understands assignments			
2. Completes assignments			
3. Tries his best			
4. Covers materials thoroughly			
5. Uses reference materials			
6. Shows good quality			
7. Shows neatness and organization			
8. Hands assignments in on time			

Comments _____

_____

_____

_____

_____

_____

_____

REPORTING (ORAL OR WRITTEN)

Contents:

1. Ideas or Information Presented

    Highly Valuable — Valuable — Little Value

2. Level of Interest

    Extremely Interesting — Fairly Interesting — Not Too Interesting

3. Evidence for Research

    A Great Deal — Somewhat — Very Little

4. Organization of Materials

    Extremely Well Organized — Fairly Well Organized — Shows No Organization

(continued)

Presentation:

5. Speaking

                                       Very   Can't Hear

                                         Clear   Audible   Too Well

6. Delivery

                                         Very   Somewhat

                                         Smooth   Hesitant   Stilted

7. Timing

                                                           Just About

                                     Perfect   Right   Stilted

8. Contact with Audience

                                    At All Times   Sometimes   None

9. Personal Interest or Enthusiasm

                                    Very High   Moderate   Not Evident

Comments: _____

_____

_____

_____

C. THE PROBLEM OF "GRADING ACCORDING TO THE CURVE"[2]

There is a system of grading that has gained many adherents during recent years, popularly called "grading according to the curve." The curve mentioned is the normal curve, which is bell-shaped and is said to represent the typical distribution of any trait that can be measured in a continuous series. The assumption underlying the use of the normal curve for grading purposes is that, in any typical sample, pupils will range in mental ability from inferior to superior. It is further assumed that a certain percentage of pupils will fall into each category of mental ability: a very small percentage will be found to be inferior, and an identical percentage will fall into the superior category. Between these two extremes, a larger percentage will be found who are below average or above average, and the largest number, those of average mental ability, will be found in the middle of the distribution.

Those who employ statistical procedures in using this grading system make up a frequency distribution of the pupil's grades, compute the mean and the standard deviation, and then use the standard deviation to assign grades. In some cases statistical procedures have been bypassed, and grades have been assigned according to predetermined percentages of As, Bs, and so on. There are many variations of the percentage to be included in each grade. The following are illustrative of this practice.

[2] Adam M. Drayer, *Problems and Methods in High School Teaching*, 1963. p. 147. Reprinted by permission of the author.

ARBITRARY DISTRIBUTIONS OF GRADES

A – 7%	A – 10%
B – 24	B – 20
C – 38	C – 40
D – 24	D – 20
E – 7	E – 10
100%	100%

Why, then, has this system of grading received such wide acceptance? Apparently, because some educational statisticians have been overzealous in interpreting and applying the concept of the normal curve of distribution. One of the paradoxes in education is that some authorities in the field dwell at great length on the desirability of recognizing each pupil as an individual; but then, apparently ignoring their own admonitions, they recommend that the pupil's progress be evaluated by converting him into a statistic in a frequency distribution.

D. GENERAL SUGGESTIONS ON GRADING

1. At the beginning of your course, explain your policies on grading to the students. Let your students know specifically what is expected of them. You may certainly work with students cooperatively in formulating your grading policies (contract grading, handing in assignments on time, number of quizzes and tests, distribution of weights, and so on).
2. Inform your students of their progress periodically through individual conferences, check lists, or progress reports. You may use these devices to supplement the regular report cards. It is educationally sound and constructive to let the students know where they stand in terms of their progress prior to their receiving grades at the end of a quarter or semester.
3. Be objective and impartial in grading the students' work. It is unethical and unprofessional to overgrade the students' work when they do not meet the given standards.
4. It is best not to change the grade unless the teacher has made clerical errors. This can be avoided by informing the students periodically, preferably in writing.
5. Do not argue with the students about grades. Discuss and reason with them to the extent appropriate. Encourage them to do better work in the future. Communicate to your students that a grade is earned, not given.

EXERCISE 18.1 PREPARATION FOR GRADING

1. Prepare a grading system and criteria for a course you intend to teach. Be prepared to defend it in class.
2. Be prepared to discuss in class the pros and cons of use of this *assignment grade memo* form.

ASSIGNMENT GRADE MEMO

_____
Student

_____
Assignment

Your grade on this assignment is _____

For possible grade improvement you may make relevant changes and resubmit the assignment no later than _____
Important: If you resubmit, please include the original marked assignment as well as your revised one, plus this memo.

3. Be prepared to discuss in class the pros and cons of frequent use of this *progress report form* in secondary school teaching.

PROGRESS REPORT
OR
"HOW I AM DOING SO FAR"

Grade to date

A   B   C   D   F

_____
Student

_____
Date

_____
Absences

E. SOME ALTERNATIVES IN GRADING

The competent teacher is familiar with the advantages and limitations of traditional grading procedures and with the alternatives available. Although it is beyond the scope of this textbook to go, in depth, into grading and evaluation systems, we would like to refer you to a well-written book that focuses on grading, its effects upon students, advantages and disadvantages of alternative systems, and that has an extensive bibliography of sources dealing with the history, research, and arguments about grading. The book is *Wad-Ja-Get? The Grading Game in American Education*[3]. Appendix B of *Wad-Ja-Get?* provides descriptions of the advantages and disadvantages of particular grading systems such as: narrative evaluations using all letters of the alphabet; self-evaluation and self-grading; pass/fail and credit/no credit systems; and, blanket grading. We will include here their description of "The Mastery Approach," which, in reality, is "the traditional grading system, done effectively."

The Mastery Approach to Grading[4]

The mastery approach begins with the teacher deciding what his operational or behavioral objectives are for his students, that is, what exactly he wants them to be able to *do* as a result of their learnings. He then organizes these learnings into units of study and arranges the units in a logical sequence, each unit serving as a necessary or logical building block to

[3] Howard Kirschenbaum, Sidney B. Simon, and Rodney W. Napier, *Wad-Ja-Get? The Grading Game in American Education* (New York: Hart, 1971). May be ordered from A & W Publishers, 95 Madison Avenue, New York, N.Y. 10016.
[4] *Ibid,* pp. 301–304. Reprinted by permission of A & W Publishers, 95 Madison Avenue, New York, N.Y. 10016.

the unit succeeding it. Then the teacher determines how he will measure the extent to which his students have mastered the body of knowledge and skills in each of the units.

For each unit, the teacher designates levels of mastery or proficiency. Thus, if a math teacher wants his students to be able to solve a quadratic equation, he stipulates what the student must do to demonstrate a *C* level of proficiency, what he must do to demonstrate a *B* level of proficiency, and so on.

At the very beginning of the course, the teacher provides the students with all this information—what they are expected to learn, how their learnings will be tested, what the criteria are for the different levels of proficiency and what level of proficiency is required before they can move on to the next part of the course. In addition, he explains to the students what resources are available to help them achieve the levels of mastery they desire.

Students are then free to master the course content in their own fashion. Some students will attend class lectures and discussions. Others will work independently. Many students will utilize the various resources the teacher has provided—learning packages, programmed texts, films, tapes, speakers, field trips, etc.

Each student proceeds at his own pace. One student may take a semester to accomplish what is normally done in a year. Another student may take a year to do a semester's work in a particular subject. Under this system the course is oriented much more to the individual student, and the professor spends most of his time in review seminars and in individual tutoring, rather than in large group lectures.

Students ask to be examined when they think they are ready to move on. Usually, when a student has achieved a *C* level of mastery in one unit of a course, he can choose to go on to the next unit. However, students who want to earn *B* or *A* grades will stay with each unit until they have achieved that level of proficiency. A student may take an exam (a different form each time, of course) over again until he is satisfied with his grade.

Using the mastery approach, several teachers or an entire department can get together and plan their courses sequentially—one course building upon the next. This is sometimes called a performance curriculum, since course credits are no longer determined by the length of *time* a student spends with a given subject ("I had three years of French.") but by the level of *performance* he has achieved in a given area.

ADVANTAGES:

a. A student's grade becomes more meaningful to him because it is tied to a performance level. In the performance curriculum, grades become more meaningful because, in several different classes, the same grade now means the same thing.
b. Much of the teacher's subjectivity in grading is eliminated.
c. When students know where they are heading, they are likely to get there faster.
d. The focus of this system is on success, not failure.
e. The student has freedom to pursue his own path in mastering the course content.
f. The teacher is held accountable for stating his objectives, providing many resources and helping his students achieve mastery. Sloppy organization and ill-prepared teachers are readily noticeable.
g. In the performance curriculum, the cooperation among teachers can generate better morale and the sharing of resources.

DISADVANTAGES:

a. To utilize the mastery approach properly requires considerable skill on the part of teachers and administrators. Most educators were not trained in this method and a great deal of re-training will be necessary. The funds are not easily available.

b. The performance curriculum somewhat limits a teacher's freedom to run his classes in just his own way. In some cases this might be desirable; in other cases some creative teachers might be hampered.

c. It is possible for teachers to use the mastery approach without allowing students to pursue their own ways of achieving the levels of proficiency. When this happens students might feel, more than many do now, that all their education means is jumping over a series of prescribed hurdles.

d. Even when students have freedom to choose *how* they will achieve the teacher's goals, the mastery approach discourages them from setting and working toward *their own* goals.

e. The total faculty must be involved in setting up a performance curriculum. The teachers in each subject area would have to carefully study goals and methods and explore new approaches to the subject matter. This could take a very long time and might normally be impossible, since most teachers teach 5 classes, have supervisory duties and are involved in one or more student activities. A long-term grant might be needed to hire additional personnel to free teachers to do the necessary research and curriculum development.

STATEMENTS FOR CLASS DISCUSSION

1. Evaluation is for the purpose of growth.
2. Evaluation, because of the many variables, can be negotiable.
3. What a student says and does is at least as important as what he writes.
4. The best evidence is a *variety* of evidence.
5. The best evidence of learning is a change in behavior. But, remember, some people who know the most about having babies have themselves never had babies.
6. Most of us probably know much more than we have learned to communicate to others. I will come closest to communicating to you what I know when you provide me with a variety of opportunities to do so.
7. I'm not "playing God" when I tell you what I think of what you are doing. I'm just telling you what I think. If you don't like what you hear, then don't listen.
8. The "average student" is a statistic, not a person.
9. "I can really do better than my grades show. I know I can."
10. "I'm no Socrates, but for $12,000 a year what did you expect?"

19

What Should I Know About Tests and Their Construction?

Constructing a good test is one of the teacher's most important and most difficult responsibilities. Some type of test can be designed for almost any purpose, and a variety of test types can keep a testing program interesting.

A. PURPOSES FOR WHICH A TEST MAY BE ADMINISTERED

1. To serve as a means of instruction and learning by providing review and drill.
2. To motivate.
3. To aid in the promotion and classification of students.
4. To provide information for student counseling and guidance.
5. To gauge teaching effectiveness.
6. To evaluate the curriculum.
7. To provide information for case conferences, parent conferences, student employment and college entrance.
8. To determine student achievement.

Can you add to this list? _____

_____

_____

_____

This chapter will provide you with basic information regarding a variety of test types. For more in-depth information on testing and measurement, please see the references at the end of this chapter.

B. ESSENTIAL STEPS IN TEST CONSTRUCTION

There are at least three essential steps in constructing a good classroom test. These are:

1. To identify the purpose for which the test is being administered.

2. To list the specific objectives (goals) of the lessons involved in the test. Be sure the objectives are *behavioral*, and also that they are specific and definite enough so that the teacher can determine whether the student has achieved them.

3. To prepare test items that will measure how well each objective has been achieved. Specific questions should require the student to do those things—recall information, apply information, interpret information, etc.—specifically called for by the objectives for which the test is being developed.
    a. Be sure the coverage is adequate, that all objectives are included.
    b. Be sure the test is balanced; that is, the items should test the objectives in proportion to their importance.
    c. Be sure each item is appropriate. Is it the type of item that will in fact measure the achievement of the particular behavioral objective that it is designed to measure?
    d. Be sure each objective item is clear and unambiguous.
    e. Each objective item should have one and only one correct answer.
    f. Each item should be difficult enough so that an unprepared student will get it wrong but easy enough for a prepared student to get it right.

C. TYPES OF TESTS

The majority of your test construction time will undoubtedly be taken by Step 3—preparation of the test items. A teacher needs to know about the variety of test items available, otherwise there may be a tendency to rely too heavily upon one or two types.

Test items can be divided into three categories—purely verbal tests, tests that involve pictures and diagrams, and tests that make use of actual materials. Each type has its own values and each has serious limitations. The third type named most closely approaches reality and can measure learnings that verbal and picture tests cannot evaluate at all. However, these tests generally are difficult to set up and administer. Verbal tests depend upon the interpretation of words. Students who lack fluency with words are penalized by them. However, when verbalization is considered an important outcome, these tests are valuable. Picture tests represent something of a compromise between verbal tests and tests based on actual materials. They are several steps removed from reality, but they do reduce some of the emphasis that is put on words in the purely verbal tests.

What follows is a review of 14 types of tests[1] defined by the nature of the test items. (We encourage you to practice writing these different kinds of test items when appropriate for your own subject field.) Within our discussion of each item type we will attempt to provide a sample item, designed each time to measure the same desired learning outcome. The objective we have frequently selected is one regarding your understanding of the importance of set induction, body, and closure to

[1] Our appreciation to Professor Alfred T. Collette who granted permission to use in this chapter some material originally printed in his out-of-print textbook, *Science Teaching in the Secondary School*, Allyn & Bacon, 1973, pp. 598–610.

a good lesson plan. This objective may not fit so well with certain item types, but its use is meant to give you a basis for comparison.

OUTLINE OF TEST TYPES WITH SAMPLE ITEMS

I. PERFORMANCE TESTS

Performance tests measure a pupil's ability to carry out certain operations. The needed materials are placed before the student together with a statement of the problem to be solved. The student is expected to solve the problem and demonstrate the end result. He may or may not be expected to explain the reasons for his operations. He may be scored on the end product only, or on each step, or on his explanations, or on all three. Performance tests come closer to measuring certain desirable outcomes of the program than do most other tests. Unfortunately, not much experimentation with this type of test has been carried out.

Sample Item

Objective:

The student is to show understanding of set induction, lesson body and closure.

Performance Test

Student is given a class of 10 students and asked to prepare and implement an effective lesson with three components.

Advantages:

Little or no verbalization is required. Manipulative ability is tested. Understandings that are difficult to verbalize are tested. Students who do poorly on verbal tests may receive recognition for their achievements.

Disadvantages:

This type of test is difficult to administer to large groups. If duplicate sets of equipment are used, a large amount of materials is needed. Otherwise, cumbersome rotation systems must be used so that each student gets a turn.
Common to the arts and physical education.

II. IDENTIFICATION TESTS

This type of test measures a student's ability to carry out identification procedures. He is given one or more unknown specimens and the materials he will need to test their properties. He is scored on the accuracy of his identification.

Sample Item

Identification Test:

When viewing a teaching demonstration, the student is to correctly identify the beginning and end of each component.

Advantages:

As with performance tests, students are working with actual materials. The test measures their true understandings of procedures. Verbalization has little place in the test.

Disadvantages:

As with performance tests, adequate materials must be provided. To be fair, the specimens must be unfamiliar to all students; this may be difficult to arrange.

Common to biology.

III. COMPLETION DRAWINGS

Students are given a drawing that is incomplete and they are asked to add the proper lines to complete the drawing.

Sample Item

An electric bell, a push button, and a dry cell are pictured on the question sheet. Accompanying directions read, "Draw lines to represent the wires needed for making the bell ring when the button is pushed.

Advantages:

This type of test requires less skill than a standard drawing test. Time needed for completion is short. The answers are usually simple to correct.

Disadvantages:

Students may misinterpret the diagrams provided for them. Students need prior practice in completing the same types of drawings.

IV. THE ESSAY ITEM

In constructing the essay item, the teacher asks a question or presents the student with some type of *problem;* the student composes the response in the form of some kind of sustained prose. The student is free to choose his own words and to organize his ideas in his own phraseology *within the limits of the question posed.*

The essay item is still widely used by high school teachers although it has been the object of much criticism, especially by experts in the field of testing.

Advantages:

1. It measures the higher mental processes, such as ability to think, to understand large concepts, to organize information and to express ideas clearly and concisely in good English.
2. It requires a useful and rewarding kind of study on the part of the pupil and stimulates creativity and freedom of expression.

Disadvantages:

1. It requires a great deal of time to read and score, if the teacher is conscientious and the results are to have any significance.
2. It tends to provide an unreliable sampling of student achievement. Because the number of essay test items must be small owing to the time factor, the teacher must draw inferences as to the student achievement from a limited sample.
3. It tends to be vulnerable to unreliable scoring.
   a. Different teachers tend to assess the same response differently.
   b. The same teacher tends to assess the same response differently at different times.
   c. The essay item is especially vulnerable to the "Halo Effect."
   d. The scorer may be unduly influenced by legibility, beauty of handwriting, quality of grammar, punctuation, diction, spelling, general neatness, and verbose answers.
   e. Teachers are prone to write essay items hurriedly, without careful thought.
4. The student who writes slowly and laboriously may not be able to complete the test although his achievement is high and his learning profound.

Suggestions for the Construction and Scoring of the Essay Item

1. The teacher must devote a good deal of time and thought to the construction of an essay test item. Unfortunately, too many teachers strongly favor the essay test over the objective test simply on the grounds that it is "easy" to construct.

244 Evaluation of Performance and Achievement

2. The question should *precisely define* the *direction* and *scope* of the response desired. It should include instructions on how much coverage the student should give the item and how much detail is desired. If the question is not clearly defined, the students "are not running the same race."

Faulty:

Discuss standardized and teacher-made tests.

(The student very likely will write in an aimless fashion, not knowing how the item will be evaluated, until he feels that he has used up enough space or has consumed his time allotment. What does "Discuss" mean? "Explain"? "Evaluate"? "Define"? "Compare"? "Contrast"? "Describe"?)

Improved:

Explain two (three, four) essential similarities and two (three, four) essential differences between standardized tests and teacher-made tests.

Faulty:

Discuss the steps in processing milk.

Improved:

What are the important steps in processing milk from dairy farm to consumer? Describe each step and explain its function.

3. A large number of questions, each of which requires a reasonably short prose response, is generally preferable to a small number of questions requiring long prose answers. (The large number of items provides more adequate sampling of the content, and briefer answers tend to be more precise.)
4. The teacher should very carefully take into consideration the time required for adequate response to the item in relation to the amount of time available in the testing period.
5. In a normal class, the practice of providing optional items is generally indefensible. Different qualities of performance are more likely to be comparable if all students face the same set of test situations.
6. When the test item is constructed, the teacher should make a tentative scoring key. The teacher should decide how many points at most will be allotted to each item. This number of points should appear to the left of the number of the item on the test so that the student will also be informed of the item's value.

    The teacher should also inform his students in advance whether he is going to include in the score an evaluation of errors in grammar and spelling, punctuation, organization, etc.
7. In order to reduce the "Halo Effect" one question should be graded seriatim for all students rather than all questions for one student. In other words, grade all Questions 1's, then all Questions 2's, etc.
8. The level of the following student performances is commonly measured by means of the essay item:

a. Comparison of two (or more) things on a given basis.
b. Comparison of two (or more) things in general.
c. Decision for or against.
d. Statement of causes or effects.
e. Explanation of meanings, uses of words, phrases, or longer portions of given passages.
f. Summary.
g. Analysis.
h. Statement of relationships.
i. Original illustration or exemplification of rules, principles, procedures, usages, etc.
j. Classification.
k. Applications of rules, laws, and principles to new situation.
l. Statement of aims of author in selection or organization of material.
m. Criticism as to adequacy, correctness, or relevance of words, phrases, or statements.
n. Outlining.
o. Reorganization of facts previously encountered in different arrangements.
p. Formulation of new questions and problems.
q. Suggestion of new methods of procedure.

V. SHORT EXPLANATION QUESTIONS

This type of question is but a shortened version of a standard essay question, the subject being limited so that the answer may be given in a single sentence.

Sample Item

Explain with one sentence the following statements: (1) The lowest string of a violin has a larger diameter than the highest string. (2) A trombone player lengthens his horn to play a low note.

Advantages:

This type of question tests a student's understandings in the same fashion as an essay question but is more economical of time for both the student and the teacher. By using several of these instead of a single essay question, a greater coverage of material is possible.

Disadvantages:

Some students cannot express themselves well enough with single sentences and many have difficulty in writing concisely enough to give an answer in such a limited fashion.

VI. COMPLETION STATEMENTS

Students are given a set of statements that lack a word or phrase for meaning. The student is supposed to add a word or phrase in the blanks provided, either within the sentence or at the side.

Sample Item

    1. Fill in the blank in each of the following with the proper word:
       a. An explosive gas that is lighter than air is _____.
       b. The product resulting from the combustion of sulphur and oxygen is _____.

Sample Item

    2. Write in the space in the left-hand margin the word that best completes the following sentence.
       1. _____ The part of the automobile engine where air and gasoline are mixed is the __(1)__ .

Advantages:

    These tests measure how well students can recall words or phrases, and when recall is important they make an excellent testing device, easy to take and relatively easy to score. Wider coverage is possible in a short time.

Disadvantages:

    The test does not measure understandings, only recall of words. It cannot be scored mechanically; the teacher must be alert for the possible significance of each separate answer.

VII. MULTIPLE CHOICE

    A multiple choice test is somewhat like a completion test in that statements are presented in incomplete form. Several possible suggestions are given and the student is to choose one or more from them. This format stresses recognition rather than recall.

Sample Item

    1. Underline the word that best completes the following statement.
       The alloy of copper and tin is called (solder, zinc, bronze, brass).

Sample Item

    2. Write in the space at the left the letter of the word that best completes the following:
       _____ 1. The portion of the sun's spectrum that causes sunburn is
       a. infrared
       b. yellow
       c. ultraviolet
       d. Hertzian
       e. orange.

Advantages:

Multiple choice items can be answered and scored rapidly. A wide range of subject matter can be tested in a short time. The questions are fairly easy to write. By using four or five alternates in each question, the effect of guessing is relatively unimportant. These tests are excellent for all purposes—motivation, review, and evaluation.

Disadvantages:

These questions measure only on the recognition level. Because the scoring is mechanical, there is danger that the problems of the students will be overlooked.

Suggestions for Constructing the Multiple Choice Item

1. If the item is in the form of an incomplete statement, it should be meaningful in itself and imply a direct question rather than merely lead into a collection of unrelated true/false statements. For example:
Faulty: The United States of America
   a. has more than 200,000 people.
   b. grows large amounts of rubber.
   c. has few good harbors.
   d. produces most of the world's automobiles.
Improved: The population of the United States is characterized by
   a. an increasing birth rate.
   b. varied nationality backgrounds.
   c. its even distribution over the area of the United States.
   d. an increasing proportion of young people.

2. Use a level of English that is simple and clear, easy enough for even the poorest readers to understand. Avoid unnecessary wordiness. For example:
Too Wordy: Which of the following metals is characterized by extensive utilization in the aircraft industry?
   a. Chromium.
   b. Uranium.
   c. Aluminum.
   d. Beryllium.
Improved: Which of the follwing is most often used in making airplanes?
   a. Chromium.
   b. Uranium.
   c. Aluminum.
   d. Beryllium

3. The length of the alternatives—that is, the number of words each contains—should not vary significantly. Otherwise students may note that long alternatives tend to be correct, or vice versa.

4. The distractors should be plausible. They should be closely related to the same concept as the correct alternative and should be as resonable and natural as the correct response. Humorous and absurd distractors have no measuring value.

5. The arrangement of the alternatives should be uniform throughout the test. If the incomplete-statement form of stem is used, the alternatives should come at the end of the statement. All alternatives should be listed in column form rather than in paragraph form. For example:

   Faulty: The cheapness of land and scarcity of labor in the West created a. an aristocratic class of landowners, b. a large class of wage-earning men, c. a system of servitude, d. a large class of small freeholders.

   Improved: The cheapness of land and scarcity of labor on the West created
   a. an aristocratic class of landowners.
   b. a large class of small freeholders.
   c. a system of servitude.
   d. a large class of wage-earning men.

6. Every item should be grammatically consistent. If the stem is in the form of an incomplete sentence, it should be possible to form a complete sentence by attaching any of the alternatives to the stem. For example:

   Faulty: One of the basic essentials in experimental research is
   a. the researcher should have a science background.
   b. the identification and statement of the problem.
   c. animals must be avilable for experimentation.
   d. variables which need to be clarified.

   Improved: One of the basic essentials in experimental research is
   a. the researcher's background in science.
   b. the identification and statement of the problem.
   c. the availability of animals for experimentation.
   d. the need to clarify variables.

7. Generally, there should be four to five alternatives to reduce chance responses and guessing. However, occasionally the number of alternatives might be reduced to three if it is impossible to construct more without including absurdities or obviously false distractors. It is not necessary to maintain a fixed number of alternatives for every item. But the use of fewer than three alternatives is definitely not recommended.

8. As a general principle, the stem should be expressed in *positive* form. The negative stem presents a psychological disadvantage to the student, often confusing and irritating him at a time when he is already under great stress. Negative items are those which ask what is *not* characteristic of something, what is the *least* defensible reason for something, what is the *least* frequent occurrence, etc. It is good practice to discard the item if it cannot be expressed in positive terms.

9. Responses such as "all of these" or "none of these" should be used *only* when they will contribute more than another plausible distractor. Care should be taken that such responses answer or complete the stem. "All of the above" is a poorer response than "none of the above" because items that use it have four or five correct answers; also, if it is the right answer, knowledge of any two of the distractors will cue it.

10. There must be only one correct or best response.

11. The stem must mean the *same thing* to everyone who reads it. For example:
    Ambiguous: Which of the following household appliances would use the most electrical power?
    a. the vacuum cleaner.
    b. the electric fan.
    c. the electric iron.
    d. a fluorescent tube.
    (Does the test-maker refer to frequency of use, duration of use, or power used by each appliance over the same period of time?)
    Improved: In one hour of operation, which one of the following household appliances would use the most electric power?
    a. a vacuum cleaner.
    b. an electric fan.
    c. an electric iron.
    d. a fluorescent tube.

12. Understanding of definitions is better tested by furnishing the name or word and requiring choice between alternative definitions than by presenting the definition and requiring choice between alternative names or words. For example:
    Faulty: Water enters the air by a process called
    a. osmosis.
    b. filtration.
    c. condensation.
    d. evaporation.
    Improved: Evaporation is a process in which
    a. vapors turn into liquids.
    b. liquids pass between the porous surfaces.
    c. solids dissolve in liquid.
    d. liquids turn into vapors.

13. The stem should state a single, specific problem.

14. The stem must not *include any clues* which will indicate the correct alternative.
    Faulty: A four-sided figure whose opposite sides are parallel is called
    a. a trapezoid.
    b. a parallelogram.
    c. an octagon.
    d. a triangle.

VIII. THE MATCHING ITEM

The matching item consists of three parts: (1) the directions, (2) a list of stems or numbered items (statements, incomplete sentences, phrases, or words), and (3) a list of lettered choices or items (words, phrases, or numbers).

Sample Item

Directions:

Identify by using the associated letter the name of the man who accomplished each of the following:

—— 1. organized the Standard Oil Trust.

—— 2. became a millionaire steel industrialist.

—— 3. contributed to consolidation and efficiency in railroading.

—— 4. invented the light bulb and phonograph.

—— 5. laid the first transatlantic cable.

—— 6. discovered a process to make steel cheaply.

A. Edwin L. Drake

B. Cornelius Vanderbilt

C. Cyrus W. Field

D. Alexander Graham Bell

E. John D. Rockefeller

F. F.W. Woolworth

G. Henry Bessemer

H. Thomas Edison

I. Andrew Carnegie

Advantages:

1. When properly constructed, it can effectively measure the ability to judge simple relationships between somewhat similar ideas, facts, definitions, and principles.
2. It is relatively easy to score because students do not construct their own responses.
3. The range of material tested can be broad.
4. Guessing is reduced, especially if one column contains more items than the other.

Disadvantages:

1. The matching item is not well adapted to the measurement of the understanding of concepts and conceptual schemes, the ability to organize and apply knowledge and other elements of higher learnings.
2. It emphasizes the identification of relationships between or among memorized content.
3. Because all parts of a matching item must be homogeneous it is difficult for the test maker to avoid giving clues which tend to reduce validity.
4. Too many items become confusing.

Suggestions for Constructing Matching Items

1. The number of items in the column from which matching items are to be selected should always exceed the number of items in the stem column. (See the prior example.)
2. The number of items to be identified or matched should not exceed ten or twelve.
3. There should be a high degree of homogeneity in every set of matching items. All items in both columns should be in the same general category. For example, events and their dates should never be mixed with events and the names of famous men.

4. If choices are to be used more than once, the directions should so state.

IX. CORRECTION TESTS

Students are given sentences or paragraphs with a number of italicized words which reduce the meaning of the statements to absurdity. Students are to replace the italicized words with others that make sense of the statements.

Sample 1.

Change the italicized words in the following paragraph so that the paragraph has meaning:
Tom went down to the *garden* to go fishing. The fish were swimming about with their *hands* and *feet* looking for *chickadees* and other insects. Tom baited his hook with a *carrot* and tried to catch one of the trout.

Advantages:

This type of test is a welcome variant to standard tests and students like its absurdities. It measures recall in the fashion of completion tests.

Disadvantages:

This type of exercise has the same disadvantages as completion tests with the added problem that the wrong words may distract the thinking of the students. Perhaps it should not be used for determining grades.

X. GROUPING TESTS

This type of test requires students to recognize several terms that are associated with each other. In a list of several items the students are to select those that are related in some way and to discard those that are not.

Sample Item

Below are sets of four terms, only three of which are alike in some way. Cross out the word that does not seem to belong with the others:
set induction
closure
insight
introduction

Advantages:

This is an interesting type of test and it stimulates discussion. It tests knowledge of groupings.

Disadvantages:

Alternative groupings may suggest themselves to students unless suggestions are given.

XI. ARRANGEMENT EXERCISES

The students are given a list of terms that are to be arranged in some specified order.

Sample Item

The names of the planets are given below.
List these in order of their distance from the sun, beginning with the closest:

Mars	Earth	Uranus
Pluto	Saturn	Jupiter
Mercury	Neptune	Venus

Advantages:

This type tests knowledge of sequence and order. It is good for review and for starting discussions.

Disadvantages:

It is difficult to give partial credit in scoring this test. Probably it should not be used in determining grades.

XII. TRUE-FALSE ITEMS

In this familiar type of test, students are given a number of statements which they are to judge for accuracy. They may accept a statement or refuse to accept it, signifying their decisions with *true* or *false, yes* or *no,* or a plus or minus sign. Sometimes a student is permitted to qualify his answer with a sentence telling why he cannot answer either way.

Sample Item

Write the word *true* or *false* in the blank at the left side of each statement:

———— (1) White pines have five needles in each cluster.

Sample Item

Read the following statement. Circle the letter T at the left if you believe it to be true. Circle the letter F if you believe it to be false.

T F   (1) A ship will sink deeper as it passes from the Hudson River into the Atlantic Ocean.

Advantages:

A great number of items can be answered in a short time, making broad coverage possible. The answers can also be checked rapidly, particularly with the use of a key. This type of test is good for initiating discussions and makes a good pretest.

Disadvantages:

It is very difficult to write items that are strictly true or false without qualifying them in such a way that students can guess what is expected of them. Much of the material that lends itself to this type of testing is relatively unimportant. If students guess the answers, they have a one to one chance of selecting the right answer. Mechanical grading makes it impossible to know why a student made his choice. True-false items are not well suited for determining grades.

XIII. MODIFIED TRUE-FALSE ITEMS

True-false tests may be modified to reduce the guessing prevalent in standard true-false tests and to encourage students to think more. The statements made are the same but students are to rewrite false statements so that they are true. Usually some clue as to the desired change must be given.

Sample

If you judge the statement below to be true, write true in the space at the left. If you judge it to be false, rewrite it so that it is true.

—— 1. Chlorine added to drinking water removed dissolved minerals.

_____

_____

Sample

Below are some statements, some of which are true and some of which are false. If you believe a statement is false, change the underlined word to make the statement true, by writing the correct word in the space at the left.

—— (1) Butterflies have <u>four</u> wings.
—— (2) Houseflies have <u>four</u> wings.

Advantages:

This modification of a true-false test is useful in stimulating discussion.

Disadvantages:

The time needed for checking the answers is increased. It is also difficult to assign credits for giving grades.

XIV. SOMETIMES-ALWAYS-NEVER ITEMS

This type of test is much like the true-false test but with a third alternative offered.

Sample Item

If you believe one of the statements below to be *always true*, circle the letter A at its left. If you believe it is *never true*, circle the letter N. If you believe that it may *sometimes* be true, circle the letter S.

A S N   1. A magnet has two poles.

A S N   2. An electric current sets up a magnetic field.

A S N   3. Like magnetic poles attract each other.

Advantages:

The addition of the third alternative reduces the chances for guessing to one in three. The test is speedily answered and scored. The questions may stimulate a good deal of discussion while being scored.

Disadvantages:

When writing the items it is difficult to avoid giving clues to the answers expected. The fairly high chances for guessing correctly reduce the value of these items for giving grades.

Suggestions for the Construction of True-False Items

1. Write the item out first as a true statement; you can then make the statement false by changing a word(s) or phrase(s).
2. Avoid negative statements wherever possible. If they must be used, the word or phrase that makes the statement negative should be emphasized by underlining.
3. Do not include more than a single idea in one true-false item, particularly if one idea is true and the other is false. Example:
   a. *Clear:*   (F) Lincoln spent six weeks planning his Gettysburg Address.
                  (T) Lincoln delivered his Gettysburg Address on November 19, 1863.

b. *Confusing:* (?) Lincoln spent six weeks planning his Gettysburg Address before delivering it on November 19, 1863.
4. Use approximately an equal number of true and false items.
5. Avoid long, involved statements, especially those containing dependent clauses, many qualifications, and complex ideas.
6. Avoid specific determiners, that is, strongly worded statements containing words such as "always," "all," or "none," which may indicate that the statement is likely to be false.
7. Avoid words that may have different meanings for different students. The word "often" may mean once a week to one student; three times a year to another.
8. Avoid using the exact language of the text with minor changes to give the true-false pattern; this puts a premium on rote memory.
9. Avoid trick items that appear to be true but that are false because of some inconspicuous word or phrase. Example:
a. *Tricky:* (F) The Battle of Hastings was fought in the year 1066 B.C.

FINAL POINTS ON TESTING

1. Exercise caution with verbal tests measuring broad outcomes, i.e. application of principles, critical thinking, discrimination. The only reliable way to measure these is to observe reactions in a real situation.
2. The essay is best for measuring mastery. Completion is good for recall.
3. For major tests, use a variety of types of items.
4. Writing:
    a. Keep questions simple and direct.
    b. Avoid many adjectives, adverbs, qualifying clauses.
    c. Use words common to them.
    d. Use caution with essay questions.
    e. Use caution with completion questions.
    f. Improve your tests each year.
5. Administering:
    a. Check room temperature and ventilation. Room should not be too warm.
    b. Give test at beginning of period, promptly.
    c. Give clear directions as to what to do when finished with test while others are still working.
    d. Consult students individually when they have questions during test.
    e. Keep room as quiet as possible during test.
6. Checking and grading should be done by the teacher.

EXERCISE 19.1   PREPARATION OF A TEST

For your Subject Field:

1. State the purpose(s) for which your test is intended. (Refer to beginning of Chapter 19) _____

2. List one specific objective the test is designed to measure. _____

_____

_____

3. Write test items designed to measure this objective—one item for each of the types listed below and discussed in the preceding section.

Performance item: _____

_____

_____

_____

Identification item: _____

_____

_____

_____

Completion Drawing item: _____

_____

_____

_____

Essay item: _____

_____

_____

_____

Short explanation item: _____

_____

_____

_____

Completion statement item: _____

_____

_____

_____

Multiple-choice item: _____

_____

_____

_____

Matching item: _____

_____

_____

_____

Correction item: _____

_____

_____

_____

Grouping item: _____

_____

_____

_____

Arrangement item: _____

_____

_____

_____

True-false item: _____

_____

_____

_____

4. Share and discuss your test with your classmates and/or instructor.

Selected References

Anderson, L.W. and C.C. Scott. "Relationships Among Teaching Methods, Student Characteristics and Student Involvement in Learning," *Journal of Teacher Education.* Vol. 29, No. 52, May-June 1978.

Bloom, Benjamin S., et al. *Handbook on Formative and Summative Evaluation of Student Learning.* New York: McGraw-Hill Book Co., 1971.

Casciano-Savignano, Jennie C. *Systems Approach to Curriculum and Instructional Improvement.* Columbus, Ohio: Charles E. Merrill Co., 1978.

Gronlund, Norman E. *Preparing Criterion-Referenced Tests for Classroom Instruction.* New York: Macmillan Publishing Co., Inc., 1973.

Hass, Glen, et al. *Readings in Secondary Teaching,* Chapter 17: "Evaluating Learning Progress." Boston: Allyn & Bacon, Inc., 1970.

Hoover, Kenneth A. *The Professional Teacher's Handbook: A Guide for Improving Instruction in Today's Secondary Schools.* Second Edition. Boston: Allyn and Bacon, 1976.

Master, J.R. "High School Student Ratings of Teachers and Teaching Methods," *Journal of Educational Research.* Vol. 72, No. 219, March–April 1979.

Nelson, Clarence H. *Measurement and Evaluation in the Classroom.* New York: Macmillan Publishing Co., 1970.

Newton, R.R. "Teacher Evaluation: Focus on Outcomes," *Peabody Journal of Education.* Vol. 58, No. 45, October 1980.

Patton, M.Q. "Truth or Consequences in Evaluation," *Education and Urban Society.* Vol. 13, No. 59, November 1980.

Reiff, J.C. "Evaluating Student Teacher Effectiveness," *College Study Journal.* Vol. 14, No. 369, Winter, 1980.

Sturn, F.D. "Relationships of Student Teacher's Bureaucratic Orientation to Verbal Classroom Behavior, Flander's Interaction Analysis System," *College Study Journal.* Vol. 13, No. 398, Winter 1979.

Weil, Marsha, et al. *Personal Models of Teaching.* Englewood Cliffs, N.J.: Prentice Hall, 1978.

Whitman, N. "Evaluations Can Isolate Teaching from Learning," *Instructional Innovations.* Vol. 26, No. 35, March 1981.

Younger, Evelle J. *The Law in the School.* Third Edition. Montclair, N.J.: Patterson Smith Publishing Corporation, 1980.

Part VI

What Should I Know About The Practice Teaching Experience and Beyond

20

What Should I Know About the Practice-Teaching Experience?

One of the most, if not *the* most, significant and important aspects of teacher training comes under the heading of "student teaching." We prefer to call this *practice teaching*, and the experience is usually the "terminal" experience in pre-service training. The reason it comes last is because professional educators believe there are things a pre-service teacher should learn before actual practice on live students, just as there are training experiences as an intern in law or medicine before the trainee is provided opportunity to practice in "live" situations.

At some universities the practice-teaching field experience is, over a two- or three-semester period, carefully blended with classroom instruction in theory. In others, the university instruction may come first followed by a one-semester immersion in field practice. In either case the field practice-teaching experience is an important aspect of teacher training and affords the trainee the opportunity to field test his skills and knowledge in a supervised real teaching situation.

Seldom is it or should it be a "sink-or-swim" situation but rather an opportunity for the trainee to obtain and improve his teaching skills in a setting carefully supervised by trained university supervisors and carefully screened experienced cooperating teachers from the host school. Sometimes these teachers are referred to as *master teachers*.

We think it is important to emphasize to all concerned that this experience is *practice* teaching.

The practice teacher will, as expected, make mistakes and will learn from mistakes. Frequently the experience provides learning reciprocation whereby the cooperating teacher learns from the student teacher. And, it is important for all to remember that the public school children should not suffer but benefit educationally from having a student teacher.

We offer the following general guidelines to both the student teacher and to the cooperating teacher to help make these experiences beneficial to all concerned.

A. PRIOR CLASSROOM EXPERIENCE AS A PARAPROFESSIONAL

Prior to practice teaching we believe the preservice teacher should have had classroom experience as a paraprofessional. The following list provides information as to the kinds of experiences a preservice teacher might have while serving in this capacity as a paraprofessional. These help to familiarize the trainee with the many exhaustive facets of a teacher's real life, before the trainee actually begins the phase we call "practice teaching."

Clerical

1. Sending for free and inexpensive classroom materials.
2. Keeping attendance records.
3. Entering evaluative marks in the teacher's marking book.
4. Averaging academic marks and preparing report cards.
5. Keeping records of class schedules.
6. Keeping inventory of classroom stock-equipment, books, instructional supplies.
7. Managing classroom libraries.
8. Setting up and maintaining seating charts.
9. Typing, duplicating, and collating instructional materials.
10. Typing and duplicating class newspaper.
11. Duplicating students' writings and other work.
12. Typing and duplicating scripts for plays and skits.
13. Finding resource materials for various teaching units.
14. Compiling information for teacher reports.
15. Preparing bulletins for parents to explain school programs, events, and rules.
16. Managing instructional materials for accessibility.
17. Keeping bulletin boards current and neat.

Noninstructional

18. Gathering supplementary books and materials for instruction.
19. Distributing books and supplies.
20. Collecting homework and test papers.
21. Checking out library books in central library for students and teacher.
22. Assisting committees engaged in special projects—constructing, researching, or experimenting.
23. Helping settle student disputes and quarrels.
24. Setting up special classroom exhibits.
25. Accompanying a student to the office, nurse's room, etc.
26. Monitoring study hall.
27. Helping teacher supervise students on field trips.
28. Running errands relevant to classroom work.
29. Read student bulletin to class.

Audio-Visual Assistance

30. Ordering and returning films, filmstrips, and other A-V materials.
31. Procuring and returning A-V equipment.
32. Setting up and operating overhead projectors, slide viewers, and other instructional equipment.
33. Previewing films and other A-V materials.
34. Preparing introductions to give students background for viewing A-V materials.

Instruction-Related
(under teacher direction)

35. Correcting standardized and informal tests and preparing student profiles.
36. Correcting homework and workbooks, noting and reporting weak areas to teacher.
37. Interviewing students with specific learning problems.
38. Observing student behavior and writing reports.
39. Preparing informal tests and other evaluative instruments.
40. Preparing instructional materials—cutouts, flash cards, charts, transparencies, etc.
41. Collecting and arranging displays for teaching purposes.
42. Preparing special learning materials to meet individual differences—developing study guides, taping reading assignments for less able readers, etc.
43. Teaching a small class group about a simple understanding, skill, or appreciation.
44. Tutoring individual students—the faster as well as the slower learners.
45. Supervising and assisting students with library assignments.
46. Teaching students who miss instruction because they were out of the room for special work—remedial reading, speech therapy, etc.
47. Preparing and teaching a short lesson to the class.
48. Repeating lessons for slower learners.
49. Helping students who were absent to get caught up with others in their group.
50. Listening to the student's oral reading.
51. Assisting students with written compositions—especially with spelling, punctuation, and grammar.
52. Instructing in the safe and proper use of tools.
53. Teaching etiquette and good manners.
54. Assisting the teacher in special demonstrations.
55. Providing accompaniment in music classes.
56. Reading and storytelling.
57. Helping students find reference materials.
58. Preparation of reading, spelling, or vocabulary lists.
59. Supervising laboratory work.
60. Putting written work on the blackboard.
61. Assisting in drill work with word and phrase flash cards (e.g., remedial reading).
62. Assisting and checking students in seat work.

Some of the Paraprofessionals' Duties

63. Supervising the halls between classes.
64. Supervising recess.
65. Supervising extracurricular activities.
66. Visiting the teachers' lounge.
67. Visiting the principal's office.
68. Visiting the attendance office.
69. Visiting the counselor's office.
70. Observing in non-standard classes (i.e. shop classes, special education, student government, agriculture, etc.)
71. Observing assemblies, student government.
72. Observing teacher meetings, department meetings, etc.

The Paraprofessionals should not be expected:
1. to take work home, i.e., to grade papers at home.
2. to do work of a personal nature for cooperating teachers unrelated to classroom assignment.
3. to bring coffee to the teacher.
4. to be left alone with class.
5. to do the entire routine for regular teachers, i.e., filing, typing dittos, duplicating, etc.

B. FOR THE STUDENT TEACHER: WHAT I NEED TO KNOW TO MAKE PRACTICE TEACHING A SUCCESSFUL EXPERIENCE

1. Is practice teaching like "real" teaching?
   The answer to this is both yes and no. *Yes*, because you will have real live students and the opportunity to try your skills at teaching. *No*, because your cooperating teacher still has the ultimate responsibility for the class.
2. How do I prepare for it?
   By preparing well! Learn all you can about the school, community, the students. The nature of the course(s) you will be teaching, what is expected of you, how you will be supervised. And plan your lesson well.
3. What kind of experiences can I anticipate?
   Rewarding, frustrating, and neutral. You will perhaps have fewer neutral days. Most will be good, bad, or a combination of both. You will become emotionally spent, elated, and tired. Students will give you a "honeymoon period," then test you, try you, go along with you, and like you. You will be scared, anxious, insecure, but will overcome. Confidence will develop. You might be mistaken for just another senior in high school. You will earn your "status." Parents will ask questions. You will be expected to attend games, dances, and faculty meetings. You will spend hours preparing lessons that might flop or go untaught. Textbooks will be outdated. Films will be late in arriving. Guest speakers may not show. You will laugh and cry and find out what makes teaching exciting, frustrating, enriching, and dull—simultaneously. There are no two days alike.
4. What kind of support can I expect?
   Perhaps little, one hopes, a great deal. But be prepared to stand alone. Be thankful when it is there, perhaps from the master teacher, or the librarian, the custodian, the student who smiles with you.
5. What kind of supervision can I expect?
   Your students are there every day. You will know from their responses how you are doing. Your cooperating teacher will offer critiques, and occasionally or perhaps often your college university supervisor will observe and offer critiques. Except for, perhaps, a drop-in by another teacher or administrator, you are alone with your class. If you don't believe you are getting proper help then seek it out. There are many people around who will be most happy to offer suggestions if asked.
6. What kind of criticisms can I expect?
   The more the better. Some will be helpful, others not so. Listen to all! Try new ideas and suggestions. Practice teaching is the time to try new skills and to get feedback. It is important for you to take the initiative in soliciting feedback. Don't wait until someone comes and offers you criticism.
7. What dangers should I be on the watch for?
   Student restlessness, inattentiveness, poor attendance. These symptoms might be a reflection on you or they might not. Investigate and find out. Be cautious of starting out trying to be too "buddy-buddy" with students. Respect and friendship are earned and occur gradually and slowly. Your students may tell you that they like you better than some other teacher. That sounds good for your poor ego but it may also mean little. If you must decide between being on the "tough" side or the "easy" side, then choose the tough.

C. FOR THE COOPERATING TEACHER: HOW I CAN HELP MY STUDENT TEACHER

1. What is my role?
   To assist when necessary. To provide guidance. To look at lesson plans before presented. To facilitate the learning by the student teacher. To help the student teacher become and feel like a member of the profession.
2. How can I prepare for it?
   Get to know your student teacher ahead of time. Develop a collegial rapport with the student teacher.
3. Who is my student teacher?
   One who is making the transition from being a college student to a professional teacher. He is perhaps in his mid-twenties and scared to death, anxious, knowledgeable, and somewhere between being a romantic idealist and a pragmatic realist. Don't destroy the idealism—help him with understanding and dealing with the realism.
4. What kind of support, criticism, and supervision should I give?
   You will have to judge this yourself. Generally speaking, lots of support, helpful criticisms, and supervision are wanted by the student teacher. But, by all means, try not to put him into a total "sink or swim" situation. Your students deserve more.
5. What dangers should I look for?
   Your student teacher may be very different from you in both appearance and style, but may be potentially just as effective. Judge his effectiveness slowly and cautiously. Offer suggestions, but not demands. A student teacher who is not preparing well is likely heading for trouble. As also is one who seems to show no interest in the school outside of the class. The student teacher should be prompt, anxious to spend out of class time with you, and aware of the necessity of school clerical tasks.
   If you feel there is a lurking problem then let him know your feelings. Poor communication between cooperating teacher and student teacher is a common danger signal.
6. What else should I know?
   Your student teacher is likely to be partially employed elsewhere and to have other demands on his time. Become aware of the situation.
   Be sure that the student teacher becomes a member of the total faculty, is invited to faculty functions, has his own mailbox, and has total awareness of school policies, procedures, curriculum guides, and so forth.
   Once your student teacher is well grounded then he should be left alone with the class most of the time. This time can afford you the opportunity to work on papers and curriculum matters.

EXERCISE 20.1   STUDENT TEACHING EVALUATION

1. Repeat Exercise 17.3, Item 1.
2. Have your secondary school students complete a form similar to those of Section E of Chapter 17.
3. Share and discuss the results of 1 and 2 above with your cooperating teacher and college supervisor.

21

What Should I Know About Getting the First Teaching Job?

You have spent four or five years in a college or university preparing yourself for a teaching credential. But what good will having the credential be if you cannot find a teaching position? Perhaps you will find the following guidelines beneficial as you set out in pursuit of your first job.

A. GENERAL GUIDELINES TO ASSIST YOU IN GETTING A JOB

1. The *personal interview* is perhaps the most important factor once you are a candidate for a teaching position. During the interview you are going to be observed carefully in (a) motivation for teaching, and (b) your ability to communicate. Be prepared in both areas; among other things "ability to communicate" probably includes your initial physical appearance.
2. Your *area of preparation* and the extent of preparation is important. You are most likely to be hired if you are a "total English teacher" rather than a specialist in Elizabethan literature. As an example: the prospective science teacher should be prepared to teach at least three of the five common science courses taught in secondary schools. In other words, the principal of a school with an opening is more likely to want a teacher with academic mobility. If you can teach history that is fine, but if you can also coach swimming that may be even better.
3. A third area of major importance has to do with *student-teaching recommendations*. The potential employer wants to know that: (a) you are an effective teacher, (b) you have good rapport with students, (c) you can manage a classroom.

In summary, you can help yourself in getting a teaching job by (1) preparing yourself to teach in several areas, (2) doing a good job in your practice teaching, and (3) preparing and showing well in the personal interview.

B.   SOME SPECIFIC GUIDELINES FOR FINDING A JOB

How to Go About Looking for a Position

1.   Find out what kinds of placement services your college or the university offers.
2.   Obtain information about new positions and vacancies and also lists of school districts in your state. (Some institutions have a job phone, a recorded message announcing weekly the various vacancies and new positions.)
3.   Read newspapers, good general periodicals such as *Saturday Review,* newsletters from teacher organizations such as *California Teachers' Association Newsletter,* and also journals in your subject matter area. You often find jobs overseas, private school teaching positions, etc.
4.   Apply through commercial teacher employment services even if it will cost you a little. For example, try Global Teacher Placement Services, 2100 Culver Blvd., Baltimore, Maryland 10021.
5.   If you know teachers or administrators in the area where you want to teach, keep in touch with them from time to time and find out the job possibilities.
6.   Write to as many schools or school districts as you want, expressing your strong interest to teach. A brief letter of inquiry and a resume will suffice for initial contact (a shotgun approach).
7.   If you do not find a regular teaching position, apply for a substitute teaching position. Most schools have two kinds of substitute teaching positions; short term (daily) and long term (weekly, monthly, or the whole quarter). Competent substitute teaching often leads to a regular position. Consider teacher aide or teaching assistant position also.
8.   When you have exhausted all possibilities for a regular position, then apply for a position in the Peace Corps, Teacher Corps, Job Corps or VISTA (Volunteers In Service Through America). Most schools look favorably upon the services you render for these organizations, and your teaching experience there will be counted as a regular teaching experience.
9.   Avoid schools or school districts where many applicants are interested in applying. Look for areas where not too many people want to apply; severely cold countries, desert areas, isolated areas, or high crime areas, etc. Chances for a position in those areas may be better.
10.   Don't trust the general statistics about teachers supply and demand situations—for example, "secondary schools are 80 per cent oversupplied, no new teachers are needed for the next five years," etc. There are exceptions to these statistics and some schools or some school districts are not included in these kinds of statistics or predictions.

Whatever you do and however you want to go about finding a job, convince yourself that *there are jobs.* It may be just a matter of *when* and *where.* Don't expect other people to find a job for you. You do it yourself.

Letter of Inquiry (Application Letter) and Resume Preparation

1.   Remember, a letter of inquiry and a resume are advertisements of yourself—a letter and a resume can transform a job applicant to a job candidate and finally to a job holder.
2.   Address your letter to the principal, personnel director of the school district, or superintendent by name, if at all possible. Individual names can be obtained from the county Public School directory.
3.   Type each letter separately. The resume may be duplicated. Use standard English sentence structure and correct spelling. Take a businesslike approach in your letter; don't be humorous, overbearing, or too aggressive.

4. Resume should be brief (not more than one page); include:
   a. Experience in chronological order (last employment first, paid as well as nonpaid jobs).
   b. Education (again in the same manner suggested as for experience).
   c. Types of credentials you hold and areas of specialization.
   d. Student teaching experience (just the school and the subject matter and the grade level).
   e. Special interests or activities you can sponsor (coaching, club activities, and adult education classes for the community, etc.) and travel experiences.
   f. Professional or fraternity organizations.
   g. Personal references. Be certain to give correct names, addresses, and telephone number.
5. It is not necessary that you write both a letter of inquiry and a resume. You may request an official application form if you are not including a resume.
6. Indicate the exact name and address of placement office where your credential file is kept.
7. Express a desire for an interview.

Hints on the Interview

The interview may be the most decisive step in your job search. This is where most likely you will get the job and not from the resume. Keep in mind the following for a successful interview:

1. Arrive at the interview place about 15 minutes early. Do some homework about the school, school district or community; cultural, socioeconomic or any other things by which you can demonstrate to your interviewer that you have some knowledge about the school/community.
2. Present a neat appearance and good grooming. No matter what your life-style may be, the teacher interviewers are generally conservative and reserved.
3. Prepare yourself to identify your strengths and/or areas for further improvement in your personality and in your teaching ability.
4. Be courteous, confident, cheerful, act naturally, and be determined.
5. Don't talk too much or too little; don't try to be funny.
6. Don't take notes; listen attentively and make yourself understood.
7. Prepare yourself for the following most commonly asked questions by the interviewer:
   a. Why do you want to be a teacher and when did you make that decision?
   b. Briefly tell me about yourself.
   c. What are the long-range goals in your life; what do you see yourself doing 5 to 10 years from today?
   d. Can you tell me briefly how you plan to teach the subject matter for the grade level for which you are applying?
   e. What do you think are the responsibilities of an educator?
   f. What can you contribute to students and the community besides teaching your subject matter in the class?
8. Do not hesitate to ask questions about the job for which you are applying. Good questions are an indication of your enthusiasm and knowledge. Prepare questions in advance.

Finally but not least important! Don't panic. If your first interview didn't go too well, learn from your experience how to be more successful next time.

EXERCISE 21.1   GETTING A JOB

Here is an exercise that it might take courage for you and the other members of the class to participate in. If you have been working well together during the course, you might like to try it. Read the exercise, then decide as a group whether it might be beneficial to all. Change the rules in any way that seems appropriate.

Introduction

By this time you all undoubtedly know one another fairly well, have worked together in groups, and most likely have observed each other teach in microsessions at least. In other words, you have as much data about one another as anyone would have who was responsible for interviewing you for a teaching position.

Procedure

Seat yourselves in a circle so each person can see everyone else's face. Put your name on a card and place it in front of you just in case others in the class might not remember your name. We hope your instructor will join you in this activity. Now, all ready? Pretend that you are a principal of a school and have three openings for teachers for next year. Each and every one of the members of this class is an applicant for one of those three positions. List on a sheet of paper the three applicants you wish to hire. Now, as a class, decide what you will do from here. Here are some choices as made by other classes:

1. Pass the papers around for all to read.
2. Pass them to one person to tally, then distribute the results in rank order.
3. Have one person tally and identify the three persons whose names appeared most often, then as a class discuss what qualities these people have.
4. Do not share your lists, but think about why you chose the persons you did.
5. Pass them folded to one person to tally and have the complete rank-ordered list posted in the instructor's office for those who want to see it.
6. Discuss candidly your reactions to this exercise.

Epilogue to Exercise 21.1

Peer evaluation and selection are difficult. As a teacher, you might from time to time expect your students to do something similar to this. It is important you remember how difficult this experience was for you. As a teacher, you may eventually find yourself in a position where you will be asked to make judgments about your colleagues—who gets rehired, promoted, and so on. So you see, it gave you some insight about the kinds of qualities an interviewer might look for and be attracted to. It would be interesting and worthwhile to follow up this exercise with research to find out which of your classmates do in fact get hired first.

In the tight teacher market of today (see Preface) we can not assure you of immediately being hired as a teacher. We offered guidelines that might increase your chances. These were in these major areas—your area of preparation, your letters of recommendation, and your behavior during the personal interview. We wish you the very best in your new profession.

C. SOURCES OF INFORMATION ON CREDENTIAL REQUIREMENTS FOR EACH STATE

Alabama
State Department of Education
Montgomery, Alabama 36104

Alaska
State Department of
Education
Juneau, Alaska 99801

Arizona
State Department of Public
Instruction
Phoenix, Arizona 85007

Arkansas
State Department of Education
Little Rock, Arkansas 72201

California
State Department of Education
Sacramento, California 95814

Colorado
State Department of Education
State Office Building
Denver, Colorado 80203

Connecticut
State Department of Education
P.O. Box 2219
Hartford, Connecticut 06115

Delaware
State Department of Public
Instruction
Dover, Delaware 19901

Florida
State Department of Education
Tallahassee, Florida 32304

Georgia
State Department of Education
Atlanta, Georgia 30334

Hawaii
State Department of Education
Honolulu, Hawaii 96804

Idaho
State Department of Education
Boise, Idaho 83702

Illinois
Office of the Superintendent of
Public Instruction
302 State Office Building
Springfield, Illinois 62706

Indiana
State Department of Public
Instruction
Indianapolis, Indiana 46204

Iowa
State Department of Public
Instruction
Des Moines, Iowa 50319

Kansas
State Department of Public
Instruction
Topeka, Kansas 66612

Kentucky
State Department of
Education
Frankfort, Kentucky 40601

Louisiana
State Department of
Education
Baton Rouge, Louisiana 70804

Maine
State Department of
Education
Augusta, Maine 04330

Maryland
State Department of Education
Baltimore, Maryland 21201

Massachusetts
State Department of Education
Boston, Massachusetts 02111

Michigan
State Department of Education
Lansing, Michigan 48902

Minnesota
State Department of Education
St. Paul, Minnesota 55101

Mississippi
State Department of Education
Jackson, Mississippi 39205

Missouri
State Department of Education
Jefferson City, Missouri 65101

Montana
State Department of Public
Instruction
Helena, Montana 59601

Nebraska
State Department of Education
Lincoln, Nebraska 68509

Nevada
State Department of Education
Carson City, Nevada 89701

New Hampshire
State Department of Education
Concord, New Hampshire 03301

New Jersey
State Department of Education
Trenton, New Jersey 08625

New Mexico
State Department of Education
Santa Fe, New Mexico 87501

New York
State Education Department
Albany, New York 12224

North Carolina
State Board of Education
Raleigh, North Carolina 27602

North Dakota
State Department of Public
Instruction
Bismark, North Dakota 58501

Ohio
State Department of Education
Ohio Departments Building
Columbus, Ohio 43215

Oklahoma
State Department of Education
Oklahoma City, Oklahoma 73105

Oregon
State Department of Education
Salem, Oregon 97310

Pennsylvania
State Department of Public
Instruction
Harrisburg, Pennsylvania 17126

Rhode Island
State Department of Education
Providence, Rhode Island 02908

South Carolina
State Department of Education
Columbia, South Carolina 29201

South Dakota
State Department of Public
Instruction
Pierre, South Dakota 57501

Tennessee
State Department of Education
Nashville, Tennessee 37219

Texas
Texas Education Agency
Austin, Texas 78711

Utah
Office of the Superintendent of
Public Instruction
Salt Lake City, Utah 84111

Vermont
  State Department of Education
  Montpelier, Vermont 05602
Virginia
  State Board of Education
  Richmond, Virginia 23216
Washington
  Office of the State Superin-
    tendent of Public Instruction

and the State Board of
  Education
Olympia, Washington 98501
West Virginia
  State Department of
    Education
  Charleston, West Virginia 25305
Wisconsin
  State Department of Public

Instruction
126 Langdon Street
Madison, Wisconsin 53702
Wyoming
  State Department of
    Education
  Cheyenne, Wyoming 82001

D. MAJOR EDUCATIONAL ASSOCIATIONS IN THE UNITED STATES RELATED TO SECONDARY SCHOOL TEACHING

AAHPER   American Alliance for Health, Physical Education and Recreation, 1201 Sixteenth Street, N.W., Washington, D.C. 20036.

AACJC   American Association of Community and Junior Colleges, One Dupont Circle, Washington, D.C. 20036.

AAPT   American Association of Physics Teachers, 335 E. 45th St., New York, NY 10017

AASA   American Association of School Administrators, 1801 North Moore Street, Arlington, VA 22209.

AASL   American Association of School Librarians, 50 E. Huron Street, Chicago, IL 60611.

ACE   American Council on Education, One Dupont Circle, Washington, D.C. 20036.

AHEA   American Home Economics Association, 2010 Massachusetts Avenue, N.W., Washington, D.C. 20036.

AIAA   American Industrial Arts Association, 1201 Sixteenth Street, N.W., Washington, D.C. 20036.

AVA   American Vocational Association, 1510 H Street, N.W., Washington, D.C. 20005.

AECT   Association for Educational Communications Technology, 1201 Sixteenth Street, N.W., Washington, D.C. 20036.

AFSTE   Association for Field Services in Teacher Education, c/o Dr. John J. Diabal Jr., Division of Extension, Northern Illinois University, DeKalb, IL 60115.

ASCD   Association for Supervision and Curriculum Development, 225 W. Washington Street, Alexandria, VA 22314.

ATE   Association of Teacher Educators, 1701 K Street, N.W., Suite 1201, Washington, D.C. 20006.

CEC   Council for Exceptional Children, 1720 Association Drive, Reston, VA 22091.

CLR   Council on Library Resources, Inc., One Dupont Circle, Washington, D.C. 20036.

Home Ec.   Department of Home Economics, 1201 Sixteenth Street, N.W., Washington, D.C. 20036.

EMC   Educational Media Council, 1346 Connecticut Avenue, N.W., Washington, D.C. 20036.

ERIC   Educational Resources Information Center, One Dupont Circle, Washington, D.C. 20036.

IRA   International Reading Association, 800 Barksdale Road, Newark, DE 19711.

JCEE   Joint Council on Economic Education, 1212 Avenue of the Americas, New York, NY 10036.

MENC   Music Educators National Conference, 1902 Association Drive, Reston, VA 22091.

NAEA   National Art Education Association, 1916 Association Drive, Reston, VA 22091.

NASM   National Association of Schools of Music, 11230 Roger Bacon Drive, Reston, VA 22090.

NASSP   National Association of Secondary-School Principals, 1904 Association Drive, Reston, VA 22091.

NBEA   National Business Education Association, 1906 Association Drive, Reston, VA 22091.

NCEA   National Catholic Educational Association, One Dupont Circle, Suite 350, Washington, D.C. 20036.

NABT   National Association of Biology Teachers, 1515 Wilson Blvd., Suite 101, Arlington, VA 22209.

NCSS   National Council for the Social Studies, 1515 Wilson Blvd., Suite 101, Arlington, VA 22209.

NCTE   National Council of Teachers of English, 1111 Kenyon Road, Urbana, Illinois 61801.

NCTM   National Council of Teachers of Mathematics, 1906 Association Drive, Reston, VA 22090.

NSTA   National Science Teachers Association, 1742 Connecticut Avenue, N.W., Washington, D.C. 20009.

Selected References _____

Alexander, William M. *The High School Today and Tomorrow.* New York: Holt, Rinehart and Winston, 1971.

Austin-Martin, G.G. *"Effects of Student Teaching and Pretesting on Student Teachers' Attitudes," Journal of Experimental Education*, Vol. 49, No. 36, Fall 1979.

Compton, R.S. *"Beginning High School Teachers; Apprentice or Professional?"*, *American Secondary Education*, Vol 9, No. 23, November 1979.

Ellenburg, F.C., *"You Can Pay Me Now or You Can Pay Me Later," Clearing House*, Vol. 54, No. 200, January 1981.

House, Ernest R., and Stephen D. Lapan. *Survival in the Classroom: Negotiating with Kids, Colleagues, and Bosses.* Boston: Allyn and Bacon, Inc., 1978.

McCaleb, J.L. and Mead, M.L., *"Involvement of Student Teachers in Interactive Research"*, *Teacher Education*, Vol. 16, No. 41, Winter 80–81.

Scherer, C. *"Effects of Early Experience on Student Teachers, Self-Concepts and Performance"*, *Journal of Experimental Education*, Vol. 47, No. 208, Spring 1979.

School of Education, *The Handbook for Student Teachers, Cooperating Teachers and School Administrators*, California State University, Sacramento, 1980.

Name Index

Alcorn, Marvin, 120n, 121n
Amidon, Edmund, 211n

Bradfield, James M., 13n, 39n, 187n

Carmical, LaVerne, 163n
Chamberlin, Leslie J., 185n, 186n
Claus, Calvin K., 96n
Collette, Alfred T., 240n
Costa, Arthur, 122n, 167n
Cusick, Phillip A., 29

Drayer, Adam M., 234n
Dreikurs, Rudolf, 165n, 166n

Fallon, John J., 131n, 231n
Feeney, Therese, 52n
Fox, Fred W., 227n

Gibb, J.R., 165n
Glatthorn, Allan A., 18n
Gorman, Alfred, 14n, 15n
Grobman, Deborah, 54n
Gronlund, Norman E., 96n

Hunter, Elizabeth, 153n, 154n, 211n

Johnson, Rita, 73n
Johnson, Stuart, 73n

Kellough, Richard, 163n, 164n, 165n
Kensworthy, Leonard S., 128n
Kinder, James S., 120n, 121n
Kirschenbaum, Howard, 236n

Leonard, Joan M., 131n, 231n
Lindsay, Targe, Jr., 68n

Mager, Robert F., 93n
Mallery, David, 27n, 28n, 29n
Massialas, Byron G., 129n
McLain, Steve, 63n
Meeks, John, 62n
Miller, Lorraine F., 165n
Morgan, Sue, 60n

Napier, Rodney W., 236n
Netherda, Shawn, 86n
Nordberg, Orville H., 13n, 39n, 187n

O'Connell, Gerri, 80n
O'Dell, William C., 13n, 39n, 187n

Peterson, Bob, 75n
Platts, Grace N., 165n

Rodriquez, Gloria, 59n

Schunert, Jim R., 120n, 121n
Scofield, Christy, 67n

Shipp, David, 65n
Simon, Sidney B., 236n
Skinner, Patricia, 145n

Von Arx, Harold, 131n, 231n

Webb, Mary, 142n
Wells, James D., 136n
Wesley, Edgar B., 133n
Wilson, Carol, 2n, 104n, 204n
Wronski, Stanley P., 133n

Zevin, Jack, 129n

Subject Index

Please remember that this is a library book,
and that it belongs only temporarily to each
person who uses it. Be considerate. Do
not write in this, or any, library book.

DATE DUE

373.1102
K49r3   157739

JY 8 '94